AN ENGLISH DOCTOR IN JAPAN

AN ENGLISH DOCTOR IN JAPAN

Gabriel Symonds

YOUCAXTON PUBLICATIONS
OXFORD & SHREWSBURY

ISBN 978-1-913425-43-2
Published by YouCaxton Publications 2020
YCBN: 01

YouCaxton Publications
www.youcaxton.co.uk

CONTENTS

INTRODUCTION   vii

PART ONE
Early Medical Life
1.   Hitch-Hiking to India   1
2.   Medical School Experiences   8
3.   Eccentric Friend   14
4.   Studying in Japan   18
5.   Junior Hospital Doctor   24
6.   General Practice Training   27
7.   London Locum Life   35

PART TWO
The Art of General Practice
8.   Introduction   47
9.   Doctors and Drugs   52
10. Common Problems in General Practice   58
11. Smoking and Drinking   74
12. Scientific Psychiatry   80
13. Dr James Cyriax   92
14. Treating Neck and Low Back Pain   101

PART THREE
Medical Practice in Tokyo
15. Acquiring a Japanese Medical License   111
16. Tokyo Medical Misadventures   117
17. Hotel Medical Visits   125
18. More Medical Visits   132
19. Eccentric and Unfortunate People   148
20. Difficult Colleagues   162
21. Poor Treatment and Other Problems   171
22. How Much Do You Want Cut Off?   192
23. Sexually Transmitted Infections   202
24. Birth in Tokyo   209
25. Psychiatric Cases   217
26. Child Psychology   231
27. Complaints   237
28. Swindled!   247
29. Memento Mori   251

ACKNOWLEDGEMENTS   257

INTRODUCTION

I KNEW I wanted to be a doctor from about the age of fifteen. I was attracted by medicine's unique combination of intellectual and practical skills, and the knowledge that I would be able to help people. In particular, the idea of being a country general practitioner (GP) appealed to me. This was encouraged by a book I read during my medical student days, *A Fortunate Man: The Story of a Country Doctor,* by John Berger and Jean Mohr (1967). It is, therefore, somewhat ironic that I ended up, instead, for most of my professional life in two of the world's busiest cities: London and Tokyo.

For me, the great interest and satisfaction of general practice is the variety it offers. One never knows what kind of problem the next patient will bring to you. It might be something straightforward like an in-growing toenail or an ear infection, or a serious disorder like heart disease or cancer, or other problems that really stretch one's knowledge and abilities.

After I immigrated, from time to time people ask me, 'What brought you to Japan?' They don't seem satisfied with the literal answer—an aeroplane—so I tell them, 'It's a long story.' Here, that story, with some of the adventures (and a few misadventures) I have had along the way, working in the National Health Service (NHS) in Britain and as a private doctor in Japan, will be told.

Patients' and doctors' names and other details have been changed to protect their identities, except as otherwise indicated.

PART ONE

Early Medical Life

CHAPTER ONE
Hitch-Hiking to India

IN 1963 I had the good fortune to be accepted at the Medical College of St Bartholomew's Hospital, known as Bart's, in the University of London. There were, however, some months to go before the start of the course, so I took the opportunity to travel. Having hitch-hiked around Europe in my school holidays, once getting as far as Istanbul, I decided I would like to go further east, in particular to India. In the early 1960s people didn't have much money, and hitch-hiking, with staying at Youth Hostels, was a common way to see the world. I have to admit this plan caused some anxiety to my parents, especially to my dear mother, who on seeing me off at Victoria Station—I went by train and ferry to Ostend before hitching rides—made me promise to go no further than Istanbul.

Such an adventure, with a hint of danger, is a kind of initiation rite for a young man. My route took me through Belgium, Germany, Austria, Yugoslavia, and Greece. I stayed in Istanbul for three weeks, earning money by teaching English at the British Council. They had a library which contained several copies of a book called *An Introduction to Pathology* by G Payling Wright. Believing it would stand me in good stead in my forthcoming studies, I read this book right through, though at the time I understood little of it.

I then put aside the promise to my mother, as she knew I would, and with a feeling of great excitement, set off to the east. I found it easy as a young man with a Union Jack on my rucksack to get lifts. I stood at the entrance to the ferry across the Bosporus (there are now two road bridges and a tunnel) and soon had a lift deep into the Asian part of Turkey. Thereafter I would be on the road by 6.00 am, having made breakfast of tea and dates. I boiled the water for tea on a small Primus stove

I carried. Anyone who was travelling by car usually was making for the next town, and thus by a series of long lifts I made rapid progress across Turkey and Persia (as Iran was then known). People were invariably kind and generous with their hospitality, not just in giving lifts but often inviting me for meals as well.

I remember seeing the snow-capped Mount Ararat near the Persian border on which Noah is said to have arrived in his ark when the flood receded. As Youth Hostels were sparse in that part of the world I stayed mainly at cheap hotels. These usually looked clean but I would often find several bed-bugs which I had squashed flat by lying upon them in my sleep, when I arose in the mornings! I seemed to suffer no ill effects from such encounters with these parasites. I spent some days in Tehran, then proceeded south east via Qom to Isfahan. This city contains the strikingly beautiful Jahan Square at the head of which is the seventeenth century Imam (Shah) Mosque; its dome and minarets are covered with mosaic tiles and calligraphy. I was able to get permission to ascend one of the minarets of this mosque. It involved a long climb up a steep internal spiral staircase in almost complete darkness, to be rewarded by a splendid view over the city and to the mountains beyond.

From there I hitch-hiked to the attractive historic city of Shiraz, on the way visiting the famous ruins of Persepolis, now a World Heritage site, built in the sixth century BC by Darius I. Thence by bus to the town of Kerman where by coincidence the then dictator of Persia, the Shah of Shahs, was passing through. People had waited for hours to see him and I found myself in a small crowd on the route of his motorcade. I just caught a glimpse of him through his car window as he sped by. Thereafter, going towards the town of Bam the bus was escorted by a jeep full of armed soldiers as bandits were apparently active in that region. Part of the way was through the Lut desert where for a time it was like being on the ocean: for 360° the land was flat and featureless apart from the tire tracks on the dirt road stretching to the horizon.

I arrived at the frontier town of Zahedan late in the evening and discovered there was a once-weekly train to Quetta leaving that very night. At the station I fell into conversation with some English-speaking local people, and was told that if I bought gold in Persia I could assuredly sell it for a handsome profit in India. I didn't know if this was illegal but I was persuaded to part with a five-pound note (worth about £100 or $130 today) in exchange for one heavy shiny gold coin.

The ticket office was closed, so I simply boarded the waiting train. Come the morning, we were on the move and an inspector appeared. Where was my ticket? I patiently explained that I had been unable to buy one because the office in Zahedan was closed when I got on the train but I was, of course, willing to buy a ticket from the inspector on the spot. No good. I would have to pay a fine as well as the fare! This seemed unreasonable to me and an argument went back and forth until he realised that I was English. He then related that he used to be a ticket inspector on the buses in Birmingham, and finding that we had an English background in common, decided to let me off the fine and merely pay the fare.

The train, operated by steam, seldom seemed to go above about 20mph (32kph) and stopped at every little station along the way. Some of the passengers played a game of running alongside the train and then jumping back in. Once I noticed a man was left behind when the train suddenly speeded up! The other passengers were local people or returning travellers from Persia, and there was the usual assortment of sheep and chickens. The train took about twenty-four hours to reach Quetta. There was a kitchen car, but no corridor, so waiters would take your order at one stop and deliver it by walking along the platform from the kitchen car to where you were seated, at another stop. I ordered a plate of rice and chicken and was just tucking into this when a little old man on the seat in front of me, who was eyeing my food with interest, suddenly lunged forward and grabbed a handful from my plate! I said to him, 'My dear chap, if you're hungry you're welcome to share my lunch, but please use a spoon.' I handed him this eating implement and we polished off the food together. It was probably the only time in his life he had held a spoon.

A little while after crossing the border into West Pakistan (now Pakistan), customs officers descended on the train and began searching very thoroughly for contraband. They climbed on the roof and poked wires into the walls of the carriages. What if they found my gold coin? I reclined on my seat trying to look unconcerned, with the Union Jack on my rucksack prominently displayed; they ignored me. What they were looking for, it seemed, were undeclared goods like quantities of silk brought in from Persia, and a number of people were detained by the side of the track when the train eventually moved on.

I was relieved to arrive in Quetta where everything was just like England—breakfast with corn-flakes and milk, buttered toast and marmalade, and proper English tea!

Cars and trucks being more plentiful, I resumed hitch-hiking until I reached the town of Amritsar, with its famed Golden Temple. There I put up for the night and received a simple supper, courtesy of the temple guardians who have a tradition of providing food and shelter free of charge for travellers. Amritsar is the site of a notorious massacre by British troops in 1919 when India was under British colonial rule.

This was all charming but in the night I was suddenly smitten with the dreaded Delhi Belly—and I wasn't even anywhere near Delhi at that point. However, I was found prompt relief by taking a large dose of a drug, now withdrawn, called Entero-Vioform, following the advice of a fellow-traveller I had met on the road. The normal dose was two tablets if needed, but I took eight at a time. It was only later that I learnt this could have caused brain damage! This medicine, together with a quantity of flavoured milk one could buy everywhere, soon put me right.

Arriving in Delhi I made for the money changers to be found beside the historic Red Fort. After some haggling I managed to exchange my gold coin—for exactly five pounds! I had been duped about its value but at least didn't lose anything. The money-changers were disappointed I only had the one coin. In Delhi I was struck by another ailment: a form of conjunctivitis. This was intensely irritating but was immediately relieved by going inside an air-conditioned building. Eventually I found an eye specialist who cured the problem with eye drops. He didn't want to charge me but I insisted, since I could claim back the cost on my travel insurance.

In Delhi there were many street hustlers. Once I noticed several men squatting on the pavement who were manipulating an instrument into the ear of another person squatting beside them. Then it became clear. As I walked by I was accosted with, 'Ears clean, Sahib? Ears clean? No pain, no pain!' I fled.

From Delhi I decided to travel to Bombay by one of the famous steam trains on the Indian railway network, originally set up by the British. There were four classes: first, second, third, and air-conditioned, the last mentioned being as expensive, I was told, as travelling by air. When I arrived at the station it was chaotic with a great crowd of people waiting for the train. I made my way to the end of the platform where the third class carriage would stop. A porter came up to me and offered to assist me board the train for a small fee. I couldn't understand why I should need his help in that way, but when the train arrived I soon saw what he meant. It was packed with people, like sardines. There was no question of opening the door and entering the carriage in the normal way. The window of the door, however, was open and the porter used my rucksack as a battering ram to create a small space into which he then pushed me. I was glad to give him his rupee. Eventually, I found a space to sit on the washbasin in the lavatory but it was impossibly uncomfortable for a long journey, or even a short one.

After about half an hour we arrived at a station where the train made a scheduled longish stop. I went to get some breakfast at a restaurant fronting the platform. Then an Indian gentleman got into conversation with me. He was appalled to learn that I was travelling in the third-class carriage and, over my protests, insisted on paying the difference so that I could travel the rest of the journey in the second-class carriage. There I had a seat to myself. I later discovered that the third class was officially designated as 'unsuitable for Europeans'.

Another touching incident indicative of Indian people's great friendliness occurred when I wanted to buy a stamp at a post office to send a letter home. It was in the countryside and there was a queue of some dozen people ahead of me at the single window for postal services. I was drawn into conversation with some of the people nearby. When they heard I was English and furthermore came from London ('London proper?' they asked) they insisted, in spite of my embarrassment, that I should go to the head of the queue to buy a stamp!

On the return journey I travelled by bus via Peshawar and the Khyber Pass to Kabul. It would be suicidal to attempt that today, but then (1963) all was peaceful. There was one main place to eat that I recall in Kabul, called *Le Restaurant Khyber* which reminded me of a Lyons Corner House. All the way through Afghanistan I received unfailing courtesy and hospitality. The problem of hitching in a country with very few cars was solved by getting lifts on buses. This was organised by presenting myself at the main bus depot and explaining as best I could that I was an impecunious English student trying to make my way home. The bus people were very kind and gave me a hand-written pass allowing me to travel free of charge. I took the southern route via Kandahar and thence to Herat. The buses, which ran all night, were very crowded and uncomfortable; sometimes I would sit on the roof where at least there was some fresh air. From Herat I crossed the border into Persia and from the town of Mashhad travelled the rest of the way home by train.

I had been away four months and felt invigorated to start my new life as a medical student.

CHAPTER TWO

Medical School Experiences

I HAD NEVER seen a dead body before.

When I started my studies at Bart's I had to get down to the task of acquiring what seemed like a mountain of knowledge about normal human anatomy and physiology. We also studied pharmacology (the uses, effects, and actions of drugs) and had to pass examinations in these subjects before moving on to learn about diseases.

On the first day of the anatomy class we were allocated in small groups, each to one body for dissection. It was covered with a white waterproof sheet and lay on a table around which we gathered. The anatomy Demonstrator (tutor), a doctor who was studying for a higher qualification in surgery, sat with his crossed arms resting on the sheet over the head of the body. I thought this posture showed perhaps over-familiarity with corpses. But he then emphasised that the people who had donated their mortal remains for the edification of medical students were motivated by altruism and that we should show them proper respect in our demeanour and how we handled their tissues. This injunction helped to relieve any apprehension we may have felt about what would be revealed when the sheet was removed.

The body bore little resemblance in its external appearance to someone in the living state. The person had died about six months previously and the corpse was preserved with formalin. The colour of the skin was grey and the arteries and veins had been injected with a red and blue dye, respectively, to assist us in distinguishing them. I was assigned to a leg. We had all brought along a small textbook, *Cunningham's Manual of Practical Anatomy*, which thoughtfully had been issued with a waterproof cover. We were expected to use this while dissecting. I had at school acquired familiarity with dissection on frogs and a rabbit and these skills were useful in our task. Soon we were engrossed in this fascinating activity. We were instructed that the object was to acquire knowledge and understanding of the structure of the human body in three dimensions, and not just to 'prove the textbook is right'! In the following terms we dissected the arm, chest, abdomen, and lastly, the most difficult area, as you can imagine, the head and neck. Our studies were supplemented by working with the bones from a disarticulated skeleton—a real one, apparently sourced from India—as well as with lectures and *viva voce* (oral) examinations.

What I found disturbing, however, was that in a side room where we had to wrap and return to a box the separated arms or legs (by that time we had detached them from the rest of the body as we explored the intricate structures holding everything together), one or two boys—I have to call them boys rather than young men—were fooling around using a disarticulated leg as a pretend cricket bat! Not surprisingly, one of the culprits failed his preliminary examinations and did not go on to study medicine at the hospital. This experience cured me of any philanthropic idea I might have had, when the time comes, of leaving my own body for dissection.

One of the same boys, during an impromptu viva in the dissection room, was asked by the professor whether a certain spinal nerve tract was motor or sensory. He held a scalpel near the hapless student's groin and said he was going to castrate him if he got the answer wrong! Luckily for him, he guessed the right answer.

The professor—his name was A J E Cave—was a splendidly eccentric man, brilliant in his knowledge of the subject, who wore a skull cap and took snuff. His attitude to the female students would not be tolerated these days; he would pick on a pretty girl, look her up and down and sometimes make suggestive remarks. There was another professor of anatomy whom I remember,

O J Lewis. I think he was from New Zealand. He taught us embryology (the development of the foetus into a baby)—a branch of anatomy I found quite difficult. He was quiet spoken, and without any notes would start at the left hand side of the large blackboard at the front of the theatre, and with a series of coloured chalks would lecture and draw lucidly until the board was filled with wonderfully intricate but beautifully clear pictures. When everything was finished he would rub the blackboard clean!

Inspiring teachers

After passing the pre-clinical examinations, called Second MB, in anatomy, physiology, and pharmacology, we moved to the hospital itself where we learnt on real patients.

I was fortunate to be taught by an outstanding ophthalmologist, Dr M A Bedford, whose tutorials I attended in a group of half-a-dozen students. He would put up a slide showing a bloodshot eye, or one which was in some way obviously (or not so obviously) diseased or injured, and say: 'You're the GP in Budleigh Salterton[1] and a patient comes in with an eye looking like *this* (showing slide)—what are you going to do about it?' You had to think! And read up about it afterwards. Then sooner or later one would indeed see a patient with that very condition and have some idea of what to do. GPs are not meant to be able to treat everything themselves, of course, but one must be confident in one's ability to recognise what is within one's competence and what isn't, and know when to refer the patient to a specialist.

Another notable specialist by whom I had the privilege of being taught was the distinguished physician, Sir Anthony

---

[1] Budleigh Salterton is a picturesque small town in Devon on the south coast of England. It was mentioned by Dr Bedford as a typical out-of-the-way place without the assistance of a large hospital nearby.

Dawson. He later became physician to the Queen. Once in a busy out-patient clinic a nursing sister approached him for approval to admit a patient into the hospital. She said it was a 'social admission'. Sir Anthony duly gave his assent and then turned to the group of observing students, of which I was one, and said: 'There is *no difference* between medical and social admissions.' This was typical of the humanity of the man, and his view, as was perhaps more common in those days, that the patient must be considered as a whole person: his or her medical, social, and psychological needs are all equally important and deserving of the highest standards of concern and treatment.

It's rather different today. For a start, there's the common use of the neologism Healthcare, or worse, HealthCare. You can hardly get away from it. For example, there was a UK governmental organisation called the National Institute for Health and Clinical Excellence, which fitted rather awkwardly into the smug acronym NICE, and which is now known as the National Institute for Health and Care Excellence.

A lament over the dichotomy between health and care appeared in the *British Medical Journal* (BMJ) in August 2014.[2] In medical practice often the emphasis is on various activities to try to restore physical health by tests, prescriptions, operations, etc., and not enough on the 'care' part, the 'looking after' which, for example, an elderly and infirm person with various chronic (long persisting) ailments may need in his or her own home, or in a care home (there we go again), as if this is something distinct from the normal medical services offered to a sick person. If one allows such a word, the plea was to put the care back into healthcare.

Is such a dichotomy really needed and valid? It seems to have had its roots in a drive against a perceived elitism: in the old days there were doctors, assisted by nurses, who treated patients. Now we have healthcare professionals who, in partnership

[2] BMJ 2014;348:g4210

with patients, deliver interventions. Certainly, for Sir Anthony and those who trained under him, care was an inherent and inseparable part of medical treatment. So it should be still.

Another out-patient clinic that we attended as observers was in psychiatry. One patient's consultation in particular made a strong impression on me. He was a middle-aged man and had been allotted a whole hour for his first appointment. I was intrigued by the way in which the doctor—he was of the senior registrar grade—took the psychiatric history. With skilled and empathetic questioning, he obtained an overview of the man's life with his family and work situation, and his symptoms of anxiety: how they had started and varied over time, what made them better and what made them worse, and so on.

At the end of the session he prescribed Librium, an anti-anxiety drug that had recently become available; it was supposed to be an improvement on older drugs, such as barbiturates, which are no longer in use. Barbiturates were notorious for their addictive potential and soporific side-effects. It was said you can't feel anxious if you're half asleep!

The patient expressed his gratitude to the doctor, and departed clutching the prescription. We were then asked if we had any questions or comments. I spoke up and said I was impressed with the way the doctor had elicited the history so that we now had a complete picture of the man's life-situation and his problems. But, after all that effort, it seemed to me that merely to prescribe a pill was something of an anti-climax. Was there not, perhaps, more that could be done with the information so painstakingly obtained? The doctor agreed with me. He admitted that prescribing a pill was the only or best thing that could be done under the circumstances, but he also pointed out that he believed, and it was shown by the patient's demeanour and profuse thanks, that the fact he had taken the trouble to listen to him in a supportive and non-judgemental way, *of itself* probably had a therapeutic effect. I thought he was right and always remembered this, endeavouring to use a similar approach with my own patients after I qualified.

Final word after graduating

At a ceremony to mark our success in the final examinations, I remember the Dean of the medical school saying something along these lines: 'Now that you are being let loose on the public, we hope we have trained you to be good doctors. But at least we are fairly sure that you won't be *dangerous*.'

CHAPTER THREE
Eccentric Friend

I HAVE PROBABLY acquired the habit of 'collecting' eccentric people from my father.[3] He would talk to everybody, from the road sweeper to upper class friends, to gain material for his novels. He always carried a notebook with him and would write down memorable phrases from their talk—then some of it would appear in his novels.

When I was a medical student there was a man in the year above whom I got to know. I'll call him Evelyn. He didn't seem to have many other friends. This may have been because, in spite of being highly intelligent, he was socially inept. For example, on one occasion when we hadn't met for a while, he said, 'Hello Gabriel. Mmm, there was something I wanted to ask you…it wasn't anything important. Oh yes! By the way, how are you?' Then again, years later after an interval in which we had had no contact, he exhibited another solecism when we spoke on the phone: 'Have you *managed* to get married?' This was, no doubt, a projection of his own difficulties in marrying, of which more will be described later. (I didn't bother with him anymore after that.)

During one of the university holidays he wanted to take a tour of Yugoslavia in his car, and he asked me to go with him. Having no other plans, I thought this would be interesting and agreed to accompany him. We would share the driving and stay at camp sites. In the beginning all went well. We visited the picturesque towns of Dubrovnik and Mostar (with its famous bridge), among other places, and it was a pleasant way to spend a

---

[3] John Symonds (1914–2006) was a writer of novels, biographies, children's book, and plays. He was perhaps best known for his definitive biography of Aleister Crowley, the self-styled 'wickedest man in the world'.

holiday. That is to say, it was pleasant until an incident occurred which taught me something about human nature, and about Evelyn's nature in particular.

It was a warm sunny afternoon in Yugoslavia and we were cruising along with the top down of Evelyn's convertible car. He was driving when we stopped for two young girl hitch-hikers. They seemed to be in their late teens. It was a bit vague where they wanted to go, but it was in our direction so we took them along. One sat in the back with me and the other in the front. We had no language in common, but another, much older language provided all the communication we needed, and a pleasant flirtation developed in which they were very much willing participants.

As the time passed, and they seemed in no hurry to get out, the question arose of where we would spend the night. We were making for a camp site, and I was much looking forward to the two girls staying with us in our tent, if this was agreeable to them. However, it suddenly dawned on Evelyn that this was where things were heading—and at that point he panicked. And went into hysterics. I had never seen such behaviour before. He started shouting that he couldn't do this, it was a sin (he was active in the Christian Union). He was literally shaking with fear and almost in tears. The girls, up till then delightful company and trustful of us as English gentlemen, naturally became alarmed. I had to take over. There were two urgent tasks: calm Evelyn down, and reassure the girls. The only thing to do then, much to my regret, was let them out at a small town through which we were passing. A few years later I discovered the reason why he had such a fear of intimacy with women.

Shortly after I had qualified and was doing my general practice training, I heard that Evelyn had, indeed, managed to get married, and I was pleased to be invited to the wedding. Or rather, I was pleased to avail myself of the opportunities such an event might provide.

A certain woman had been jilted at the church door and,

being on the rebound (as the expression has it) was desperately in need of a replacement. By an unexpected change in her fortunes just at that unhappy time, she was introduced through mutual friends to Evelyn. He proposed and was accepted. The wedding took place shortly after at the chapel on his wealthy parents' estate in Surrey.

I drove there in my car, bringing a small gift. However, I had mistaken the time and arrived around noon instead of 2.00 pm as stated on the invitation. It was pouring with rain as I proceeded up the drive. A man carrying an umbrella came to meet me. He was Evelyn's younger brother. I introduced myself. Younger brother said, in his upper class drawl, 'Oew, you're rather too early. Please go away, and come back a bit before two o'clock and then yew can be an usher for the other guests.'

I turned around and drove to the local village pub. While I ate a ploughman's lunch, washed down with a half of bitter, I debated with myself whether I should never have anything more to do with that family, but opportunism got the better of me. I'm glad it did because at the reception I met the bride's younger sister with whom I subsequently had a pleasant, though brief, affair.

My feelings towards Evelyn and his family being thus mollified, we kept in touch. Then a few years later an incident occurred which reminded me of Édouard Manet's famous painting, *Le Déjeuner sur l'herbe*, in which two fully dressed men are having a picnic with a nude woman.

I was having tea one day with a male friend at my London flat when the doorbell rang. It was Evelyn come to call, self-invited and unexpected. I showed him into the sitting room, introduced him to my friend, and made another cup of tea. After exchanging a few pleasantries, Evelyn suddenly said, 'I think I'll just strip off.' Being used to his eccentricities, and my friend (a heterosexual) making no objection, we were then in the unusual situation of two fully dressed men drinking afternoon tea with another man being stark naked. A few minutes later there was a slight commotion—he had ejaculated. Realising what had happened, I passed him the box of tissues which was on the table, and suggested he visit the bathroom upstairs. He did so, and while he was out of the room, my fully dressed friend commented, 'He got a bit over-excited, that chap.'

On another occasion a few weeks later, I was invited to visit Evelyn at his parent's London home where he was staying by himself. We discussed medicine and other matters of mutual interest, and then he said what was by then boringly repetitive, 'I think I'll just strip off,' and forthwith proceeded to remove all his clothes. Then it came to the point: he wanted me to undress as well. I had to tell him, 'Look, Evelyn, please understand that I have no interest whatsoever in this kind of behaviour, but if, on the other hand, your wife was to join us, then maybe…'

Of course, he didn't want that, and was terrified his wife might find out about his homosexual leanings. He was disappointed, and I was glad to get away.

Nonetheless, from what I heard indirectly later on, it seemed he had a happy marriage.

CHAPTER FOUR
Studying in Japan

THE REASON I ended up for most of my professional life in Japan started when I was a medical student. For the paediatrics (children's diseases) part of the course, which lasted three months, the department in Bart's at that time was not large enough to cope with the whole intake—there were about a hundred of us—and we were encouraged to find a placement elsewhere, preferably overseas to broaden our outlook. A couple of my friends in the year above had had a great time at the Mildmay Mission Hospital in Uganda. They had gained considerable clinical experience (meaning they had seen a lot of very sick people) as well as having given much needed helping hands to the hospital in that part of the world. I thought I would like to do the same and wrote to apply. As it happened, the post to and from Uganda was not very efficient and, despairing of hearing from them, I looked elsewhere. Which was the most interesting country in the world? The one that came to mind was the mysterious (to me) far eastern country of Japan—the land of the geisha and samurai! That was about all I knew of the country at the time.

To get accepted for a three month attachment at a university hospital in Tokyo turned out to be surprisingly straightforward. I belonged to the International Federation of Medical Students' Associations, as it is known, through which I was put in contact with the Japanese chapter. Soon I received a courteous reply from a fellow student, Tadaaki Tokuda: they would be happy to have me at the paediatric department of the prestigious Jikei University School of Medicine in Tokyo. In addition, I was honoured to be offered the opportunity of living with his family as their guest, and I would be the first foreign medical student to be accepted on what would later become an exchange scheme. This was in 1967.

The problem was to fund the fare. It was just over twenty years after the end of the Second World War and there was little money to spare. However, I was lucky to receive an educational grant from the Foyle Foundation (of the famous Foyle's bookshop which used to be in London's Tottenham Court Road), and with this I managed to scrape together enough to travel to Japan via Siberia.

The journey, which would take a week, started from London's Victoria Station and was an adventure in itself. The train took me to first to Berlin. One had to pass through to the Soviet-controlled east part. I remember the high wire fence on both sides of the track, patrolled by soldiers with guns and dogs to prevent people escaping the workers' paradise.

Arriving at Moscow some thirty hours later, as soon as I stepped off the train, two men in raincoats approached. 'Come with us, please,' they said. It was just like a spy film. I did as I was bid. Outside the station was a small car like a Fiat 500. We drove to the airport about one hour away along an almost deserted highway. The next leg of the journey was by an Aeroflot plane for 6,000 km (3,730 miles) across Siberia. It was an old propeller-driven machine. There was a musty smell and various disconcerting rattles coming from the interior. After a few hours we arrived safely at the city of Khabarovsk. I was jet-lagged but there was an obligatory tour of the city sights. A guide showed us the sports stadium, a War Memorial, and, what was of much more interest to me, a fine natural history museum. Then at last we boarded a train for another day's journey to the port of Nakhodka, and thence twenty-four hours on a ferry to Yokohama.

At last I set foot in the land of the Rising Sun! My host, Tadaaki, with another young student, was waiting to meet me at the quayside. We had no difficulty recognising each other. We travelled in Tadaaki's father's car to central Tokyo. On the way I was asked if I wanted something to eat. Indeed I did, and was taken to a restaurant serving sushi—raw fish on cold rice! I did my best, having taught myself from a book how to use chopsticks. Later I came to enjoy sushi as a delicacy.

When we got near the centre of Tokyo in the mid-afternoon I noticed that you couldn't see the sun; the sky appeared as a yellowish-grey haze. This was because of industrial pollution which was very bad in those days. It really was true that policemen on point duty had an oxygen cylinder beside them to use when needed. Since that time, however, air pollution has steadily reduced and nowadays Tokyo is one of the cleanest large cities in the world.

I was welcomed as one of the family and enjoyed the experience of eating with them while sitting at a low table on the floor and using chopsticks. I also learnt the etiquette of the Japanese bath, the water for which was heated by a wood-burning stove. As the guest, I was invited to use the bath first. You had to wash yourself thoroughly outside the hot tub before getting into it for a pleasant soak. Then the family used the same hot water.

My ostensible reason for spending three months in Japan was to learn about paediatrics, and I certainly learnt a lot. My days were spent in much the same way as Japanese medical students, although I was excused having to attend lectures since at that time I was ignorant of the Japanese language. The main way I learnt was by attending ward rounds where interesting patients were discussed. The professor (equivalent to a consultant in the UK) and other medical staff nearly all spoke English and translated the gist of the presentations and discussions for me. Then I would read up about these patients in the hospital library—it was an extensive one with all the major English-language medical journals and textbooks.

I remember some of the patients to this day. On was a 4 year old boy with a persistent cough. The cause was confirmed and cure dramatically effected as I looked on in the endoscopy room. They didn't yet have the wonders of fibre optics to enable you to see around corners, but with the patient safely asleep under a general anaesthetic, an offending peanut which the child had inadvertently inhaled was removed through an instrument called a bronchoscope.

There were several patients with what is known as Wilson's disease—the department had a reputation for caring for them. Wilson's disease is a rare inherited disorder resulting in an excess of copper accumulating in the body, particularly in the liver and brain. There is a characteristic sign which can be seen in the eyes of such patients, the Kayser-Fleischer ring, and I was able to observe this with an instrument called a slit-lamp. If found early enough the disorder can be treated with a drug, penicillamine, to assist excretion of the excess copper, though one unfortunate young patient I saw had a severe skin reaction to it. Interesting though it was, I have never seen another case of Wilson's disease since that time.

Soon after I arrived in Tokyo I was introduced to Dr Komei Kumagai, a charming man ten years older than myself whom I shadowed in some of his medical work, and we became life-long friends. I attended some of the well-baby clinics that he conducted for the local health department. These were done rather more frequently than would happen in the UK. I was able to observe and learn the range of normal development of Japanese babies.

As well as the medical and study aspects there were many social events arranged in my honour: welcome parties, at which there was much jollification and consumption of alcohol, and a series of similar farewell parties when the time came near for my departure.

One heart warming aspect of my visit was the wonderful hospitality shown by everyone to me, including, and particularly, the head of the department, Professor Yoshiyuki Kokubun. For example, he had been engaged on a lecturing assignment in the city of Hiroshima, about five hours away on the famous Shinkansen (bullet train), and he invited me to accompany him. The city of Hiroshima has a well known tragic history. Professor Kokubun said to me, as we approached, 'Hiroshima is a very very silent city.' I had seen glimpses of the place from a moving film, a love story about a Frenchwoman and a Japanese man, *Hiroshima Mon Amour* (1959), in which there were flashbacks to scenes of the devastation after the atomic bomb catastrophe, and I remember in the film the striking upturned ends of the parapets of the Peace Bridge which are still in existence.

During the day when the professor was lecturing I explored the city, seeing the Memorial Peace Park and the museum. The city was indeed quiet and I remember thinking, 'My God, this is where the bomb exploded!' Some of the survivors were still suffering from the effects of radiation and I was privileged to meet one or two of them at a hospital which I visited with the Professor.

There was another side to my education on this trip, and that was being taken in the evenings to enjoy Japanese gourmet cooking. In one restaurant we had a private room attended by our own hostesses who assisted me in delicately picking the flesh of a fish from the bone with chopsticks. More experience of hostesses occurred in visits to night clubs—the sort of place a foreigner could not usually attend on his own—where interesting discussions occurred, accompanied by practical palpatory observations, on the difference in sizes of Japanese and western girls' breasts. I hasten to add it was all very good natured and the boundaries were well understood. I reflected that this kind of experience would never happen to a visiting foreign medical student in England!

Once, when travelling with Tadaaki and another student, we were sitting on a tram, and there was a woman opposite us quite unselfconsciously breastfeeding her baby. Tadaaki turned to me and asked, 'What do you think of the milking?' I thought this was very nicely put.

Among other noteworthy doctors at the Jikei University, one stands out: Professor Norimitsu Yoshikura, a leading Japanese paediatric neurologist of the time. I would sit in at his outpatients clinic, and he would explain to me in his fluent English about the patients we saw. I also attended his weekly tutorials with his junior staff at which we worked through a text called *Correlative Neuroanatomy* by Stephen G Waxman (now in its 28th edition). The material in the book, with its rather daunting title, was brought alive by Professor Yoshikura's enlightened guidance.

He was a doctor of what one would call the old school. In the days before MRI and CT scans, the history, clinical examination, and deductive processes required to reach a diagnosis were paramount, and in this perhaps most difficult field of medicine, neurology, Professor Yoshikura was a master. In addition to his impressive clinical skills and knowledge, he was a humane and kind doctor who, as much as he cared for his patients, inspired his students. Even though so much time has passed, I remember him well, with gratitude and affection.

CHAPTER FIVE

Junior Hospital Doctor

WHEN I QUALIFIED in 1968 the first step was to apply for provisional registration with the General Medical Council. This was granted automatically on passing the final examinations. You then had to do a year as a junior house officer, consisting of six months each in medicine and surgery.

My first post was in medicine at a large general hospital in the east end of London—a somewhat forbidding converted Victorian pile. It was a kind of baptism by fire. From being a medical student to having to take responsibility for fifty patients was a big step. There was a senior doctor whom I could ask for advice, but he wasn't around all the time, and the consultant had very little tolerance for error. The worst aspect of this job was chronic sleep deprivation. I worked a one-in-two rota. During the nights on call I would get very little, if any, sleep and hence the next day would be walking around in a bit of a daze.

One of the reasons for the disturbed nights was because I would be on what was called the crash team. This meant that if a patient suffered a cardiac arrest the nurses would send out a 'crash call' and the team would rush to wherever it was needed to attempt resuscitation. It was a dreadful business. I don't recall a single patient who survived under these circumstances. Not only that, but the winter of 1968 was very cold and many patients were admitted with severe respiratory problems only to die in hospital in spite of our best efforts. A redeeming feature, however, was a wonderful ward Sister from whom I learnt a lot about comforting bereaved relatives.

The consultant was unsympathetic. He was one of those 'In my day…' people: 'In my day I had 150 patients, and I had one day off a month,' he said. This was hardly encouraging, but somehow I stuck it out, and after three months or so had got used it. What saved me was the doctors' mess. There was a plentiful supply of Foster's Lager and a gramophone on which was played repeatedly the one record they had: the Beatles' *Get Back*. One could unwind and share one's problems with colleagues. Although not a fan of pop music this is the one Beatles' song that I have liked ever since.

The next post was in general surgery, in a smaller hospital, also in London's east end. By then I had got the hang of things so I enjoyed the work and learnt a lot about surgery. But there was one unpleasant incident. The resident junior doctors lived in bedsitters on the top floor, and there was a motherly lady called Eileen who kept house for us. There was one peculiarity about this arrangement, however. An Irish doctor near retirement, Dr Acheson, known as Achi, also lived there.[4] He had never become established in his career due to alcoholism, but was kept on as a long locum partly out of charity, it seemed, for the casualty (emergency) department. He had two lovely Irish Setters who lived with him, using a flat roof outside his room, accessible through the window, for their natural functions. I supposed Eileen cleaned it up from time to time. The problem was that at irregular though not infrequent intervals Achi would be too drunk to appear for his turn of duty in casualty. When this happened he would be asleep on the floor of his room with the dogs on the bed. Feeling sorry for him, one of us junior house officers would cover for him until he had sobered up. The problem with this arrangement was that on one occasion it showed an all too clear example of the Irish saying, 'I don't know why he hates me—I've never done him any favours!'

One evening I was on duty in the casualty department. All was going normally and I attended to the patients who came in from time to time. It was around 11.00 pm when Achi turned up, drunk. I mean, angry drunk. He seemed to think he was on duty

---

[4] I use his real name because he is now long deceased.

and that I had no business to be there. It was no use trying to reason with him and I refused to leave my post. He then he took a swing at me but fortunately missed. What was I to do? I took the only step I could think of and that was to call the police. They duly turned up. One of the officers said to Achi, 'I don't like arresting doctors, so please go to bed.' That calmed things down and he went away; but that wasn't the end of the matter. The story had got around and the next day I was summonsed to the hospital Secretary's office. Achi had been dismissed on the spot—I suspect the incident the previous night was merely the last straw in a series of complaints about him. But the reason the Secretary was upset was because in those days hospitals were run differently from the way they are now. He complained that I should have called *him*, not the police. 'It's *my* hospital,' he said, 'and *I* would have dealt with it.'

CHAPTER SIX

General Practice Training

IN THE 1970s general practice in the UK was evolving and new regulations were coming into force to try to ensure proper standards. When I qualified in 1968 one could go straight into general practice after doing the basic house jobs as a junior doctor, without any further required experience. In my case I had obtained the two degrees needed to qualify: Bachelor of Medicine and Bachelor of Surgery (MB, BS).

These qualification and the minimal mandatory hospital experience needed in order to be fully registered with the General Medical Council do not equip one to work in general practice—one needs to know considerably more than that.

The areas of medical practice that a well-rounded GP should know something about are adult general (internal) medicine, surgical diagnosis, minor surgery, dermatology, ophthalmology, otorhinolaryngology, paediatrics, obstetrics, gynaecology, psychiatry, orthopaedics, rheumatology, neurology, venereology, and geriatrics—the list is not exhaustive.

So I set about educating myself, and was accepted for one of the first UK general practice training schemes. It was voluntary in those days and was based in a provincial town some 65 km (40 miles) from London. The syllabus was flexible so I could choose the specialities I felt would be most useful to me. These were paediatrics, psychiatry, and obstetrics which were resident appointments at the senior house officer grade; and attending out-patient clinics in dermatology, ophthalmology, and ENT (ear, nose, and throat disorders).

The out-patient clinics were similar to when I was a student: sitting in as an observer in a clinic, say, in dermatology, where a succession of patients who had been referred by their GPs with a variety of disorders in the relevant speciality would turn up, one after the other, and be seen by an expert, the consultant. It was a wonderful learning experience. I would afterwards go and read up about the cases I had seen.

After the hospital part the scheme was supposed to include a year as a trainee in a local group general practice. This was useful as far as it went, but the scheme collapsed a few months after I started because the trainer left at short notice to accept a scholarship in the US in some medical-related field. The other two partners were not designated trainers and I decided it wasn't worth staying on. However, the time that I did spend with the trainer was certainly useful, but I thought a full year would have been excessive. This is because the art of general practice is something one can only learn by experience.

Emergency!

Part of the training scheme involved visiting the local cottage maternity hospital. Having just completed six months in obstetrics I was familiar with the problems that might arise during pregnancy and labour. The hospital was staffed by midwives but it had no operating theatre or resident doctors and was thus only suitable for women to give birth who were deemed to be 'low risk'.

Soon after I arrived on a routine visit on a sunny spring morning, I was summonsed urgently to the labour room. There was a woman in the middle of labour and the midwife was alarmed to see a prolapsed cord! This meant a loop of the umbilical cord had come down through the cervix (opening of the womb) in advance of the baby's head. As the cervix was only partially dilated the normal course of labour could not be awaited because the baby's head was compressing the cord, cutting off its oxygen supply. This is a rare complication of an otherwise normal labour but it is an obstetric emergency. The only way to save the baby under these circumstances is by a prompt Caesarean operation.

This couldn't be done in the cottage hospital and the district general hospital was twenty minutes away by ambulance—but the baby would be stillborn if nothing was done. The emergency procedure is gently but firmly to push the baby's head back into the womb to relieve pressure on the cord. Being young and fit it fell to my lot to travel in the ambulance with two fingers in the woman's vagina to hold up the baby's head. This was not easy as I couldn't relax the pressure for a moment, and it was particularly difficult as the woman was having contractions. Somehow, she and I were manoeuvred into the ambulance and then with blue lights flashing and the siren blaring we drove to the main hospital where they were waiting for us. We went straight into the operating theatre. The woman was anaesthetised and an emergency Caesarean operation performed. By that time I had lost all sensation in my hand.

The story had a happy ending with both mother and baby being safe and well. And my hand recovered.

Terrible training practice

I spent some fourteen years working in London, mainly in general practice, but the story of my 'training' continued.

Around the time that I was offered a place at a clinic in Tokyo, under then new regulations promulgated by the Royal College of General Practitioners, to work as an NHS GP one needed a Certificate of Equivalent Experience issued by the Joint Committee on Postgraduate Training for General Practice, as the august body styled itself. (It became defunct in 2005.)

By then I had gained considerable experience working as a locum and I considered myself competent. But the Committee in its wisdom determined nonetheless that I needed to undergo six months as a trainee in a recognised training practice. Being unsure of what the future might hold, I decided to do this training before I went off to Japan. I therefore applied for and was accepted by a so-called training practice not too far from where I lived.

It was in an insalubrious part of London with which I was familiar from my time at the grammar school where I received my secondary education, in Islington. The practice was run from a main surgery in a converted house, and from a branch surgery about 1.2 km (¾ mile) away. There were four partners and one other trainee. The following is a diary entry I made about my first day there:

> Turned up at the group practice where I was going to start my six months traineeship at 10.30 as requested. Introduced myself, and straightaway was asked by the other trainee, an attractive young woman, if I would like to sit in with her. I said I would but the practice manager interrupted to say that Dr— (the 'trainer') was coming in early for me to sit in with him, so I had better wait. I hung around for twenty minutes and he arrived. For over an hour I sat in with him and saw some ten or so patients. This was very boring for me, as I have been doing this work for years. The consultations consisted mainly of prescribing antibiotics for patients with obvious viral infections. Dr— seemed to know the patients well but didn't talk to them much, though his manner was friendly enough. For instance, he never explained to the patients how to take the medicines he prescribed, e.g., 'Take this three times a day,' but just gave the prescription. Every consultation ended in the giving of a prescription. His desk was so crowded with papers that there was hardly any space to write. Eventually he said that we should change places. This made me feel slightly nervous. I saw two patients: a baby with a sore mouth which was probably nothing but the parents' anxiety over teething, but I prescribed Nystan suspension in case it was 'thrush' and as the easiest way of dealing with the consultation; and an elderly lady with a runny nose who also got a prescription. Then Dr— said we should consult on our own, and I think he only wanted to observe

me for a token couple of patients so he could say he had done it. I went into a room on the other side of the corridor and saw two more patients, one with back pain whose back I manipulated, and a boy with dandruff of his eyelashes. Then the other trainee suddenly came into the room, not realising it was occupied. She immediately started telling me all that was wrong with the practice—badly organised, notes (patient records) in a terrible state, being worked too hard, etc. We didn't have enough time to talk and she invited me to tea at the weekend to tell me more. I was anxious to leave promptly as it was a half-day. It was already 1.00 pm, but Dr— wanted me to do two home visits. One was at a pub, difficult to find, and I saw a woman aged 60 who could easily have come to the surgery. Dr— had already seen her once on a visit. She had a long-standing mildly swollen leg. I thought this was due to circulatory impairment and prescribed elastic stockings—she should have been given these before. The next visit was a nightmare to find, in a council estate, with no names on the buildings and the flats numbered apparently in random order. It took me a good twenty minutes to find. It the end, it was a patient who only felt mildly unwell with the beginning of the flu. A visit, again, was unnecessary, and I started my half-day at 2.00 pm.

When I had completed my six months' stint in this place I found it necessary to write a report and complaint to send to the Joint Committee. This is a condensed version:

There is no doubt that from the beginning I worked in the capacity of a locum tenens, carrying a full share of the workload. I would see on average eighteen patients per nominal 1½ hour session—five minutes per patient! Extra, late requests for visits were often passed to me. There were no appointments so patients took pot-luck as to whom they saw. A frequently overheard conversation at the reception hatch was as follows:

Receptionist: Which doctor would you like to see?
Patient: Who's on tonight then?
Receptionist: Dr A, Dr B, Dr C.
Patient: Oh, well, just put me down for the one with the shortest wait.

In many cases no one seemed to be in overall charge of the patients. A pile of cards of patients I had never seen would often be handed to me by a receptionist or nurse with the expectation that I would simply sign further prescriptions for them. I always felt under pressure to get through the patients as quickly as possible. Therefore, in order to be able to finish a surgery within a reasonable time I was often forced to cut corners. This I found professionally unsatisfying and even soul-destroying.

The patients' records were chaotic. Typically, letters were folded twice and stuffed at random into the envelopes. The handwriting of Dr— (my trainer) was almost completely illegible. The records were frequently missing. All the consulting rooms were untidy and ill-equipped. Essentials like pathology forms, notepaper, and envelopes were often hard to find and were not kept stocked up. The examination couches were old and rickety and the back-rests could not safely be pulled up. There was no running hot water. The nurses' treatment room was, literally, a cupboard. No doctors' meetings took place.

The 'patient-call' system could only be described as ludicrous. There was no intercom, buzzer, or light, and the internal telephone might take minutes to be answered. This meant that unless the receptionist happened to notice your last patient go out, and usually she did not, one would be left incommunicado and twiddling ones thumbs. It was therefore necessary after seeing every patient to plod down the corridor and ask the receptionist to call the next patient. Likewise, additional trips were frequently needed if the patient was sent in without any notes, or with the wrong notes, or to go in search of stationery or pathology forms. This walking exercise was not needed, however, if one happened to be working in the room next to the reception area. Here, the recognised signal that one was ready for the next patient was a blow with the fist upon the wall! Reception duties were also regularly performed by the cleaning lady, who, it must be said, was very efficient.

Contrary to the general requirement that training practices should work to a high standard, in my opinion, the standard at Dr—'s practice was poor.

My six months' work in this practice was a good deal for them because my salary was paid by the local authority and the practice received additional payment for 'training' me! When my time was up I needed to get Dr—'s signature on a form attesting to my satisfactory performance. But would he sign? No. Why not? He refused to tell me. What was I to do?

My first port of call was the British Medical Association (BMA). This is the doctors' trade union. I had been a member since my student days. Surely they would be able to help me? It was a like a joke: I was told there was nothing they could do. Could they not at least have offered to write to Dr— and request an explanation for his refusal to sign the form? No, they couldn't.

The caring attitude of the BMA was also shown when I decided not to renew my membership; there was no point since I had left the UK. But by that time I had been a member for some twenty years. Would there have been, perhaps, a personal letter from the Chairman expressing his concern and enquiring if I was in any way dissatisfied with the services they provided? No. I merely received one standard letter warning me that my membership would be terminated unless I paid the dues forthwith.

Two years later, probably as a result of the original complaint I had made, I did receive my Certificate of Equivalent Experience from the Joint Committee on Postgraduate Training for General Practice. I must admit that after all the trouble I had been to in order to be granted this recognition, I had the certificate framed and hung it up for a while on the wall of the lavatory of my apartment, with a noticed affixed saying, 'For emergency paper, break glass'.

CHAPTER SEVEN
London Locum Life

HAVING RECENTLY COMPLETED my general practice training, or as much of it as was possible under the circumstances, I looked around for a practice partnership to which I could apply to join. There was one where I had an informal introductory chat with a doctor who was much senior to me. He told me, 'General practice is all about cheering the patients up.' Being inexperienced I had grand ideas about practising 'scientific' medicine and thought such a statement dubious. For various reasons I did not proceed in applying for that particular vacancy, but I soon realised he was right. This idea helped me to deal with a large number of patients who attend GPs who are not ill in the sense of suffering from a diagnosable illness, but are seeking reassurance—'the worried well'.

Sometimes the need for reassurance, however, did seem rather far-fetched. In one of the better practices where I worked, the following conversation was related to me by the receptionist about a patient who had called at the last minute on a Friday evening. The patient wished to be seen straightaway because she had a sore throat. The receptionist said, 'We're just going to close. Can't it wait till tomorrow morning?' The patient replied, 'No, it will have recovered by then.'

There were not many partnership openings available in the 1970s, at least in London where I wished to be. So while I looked around for a practice I had to content myself with working as a locum tenens, or locum, as we would say. Locum tenens is Latin for place holding. One could easily find this kind of work. The BMA had a bureau to which a phone call would usually produce the names and phone numbers of two or three practices in need of a doctor to provide cover while the usual doctor was away. This might be for one session, a few days, a week, a month, or even longer. The pay was good, though one had to provide one's own car and pay for petrol as there were almost always home visits to do as well as the clinic sessions. I also had to provide my own doctor's bag for these visits, containing stethoscope, blood pressure machine, torch, patella hammer, etc., and emergency drugs.

Thus, while I was looking for a permanent position, I gained experience in working as a locum in many different kinds of NHS practices, and in a few private practices. These varied from the excellent to the unmentionable.

One surgery (the word is used for the premises as well as the session itself) was a shed with a corrugated iron roof at the side of the doctor's house; not very suitable or comfortable! At another, in the east end of London, I was shown the surgery and noticed it was very untidy with many drugs samples lying around from visits from drug salespeople. But one thing was missing: an examination couch. I asked the receptionist where the couch was to be found. She didn't understand me. I tried to explain: 'You know, where do I examine the patients?' She replied, 'Oh, doctor never examines the patients. If he thinks there's anything wrong with 'em he sends 'em round the 'orspital!'

At a group practice in a lower middle class area of west London I was engaged to cover for two weeks. Two other doctors were working there including the senior partner. The usual arrangement was that you would see walk-in patients (there were no appointments) during the morning session, and then take your share of the requests for home visits—it was called 'doing the rounds'. In this practice as soon as I arrived on my first day I was told there was an urgent call to a family where someone had suddenly died, probably from a heart attack. Being relatively new to the job I was somewhat apprehensive as I drove round with my little black doctor's bag to the address. The place was in chaos. No one knew me and I had never seen anyone in the family before. The phone was ringing constantly, relatives and friends were arriving, and an ambulance had been called. I was pretty much ignored. The only thing I could think of doing was to offer a sedative injection to the wife who was in a state of shock and unable to speak. I hung around for while and then just went away, feeling not only useless but as if I was an intruder on the family's distress and grief. Why didn't the senior partner go himself? This was an obvious situation that should not have been left to the locum to deal with on his first day. (A similar situation occurred in Tokyo some years later.)

In the same practice on another day a mother brought an 8 year old boy with a swelling of his penis, under the foreskin. I thought it was harmless and advised accordingly. This is a not uncommon condition due to a collection of smegma that can be felt and seen as a mobile lump. It requires no treatment. Maybe, due to lack of experience, I didn't explain this convincingly to the mother. Two days later she came back. It was obvious there was trouble by the look on her face and the fact she was smoking a cigarette. This was to calm her nerves for the imminent confrontation. I knew better than to argue with her or to ask her to put out her cigarette. She said, 'You told me there was nothing wrong with him—and look where he ended up!', throwing onto my desk a card showing the child's attendance at the casualty department of the local hospital. They had done an 'emergency' circumcision. The mother wanted an apology from me for allegedly missing the diagnosis that the hospital made. Taking the line of least resistance, she got her apology. The alternative would have been to have pursued the matter with the hospital to find out why they had needlessly operated on the child.

In some rough parts of London where I worked as a locum, one was advised when doing home visits not to look like a doctor. So I would go wearing casual clothes and take essential equipment—torch, stethoscope, pen, and prescription pad—in my pockets rather than in the traditional black bag.

My experience of general practice in London was in the days before computers. Records were kept in what were called Lloyd George envelopes, named after the Liberal politician who was instrumental in introducing socialised medicine in Britain. They contained cards about 13 x 18 cm (5 x 7 inches) where one could write the clinical notes. Often the entry consisted of only two words, apart from the date: a symptom and a drug. For example: 'Tonsillitis—penicillin', or 'Cough—Gee's linctus'. The envelopes would be often be stuffed in random order with other records, such as letters from hospital specialists, blood test results, and miscellaneous paperwork.

If a patient was a frequent attender the envelopes would contain more records, and vice-versa. Some people were *very* frequent attenders, and they would be known, rather unfairly I thought, as 'fat envelope' patients or, even more unfairly, as 'heartsink' patients. This meant the doctor's heart would sink when old Mrs Jones turned up yet again with another undiagnosable complaint, often presented in such words as, 'Doctor, I feel all anyhow!' She had already been sent to innumerable specialists who had been unable to find anything seriously the matter. Such patients' disorders are also known as 'functional'. This is supposed to mean that though their complaints have a physical basis they are not due to any detectable disease. For example, someone might be worried about their heart because they could feel it beating in their chest and hear it when they put their head on the pillow at night, and be worried they had heart disease; even exhaustive investigations would fail to reassure them.

I liked so-called heartsink patients. It was a challenge. There must be *something* wrong with them, or maybe they just needed a sympathetic ear for loneliness or family discord. This is where the 'cheering up' came in—and how important it was! I enjoyed going through some of these fat envelopes and 'weeding' them, as we said: discarding out-of-date paperwork, and then trying to focus on what the real problems were. Often, such patients were taking a multiplicity of medicines—polypharmacy, as we say.

One had to be careful about discontinuing too many medicines too quickly, because patients sometimes had a psychological dependence on the pills: it gave them a reason to keep coming back to the doctor. Indeed, to avoid getting oneself into an invidious position while working in someone else's practice, I soon learnt the first rule of locum tenens: unless it is actually killing the patient, don't change the treatment!

Working for London Transport

While trying to decide what to do with the rest of my life I worked for about three months for London Transport. This was not, as you might imagine, driving a bus, but in the medical department to examine staff applicants. It was very interesting and I had a free pass on London buses and the tube (subway), as well as subsidised travel on British Rail.

Most of the recruits for bus crews, tube train drivers, and guards were fit working-class men and women. I got on well with boys from that kind of background at the school I attended. They looked you in the eye—and no bullshit. For most of the applicants it was straightforward and they passed the medical assessment without difficulty. One had to be careful, however, since public safety was involved.

One man applied to be a bus driver. The only matter of note in his medical history was that he had been treated for lung cancer and was in remission since five years. Surely it would be all right for him to drive a bus? Actually, no. It is a rare possibility that someone in this situation might have a recurrence years later; the cancer might spread to the brain and show itself by an epileptic fit; this might be a disaster in a bus driver, and he had to be turned down. One could imagine, in this very unlikely event, that his recruitment records would be scrutinised and London Transport wouldn't have a leg to stand on, having knowingly taken such a risk.

I tried to be fair, of course. There was a poor middle-aged

lady who seemed down on her luck. She wanted to work in the staff canteen but had filthy finger nails. I was obliged to reject her, but added that if she cared to reapply with clean hands and nails she would be sympathetically reconsidered.

The medical part was the last in the line of various stages of the application process. Once, just before a would-be tube train guard came in to see me, someone who had interviewed him sent me a message: they weren't quite happy about him but couldn't exactly say why. He just didn't feel right, and could I find some reason for failing him on medical grounds?

A young man, quite presentable on the outside, came in and sat down by my desk. I needed to check his heart and take his blood pressure so I asked him to remove his shirt. He did so. Then I asked him to put his shirt straight back on, and explained that London Transport was unable to employ him. He had needle marks at the front of both elbows and was obviously an injecting drug user. 'But I've stopped,' he protested. 'I'm sorry, but those are the rules,' I said. Train guards may need to act as emergency drivers and obviously this would be an impossible situation.

Another applicant was interesting. This was in the 1970s and attitudes were not so flexible as now. A man who was in the process of changing into a woman applied to be a bus driver. He had already been working as a driver with a provincial bus company. In those days, if one could show that one had been living successfully in the role of the desired other sex for two years, such a person could be considered for a sex-change operation on the NHS. He was smartly dressed as a woman and showed female mannerisms; but he was obviously a man. I asked a senior colleague about this unusual situation and was advised to clear it with the legal department. The legal department found no problem in principle but did raise a cautionary note that it should be clarified in advance which lavatory he would use. The application went ahead and in due course he was employed driving a bus from the Chalk Farm depot in north west London. So all should have been well? Actually, it wasn't.

This was because there were some husband and wife teams working the buses as driver and conductor, respectively. As might have been anticipated, he wanted to use the ladies' lavatory. But then there was threat of strike action. One of the drivers was reported as saying, 'If that bloke goes into the ladies' while my missus is in there, I'll belt him one!' The man who wanted to be a woman had to be let go.

Two long locums

I had a taste of how being a partner in general practice would be by doing two locums for a year each.

One was in the Notting Hill area of London, a colourful working class district now famous for its annual street festival. The practice where I was engaged was in a converted shop. Next door on one side was a Turkish restaurant, and on the other, a betting shop. I became the doctor to a small community and found it very interesting. The practice was owned by a certain Dr Mean who was never to be seen there; the practice was run entirely by locums.

Dr Mean worked in partnership with a Dr Mustard who had an NHS practice in a more up-market part of west London. As I discovered later, he spent little time there, the practice likewise being run mainly by a succession of locums.

The Notting Hill practice comprised a waiting room, consulting room, and a little cubicle adjacent to the consulting room where the records were kept. There was a pleasant lady receptionist called Susan. She didn't have much to do for me except hand me the records of the patients as they came in—there were no appointments. But the phone was ringing constantly and was answered by Susan.

I didn't take much notice of this at first but then started wondering about it. Who were the people calling all the time?

Eventually, curiosity got the better of me and I asked Susan what was going on. She told me that the phone calls were from patients of Drs Mean and Mustard who wanted to make appointments. She wrote the appointments in a book. But where were the patients seen? In Harley Street!5 But these 'private' patients were registered at the NHS Notting Hill or west London practices. The point of this arrangement was that these patients could receive private paid-for appointments in more pleasant surroundings and yet get their medicines on NHS prescriptions. This is—how shall I say it?—not quite in accordance with the rules. At least Susan was sympathetic to my situation as a keen young doctor working in such a place and she encouraged me in my desire to seek a more satisfying career. 'You're worthy of something better, Gabriel,' she said. I'll always be grateful to her for that.

Inevitably, I fell out with Drs Mean and Mustard. They expected me on occasion to visit their private patients at home and issue NHS prescriptions to them—and they weren't willing to pay me any extra for rushing around in this way! I wasn't very happy about it. These two doctors, who had a passing resemblance to Laurel and Hardy, one being very fat and the other tall and thin, were paid for running NHS practices, the income from which must have easily covered the cost of employing locums. A nice little earner for them!

Another, much better practice, was in the St John's Wood area near the Abbey Road pedestrian crossing of the Beatles fame. It was the same deal: a converted shop just off the main road, but the practice was run to a proper standard. The senior partner had just retired and the remaining partner was a very pleasant man and a good doctor with a higher qualification, Membership of the Royal College of Physicians. He was Dr Henry Garfinkel

---

5 Harley Street is in a fashionable area of west London where private doctors traditionally have their practices.

(his real name), and he worked from a large office in the back of the building, while I had a small coffin-shaped room adjacent to the street. At one point he did me the honour of asking me to join the practice. Maybe I should have accepted, but at that time I just couldn't see myself working there for the rest of my professional life, so I declined. If I had joined him in a partnership, it would have been known as that of Drs Garfinkel and Symonds. For some reason that I have never been able to understand, people used to find the juxtaposition of our names amusing.

.

PART TWO

The Art of General Practice

CHAPTER EIGHT
Introduction

IN GENERAL PRACTICE most of the patients one sees have minor medical problems which can competently be dealt with by the GP himself or herself. Then there are, as mentioned above, a fair number of the 'worried well'—those who fear disease but in whom no disease is present as far as it's possible to tell. And there is a minority who have or might have a serious problem that needs specialist attention or hospital referral.

Usually it's not difficult to decide in which category a person attending a GP's surgery belongs, but one has to be careful. Reassurance is fine if one is reasonably certain no serious disorder exists, although in practice one can never be absolutely certain. This is why medicine is called an inexact science.

One important feature of general practice is that one can get to know the patients including their family relationships, home circumstances, and medical histories. But what about patients one sees for the first time, such as when visiting a hotel guest who may be staying only a short while? Here it is more difficult. The patient can tell you their medical history, but the diagnostic equipment in a doctor's bag is necessarily limited. I carry a stethoscope, an auriscope (for examining the ear-drum, especially in children), torch, patella hammer (for testing reflexes), and a blood pressure measuring instrument. Some doctors also carry an ECG machine but I find the times when I might need it do not justify the expense and trouble of keeping it in my car. If a patient needs an ECG they can be seen the next day at the clinic or they may need urgent hospital referral anyway.

Therefore one has to rely on clinical judgement. The decision that has to be made on a home or hotel visit is whether the patient has a simple problem for which reassurance and the medicines I carry with me will suffice, or can it wait till he or she attends my clinic the next day? Or does the patient need immediate transfer to hospital by ambulance? Not everybody can be sent to hospital 'just in case', but it's best to err on the side of caution. The one thing to avoid at all costs is a hotel death; hotels don't like this. It upsets the other guests and is bad for business. There is, however, always a service lift (elevator) where people on stretchers, alive or dead, can be taken to a waiting ambulance. The following case in which I was involved in Tokyo illustrates this point.

Heart failure

I was asked to visit a hotel late one evening to see a man in his sixties because of a cough. He was a UN Ambassador from a Southeast Asian country and was passing through Tokyo. There was no history of heart problems. I found him sitting up in bed, slightly breathless. On listening to his chest I could hear what are called crepitations at the bases of his lungs. His ankles were slightly swollen but apparently had been so for some time. What to do? I had a gut feeling his condition was potentially serious— medical instinct, one might say—and advised hospital admission. An ambulance was called which took him to a hospital where I had arranged for him to be accepted.

The next day I called the hospital to enquire about the patient's condition. Unhappily, I was informed that he had been admitted to the intensive care unit with heart failure but had died in the night. This was sad news, but under the circumstances I was glad to have made the right decision to have him admitted straightaway.

Listen to your patient

In medical practice the normal way to assess a patient's problem or problems is through the time-honoured method of the medical history, followed by a physical examination, supplemented if necessary by blood tests, X-rays, scans, etc.

Sometimes doctors don't pay enough attention to the history or examination and resort too readily to tests. An egregious example of how patients can be ill-served by proceeding in this way is shown in a scholarly paper I came across in a specialised medical journal with the splendidly succinct one-word name, *Gut*.[6]

This paper gives an account of a Swiss bagpipe player with a persistent cough. The patient, a man of 34, noticed that his cough was worse on the days when he played the bagpipes and the following morning. Could there have been a connection? This question, it seems, was only considered when all other possibilities had been excluded by exhaustive and, to the patient, no doubt exhausting, investigations.

You need to be fit to play the bagpipes; it requires considerable physical effort. Now, even if you know nothing about this wondrous instrument, these days it's easy to learn what is involved, for example from YouTube. Also, doctors should keep in mind the aphorism of the great nineteenth century Canadian physician, Sir William Osler: 'Listen to your patient; he is telling you the diagnosis.'

The piper with his troublesome cough attended a Swiss hospital, and what happened? He was investigated and, when no cause for the cough was found, was investigated some more. In fact he had every conceivable type of investigation for a cough. Although one should be thorough in order not to miss a serious disorder, but as some tests are uncomfortable, time-consuming, and even hazardous, they should be used with discretion.

The patient was subjected to tests for allergies as well as for bacterial and fungal infections. He was also tested for asthma by the inhalation of methacholine (a drug that constricts the bronchial tubes) from a nebuliser and checking his lung function before and after. Methacholine may cause serious side-effects such as severe bronchoconstriction. Routinely he had X-rays

---

[6] *Gut*, December 2017. Doi 10.1136/gutjnl-2017-315420

and a CT scan, which were normal. These, however, did him potential harm by exposing him—unnecessarily as it turned out—to a not insignificant dose of radiation. Then he underwent bronchoscopy and broncheo-alveolar lavage ('washing out of the lungs') and a biopsy was taken of the lining of a bronchial tube. This required sedation and using a local anaesthetic in the throat and upper part of the airway. I wouldn't care to have this done to myself unless I could be persuaded there was a very good reason for it. The cells obtained from the 'washings' and the biopsy were examined for evidence of immunological and inflammatory disorders, and cancer, respectively. All these results were negative (normal).

Since a diagnosis has not been reached, empirical (trial and error) treatment was prescribed. First, he was treated for asthma (in spite of the negative methacholine test) with a combined steroid and bronchodilator inhaler. No good. Then, a drug to reduce acid production in the stomach, known as a proton pump inhibitor, was administered by mouth for eight weeks. No change. Now what?

Finally, the penny dropped. Maybe it was something to do with playing the bagpipes! But for some reason they felt they had to prove this before acting on it. The poor piper had to endure what is called oesophageal manometry—measuring the pressure in his oesophagus (gullet) with a tube passed through the nose down into the stomach—while he was playing the pipes at the same time. Again, this is not a test I would care to have done to myself. But there was the answer! During playing the pressures he generated in his abdomen were so high that they caused some of the acid contents of his stomach to be forced up to the throat (reflux) where some would spill into the windpipe, causing the cough.

The treatment was to prescribe softer reeds for the pipes and a smaller bag so that he could keep it inflated with lower pressures. This resulted in cure. But it should have been obvious from the start if only they had remembered Osler's dictum and listened to their patient. He could have been spared all those unpleasant investigations and avoided taking useless treatment for weeks on end.

CHAPTER NINE

Doctors and Drugs

PHARMACEUTICAL COMPANY SALES representatives are known in Britain as 'drug reps', or simply as 'reps'. In America they are called detail men.

After a long session seeing patients in general practice, and for no good reason this is sometimes called 'the front line' or even 'the coal face' (!), it can make a pleasant break to see reps. Often I would find one or two in the waiting room or they came by appointment. They were always smartly dressed and behaved politely and respectfully like the good salespeople they were. And they came bearing gifts: drug samples and useful items of desktop clutter such as pens, calendars, or even clocks and calculators. These were always emblazoned with the company's logo and names of their drugs. Reps were usually intelligent people and one could have an interesting conversation with them. Naturally, they were trained to flatter you by asking, 'Doctor, how would you treat X disease?' Then you could show off your knowledge and they would tactfully suggest that you try drug Z instead of your usual treatment with drug Y. One might think one wouldn't be influenced by this sort of thing but of course one is—at least to the extent that the name of the drug is in your mind when a patient with a relevant condition sits down in front of you, so you might well end up prescribing it.

When I was at school one of my contemporaries determined to leave at the earliest opportunity, when he was 16, so he could get a job and earn money to buy himself a motor scooter. He said he needed this to increase his chances of picking up girls at the Hammersmith *Palais de Dance*. I bumped into him some years later when I was doing my first hospital house job and he was working for a multinational pharmaceutical firm. He had come to tell me about a new drug his firm was marketing, and

I remember feeling mildly envious that he was clearly earning much more money than I at that stage of my career.

In the practices where I worked doing locums there were usually samples of prescription drugs lying around. What was one supposed to do with them? It seemed you were meant to use them as starter packs when a patient with an appropriate disorder turned up, and issue a prescription for the same drug so the patient could complete the course with the requisite number of pills obtained from the chemist.

In one practice where I worked these samples had been collected into plastic bags. The doctor for whom I was then working told me, 'If you take them round to the local chemist's you can exchange them for the equivalent value in lavatory paper or toiletries.' I tried it with the friendly neighbourhood pharmacist and—it worked! The pharmacist took this in his stride. Soon I was overflowing with lavatory paper. Then he suggested he could give me cash instead if I wished. This sounded agreeable so I started collecting more samples.

It soon got around that Dr Symonds was rep-friendly. I would listen politely to their spiel and then ask if they had any samples, or they offered me some anyway and were usually glad to give as many as I wanted. The important thing was to wait, after they had left the room, until they were out of earshot before the sound of the glossy brochures they had given me could be heard thudding into the wastepaper basket—which was where I would usually consign them. What I obtained in exchange from the chemist—I trust he made an allowance for his own profit—was a small fortune.

Yes, I did have a twinge of conscience over doing this. But it was nothing compared to the way in which a few notorious doctors gamed the system over the matter of drug company freebies in the form of lunches and dinners.

These are supposed to be educational, which they may well be, but obviously they're really a marketing opportunity for pharmaceutical companies. We called them 'drug lunches'. There was usually an educational film—I recall one on heart failure—and it would be discretely mentioned at the end of the film that their new drug was safe and effective for treating this condition.

One such drug lunch I attended at an early stage of my general practice career was held at an up-market pub called Jack Straw's Castle at the entrance to Hampstead Heath, an affluent area of north west London. There were some fifteen or twenty hungry doctors—I mean, participants. A film was duly shown, and at the end of it the presenter asked if there were any questions. Silence. He tried again: 'Surely, someone must have a question about the interesting matter shown in the film?' Nobody spoke up. 'Oh well, then I suppose we might as well have lunch.' As soon as he said the word there was what I can only describe as a stampede—to the buffet table! It was as if those poor doctors hadn't eaten for a week and were on the verge of starvation. It was so undignified I felt ashamed of my colleagues' behaviour and vowed I would never again attend a drug lunch.

There were one or two notorious doctors who regularly attended these lunches and dinners with their wives in tow. They were well known and the organisers accepted them without overtly raising an eyebrow. This also felt embarrassing, and I determined that if I ever acquired a wife—it was in my bachelor days—I would take her out to a good restaurant and pay for the meal myself.

Talking of bachelor days, I had another reason for attending these events and for seeing reps. This was because some of them, I have to admit, were attractive young ladies. After politely listening to their presentations and asking a few questions, I would suggest we continued our discussion over lunch. Sometimes interesting friendships developed in this way.

Much later, when I had my own practice, I decided never to see drug reps; they would be politely turned around at the door and no samples, brochures, or knick-knacks were accepted. If I needed a ball pen I would buy one with my own money.

Drug reps and bad prescribing

There has recently been much news about a terrible situation in America, where many people have become addicted to prescription drugs, especially an opioid called oxycodone (Oxycontin), and a large number have died from overdosing on them. Oxycodone is used primarily for the control of pain in palliative care, especially in cancer patients. It is potentially addictive as all doctors should know.

Why has there been an epidemic of opioid deaths? According to the US National Institute on Drug Abuse, it is because:

> In the late 1990s, pharmaceutical companies reassured the medical community that patients would not become addicted to prescription opioid pain relievers, and healthcare providers began to prescribe them at greater rates.

And who is to blame for this deplorable situation? The drug companies! For example, in April 2019 the CEO of a company called Rochester Drug Cooperative in the US was arrested and sentenced to jail for providing narcotics to pharmacies which were filling prescriptions for oxycodone and fentanyl (a very strong pain-killer). But the prescriptions were written by local doctors!

How can a doctor just take a drug company's word for the safety of a drug? Why do they even *see* drug company salespeople or look at their advertisements? Don't they have their own knowledge or access to independent sources of information on the proper use of pain-relieving drugs? Are they ignorant of the addictive potential of *all* such drugs? Yet as far as I could see there was not a word of criticism of the prescribing doctors.

Beware of new drugs

The curious business of blaming the manufacturers when things go wrong with heavily promoted old or new prescription-only drugs has a long history.

Take two drug that came under a cloud in the late 1990s and early 2000s, Vioxx and Yasmin, respectively. The latter is not, as you might think, a chocolate bar, but an oral contraceptive. As for the former, an anti-arthritis drug, I cannot help being reminded by the quirky spelling of the running 'guru' James Fixx, who in 1984 dropped dead at the age of 52 from a heart attack while running.

The disease that killed James Fixx was also claimed to have caused the deaths of 40,000 to 60,000 Americans who died of heart attacks while taking Vioxx. As for Yasmin, it was promoted to doctors in 2002 as an oral contraceptive which was 'truly different', with a claimed favourable effect on pre-menstrual tension, skin condition, and weight gain. However, a year later an independent review found that it had no advantages over then existing, much cheaper oral contraceptives. The Scottish Medicines Consortium advised in 2003 that Yasmin is not recommended. In spite of this it was and still is extensively prescribed.

In the case of Vioxx, when the drug was withdrawn the manufacturer, Merck, was hit with a deluge of lawsuits from patients and their survivors on the charge that they withheld information about adverse effects on the heart in order to get the drug quickly approved and on the market. Quite right they should be sued, you might say.

But just a minute. As in the case above, it was the *manufacturer* who was sued? What about the prescribing doctors? Why weren't they sued as well, or instead?

When a new drug comes out it is often heavily promoted, particularly by drug company salespeople on their visits to doctors. And what do the doctors do? *They immediately prescribe it. Like there is no tomorrow.* It is reported that nearly 107 million prescriptions for Vioxx were dispensed in the US between 1999 and September 2004.

Why, oh why, did the doctors do it? Did they assume, because the drug was been approved for marketing and was available for prescription, it was safe? Apparently, yes. Were the doctors so influenced by the blandishments of Big Pharma that their critical faculties flew out of the window? Were they bereft of judgement, of caution? Apparently, yes. Were they over-awed by a free ball-pen, or even a free dinner, so that they went right ahead and widely prescribed the new drug? Apparently, they did.

It has been demonstrated time and again that new drugs, approved after necessarily limited trials, are thought to be safe but later turn out not to be.

For me, the fact that a drug is new is a reason *not* to prescribe it immediately, but to await independent confirmation of its possible benefits and freedom from harmful effects. Certainly, if someone came up with an effective and safe cure for cancer, I would use it straightaway, but many new drugs are 'me too-ers' which are similar to existing drugs; their claimed benefits or improvements are often questionable, or marginal.

How, then, are new drugs to be tested? There is no simple answer, but in the meantime, just as there are so-called NIMBY people (Not in My Back Yard—nuclear power stations and waste disposal plants, for example, are necessary but I don't want them near where I live), I would not mind, in relation to using new drugs, being known as a NOMPY doctor: Not On My Patients Yet.

CHAPTER TEN

Common Problems in General Practice

THE USE, OR rather, overuse, of antibiotics is a vexed question in general practice, with doctors being regularly advised, or even pressured, to cut down on prescribing them. They should be avoided unless there is a good reason, or indication, as we say, for them to be offered to patients. This is because if they are used indiscriminately, or even if they are used with discretion, there is a risk that bacteria will develop resistance to them and then even life-threatening infections may become difficult or impossible to treat. This is happening with tuberculosis, for example, and the unfortunate people in this situation are said to be suffering from MDR-TB, or multidrug-resistant tuberculosis—a dire state.

When should antibiotics be used? The answer is, when they are needed and not when they are not. But it's not so simple as that.

Sometimes patients come with respiratory symptoms such as a cough with phlegm which they have had for a short time and are not very ill. While taking the history and examining the patient I would come to a conclusion about the likely cause of the trouble, and would be fairly confident it was a common viral infection which would get better by itself—what we call a self-limiting condition. Thinking the patient might be expecting an antibiotic, I would be gathering my thoughts about how best to explain why it would be unnecessary. I might even anticipate this by saying, 'You may be thinking that an antibiotic would help, but...' and the patient would imagine how I was going to continue and politely interject, 'You mean I don't need an antibiotic? Thank goodness for that! I was afraid you were going to say I did!'

Within reason one always wants to meet the patient's expectations. It's not good for anyone to have a dissatisfied patient. Perhaps I had this idea from the few occasions when I was a schoolboy and visited my own family doctor. He was a no-nonsense kind of GP who would tell you authoritatively his opinion. It was often an anti-climax visiting him; it would be over before you knew it and one felt there had been little chance for asking questions. I was determined that when I became a GP I would put myself in the patients' shoes and give them the opportunity for asking me as much as they wanted. Sometimes I would even say, 'Is there anything else you would like to ask me?' Otherwise the patient, while nearly going out of the door, might say, 'While I'm here doctor…' to reveal the real reason for coming which they had felt unable to do while sitting in front of me.

Once, when I was in my forties and very fit (or so I thought), for no obvious reason I developed a cough with sputum (phlegm). In the usual way that doctors have of ignoring their own symptoms, I did nothing about it and hoped it would go away. It didn't. And it got worse. I found I was constantly coughing up yellow sputum, and had a mild fever on and off. I also had a sinus infection. Infectious sputum would be coughed up into my sinuses, then drain down to the lungs, and a vicious cycle was established.

This was a bit embarrassing in front of patients and in social situations. I ordered myself a chest X-ray; it was normal. Then I treated myself, I regret to say, with short courses of two or three different antibiotics. In retrospect I took a too low a dose for too short a time. I consulted colleagues. Perhaps because of nervousness about treating another doctor, they weren't very effective. One thought I had an allergy and recommended antihistamines; another thought I should take aspirin. These remedies, not surprisingly, were useless. Eventually I got referred to a pulmonary (lung) specialist in London. He diagnosed bronchitis and prescribed a ten-day full dose course of amoxicillin. I could feel myself recovering after one day on this regimen. Therefore, it's not a bad idea if doctors themselves suffer from some of the disorders of their patients. This concept was recognised in antiquity: the 'wounded healer'.

Such an experience did make me more sensitive to the needs of patients with similar symptoms—not that I have ever been over-ready to prescribe antibiotics or other drugs—but if I came across patients who had a cough and sputum for a week or more, I would probably prescribe. And I am afraid I am not much impressed by the official advice that antibiotics should be avoided in sinusitis and bronchitis. It's a matter of degree, and if the patient doesn't get better naturally within a reasonable time, then one should not show undue hesitation before prescribing.

Then again, we're told antibiotics are no good for sore throats, but what is a sore throat? In many cases it's obvious the patient has a viral infection and antibiotics will be ineffective, so I don't prescribe, but what if the patient has a painful throat and his or her tonsils are grossly enlarged and inflamed, with a fever and enlarged neck glands? One can do a side-room test for the dreaded 'Strep throat', as the Americans call it—an infection of the tonsils due to the *Streptococcus* bacterium—and the answer is available within a few minutes. If it's positive, then antibiotics need to be prescribed, and old-fashioned penicillin is still the best choice unless the patient is allergic.

Cough

'It's cough cough cough cough cough, cough cough cough cough cough—all night long, doctor!'

Cough is a very common symptom in general practice. It has an important function: to expel particulate matter and bacteria and viruses trapped in the mucus produced by the glands in the bronchial tubes. This kind of cough is useful, but if there's nothing coming up it could be called a useless cough.

Once I was called to visit a young child with this symptom in a housing estate in the east end of London. It was a weekday morning. The father was at home, dressed in his under vest, and sitting at a table reading the newspaper. He said, 'I want you to prescribe penicillin for 'is corf,' indicating a child lying in a cot across the room. No further details of the history were forthcoming. I carefully examined the child and could find no obvious abnormality. What to do? I decided discretion was the better part of valour and left a prescription for an antibiotic.

On another occasion, also in a poor part of east London, I was consulted by the parents about their boy with a cough of the type mentioned at the start of this section. Neither from careful questioning of the parents, nor from physical examination was any cause apparent. Nowadays a child like this would be probably be diagnosed with asthma, for which there are effective treatments. So I referred the child to the local hospital where he was thoroughly investigated by a children's specialist. No abnormality was found and, as was entirely proper, he was referred back to my care. What was I do to?

A little time before that I had attended a week's course to learn about homoeopathy, run from the Royal London Homoeopathic Hospital. One doesn't need to work very long in general practice for it to become all too clear that there are many conditions for which there is no satisfactory orthodox treatment, or a least no curative treatment. Examples are rheumatoid arthritis, eczema, allergies such as hay fever, and many mental symptoms. I wanted to learn about homoeopathy in order to have another string to my bow for these difficult-to-treat common problems. For the same reason I later learnt about acupuncture as an additional treatment, particularly for painful conditions where there was no good orthodox alternative.

The remedy called Bryonia, derived from the plant of that name, seemed to fit the little boy's type of cough, and I prescribed it for him. In those days you could do this on the NHS. It was difficult to explain to the parents what homoeopathy meant, so I just said it was a herbal treatment.

A few days later I was curious to know the result, so I visited the patient at home. The father said to me, 'You know you prescribed 'erbs for our Johnny.' I was wondering, with slight trepidation, what he was going to say next. He continued: 'Well, we gave 'em to 'im like you said—and 'is corf just stopped! Thank you very much, doctor!'

Coincidence? Maybe. Did the remedy really work? I'm inclined to think it did.

Multimorbidity, polypharmacy, and 'deprescribing'

In the British satirical magazine *Private Eye*, there was a cartoon a few years ago under the heading *Fallen Angels*, which showed two nurses standing by a patient in a wheelchair. One nurse says to the patient, 'Nurse Pringle can't talk to you; she hasn't finished her patient communications module yet.'

I was reminded of this situation when in 2014 I came across an editorial in the BMJ headed 'Discontinuing drug treatments'.[7] Sounds like a good idea. If a patient doesn't need a drug anymore it should be stopped, right?

You wouldn't think so reading this editorial. The authors use a made-up word, 'deprescribing', to refer to reducing or stopping drugs, and express concern about the paucity of the evidence base to guide doctors how to proceed in this common situation. Well, Dr Pringle, it's obvious, innit? You just cut down slowly or stop abruptly drugs which you judge, based on your knowledge, experience, and observations are not doing the patient any good and which are doing or might do harm. This must be done sensitively and with the patient's full involvement and agreement, but as a general rule surely drugs should be stopped or at least reduced if there is no longer a clear need for them. Why should this be so difficult?

The problem of stopping drugs applies particularly in people

[7] BMJ 2014;349:g7013

with what is called multimorbidity. This jargon word is applied to those suffering concurrently from more than one chronic health problem as is often the case in the elderly. Such a person may be under treatment for high blood pressure, high cholesterol, type 2 diabetes, depression, and arthritis, and so may be taking a fair number of different drugs. This is referred to in the trade as polypharmacy. But since all drugs can cause side effects and anyway may no longer be needed, *of course* a patient's drug regimen will be regularly reviewed, and *of course* the drugs should be reduced or stopped if they are doing the patient no good or are causing harm or if there is no clear continuing need for them. What's the big deal? Surely any self-respecting GP, as an expert in caring for patients with multimorbidity, should be able to carry out such a task.

This onerous matter was revisited in an opinion piece in the BMJ in 2019, with the ominous title, 'The perils of deprescribing'.[8] This time our hypothetical patient was a 78 year old woman taking eight regular pills who was overdue for a review and for whom only twelve minutes were available.

One of the pills the good lady was taking, inevitably, was a statin.[9] Apart from some of the other medicines, the doctor had the dilemma of stopping the statin, and it was suggested this could be approached by saying that new research had shown that at her age it was unlikely to do her any good. But had it done her any good up till the present? Over the last few years she had taken thousands of these pills. Was all that really necessary? Had our elderly lady only avoided a stroke or heart attack courtesy of these pills, and now by some magical quirk of metabolism when she crossed the threshold into her seventy-ninth year she was no longer at risk?

The writer ended by saying, 'We certainly need to build our

---

[8] BMJ 2019;364:l666

[9] Statins are a class of drug now widely prescribed with the aim of preventing strokes and heart attacks. How they work is not completely understood. They reduce cholesterol levels but this is not the whole story; they also may have an effect against inflammation which is involved in the development of blood clots in the heart and brain.

confidence…to reduce the treatment burden on our patients and begin to tackle the huge waste of time and money that this overprescribing represents.'

Yes, indeed. But why were the statins prescribed in the first place? The answer is because official guidelines for doctors indicate they should be considered for patients deemed to have a certain degree of risk hanging over them for strokes and heart attacks, and that this can be reduced by taking a pill every day, indefinitely.

Another editorial[10] in the doughty BMJ on deprescribing admonishes readers that 'Careful judgement is required to optimise benefit and minimise harm.' It then approvingly refers to an eighty-five page publication by the Scottish Government called 'Polypharmacy Guidance, Realistic Prescribing, 2018', to which doctors can turn for advice on how to deprescribe. Buried in the middle of this self-important document we find a 'Structured 7-Steps patient-centred medicines review', as follows (paraphrased for clarity):

Step 1: What matters to the patient?
Step 2: Identify essential drug therapy
Step 3: Does the patient take unnecessary drug therapy?
Step 4: Are therapeutic objectives being achieved?
Step 5: Is the patient at risk of drug side-effects or does the patient suffer actual side-effects?
Step 6: Is drug therapy cost-effective?
Step 7: Is the patient willing and able to take drug therapy as intended?

This is so patronising and obvious it's almost insulting.

Medication reviews should be an inherent part of every patient contact. If there is one doctor who knows the patient and who

[10] BMJ 2019;364:l570

has been involved in all hospital referrals, he or she will have, or should have, an overview of all the drug treatments and is, or should be, in a position to adjust them as necessary. Why make what should be a routine matter needlessly so complicated?

Death by statin?
Incidentally, in the medical sense what's the difference between a medicine and a drug? They mean the same, but it has been said that if a doctor wants a patient to take it he calls it a medicine, and if he doesn't want the patient to take it he calls it a drug!

Are statins safe? The answer seems to be that they are, but in rare cases they can cause muscle pain and weakness. If this happens a blood test can be done to check for muscle damage and if this is confirmed it may be advisable to take the patient off the statin.

In December 2012 I had a letter published in the BMJ in response to an article about a patient who developed weakness of his muscles which was eventually fatal.[11] He had been prescribed a statin a few months previously because he had had a heart operation to treat angina (chest pain on exertion). On the face of it this was a good idea and normal practice. However, the patient himself thought that his muscle weakness was caused by the statin and he wanted to stop it, but was persuaded through fear (his GP is quoted as saying, 'If you don't take it you will die.') to continue. This is the letter:

It is not clear why this patient's muscular weakness progressed to death but the general opinion was that the statin was, or might have been, involved.

The obvious thing to do in this situation, since it is well recognised that statins can cause muscle pain and weakness, is to STOP THE BLOODY STATIN! The patient himself

---

[11] https://www.bmj.com/content/345/bmj.e6880/rapid-responses

wanted to do this and it doesn't require a huge body of medical knowledge to come to this simple decision. Unfortunately, by the time he was taken off the statin it was too late.

The comments of the GP who took over his care towards the end are revealing. The patient acknowledged she was a dedicated and compassionate doctor and no criticism of her is intended.

She says: 'As his GP, one of my roles was to hold an overview during his often difficult journey through the health system. He was referred to consultants from diverse specialities, each holding an important piece of the jigsaw—hepatologists (for his abnormal liver function test results), rheumatologists (for his myalgia), ENT consultants (for his hoarse voice), cardiologists (for his breathlessness), lipid clinics (for advice on statins), and neurologists (for his fatigue).' Note the plurals.

Indeed, one of the roles of a GP—I would say a major or essential role—is to hold an overview. I would add that the GP must be prepared to take decisions on his or her own responsibility, when needed, and not just defer to the presumed greater wisdom of specialists. It seems incredible that so many specialists were involved. Is it really true he was referred to more than one hepatologist, rheumatologist, ENT consultant, etc.? Specialists' advice may be helpful but surely it is the referring doctor, the GP who holds the overview, who needs to decide whether—or not—to act on the opinions given.

She continues: 'GPs' actions are often driven by guidelines, treatment pathways, and quality and outcomes frameworks. Opportunity for careful consideration and contemplation of a disease process and manifestation is a rare luxury.'

How can this be? What is sitting on the shelf behind her? The *British National Formulary*? The *Oxford Textbook of*

Medicine? Does she not subscribe or have access to internet medical resources? In a case like this she needs to research the matter to the best of her ability. No time? Then burn the midnight oil. Referral to multiple specialists can result in fragmentation of care. As for 'guidelines, treatment pathways, and quality and outcomes frameworks', these are, indeed, just guidelines and are not set in stone; they should never replace clinical judgement. Are GPs now reduced to being merely referral agencies? Something wrong with your liver tests? See a hepatologist. Your muscles are weak? See a neurologist. Whatever your complaint, there's an 'ologist to deal with it.

It's time for GPs to say enough is enough. Throw off the shackles of rampant guidelineitis. Have confidence in your own opinions. Keep in mind that unexplained symptoms may be drug-induced. *This is especially important when so many patients these days take drugs to prevent something that may never happen.*

Doing more harm than good?

The situation where doctors get carried away by their enthusiasm is also illustrated in the following situation.

Some time ago a new patient came to register at my practice. He was an elderly Chinese man who had previously lived in America. He hadn't brought his primary care physician's records because he had baulked at the large fee the doctor wanted for the privilege of providing them. He did bring, however, an envelope full of copies of the reports of various specialists to whom he had been referred: a neurologist, an orthopaedic surgeon, and radiologists.

Allowing for some Americanisms and carelessness in proof-reading, it must be said these reports were impressive in their thoroughness and comprehensiveness, including reference to problems of 'cognitive dissonance' and 'executive functions'. It is recorded that he suffered a mild head injury but there was 'no loss of conspicuousness' (*sic*), that he 'ambulated without assistance', and that 'his mood was euthymic'.

Why had he been referred to a neurologist? This was because of the above-mentioned injury. It occurred when he had been skiing and slipped on the snow, striking the back of his head on the ground. He did not lose consciousness but picked himself up and carried on, though he had headaches and didn't feel very well for a little time thereafter—hardly surprising and not in itself a cause for concern. But he also had memory loss and dizziness. Off to the neurologist! Predictably, brain scans (note the plural) were ordered. One scan was declared to be normal, but the other apparently showed changes that were compatible with and suggestive of some possible brain abnormality. Thus a label was applied. Labels tend to stick. He was a stroke patient! Therefore he was prescribed a statin and aspirin.

As for memory loss, a former British Ambassador to Japan to whom I was once chatting at a party expressed mild concern that he sometimes found it difficult to remember names when introducing people at social functions. Before I could comment he provided the explanation and appropriate reassurance himself: 'Well, I suppose that's just normal forgetfulness,' he said, 'but if I were to go around believing that I was the French Ambassador, rather than the British one, then that really would be a problem!'

Back to this patient. He also had a vague feeling of heaviness in his left arm. It was previously noted that he had a painful left shoulder—which was the likely explanation for the arm symptoms. But, just to be on the safe side, nerve conduction studies were done. Abnormal! Motor and sensory neuropathy! And while we're about it, what about measuring his HbA1c (a test for diabetes) and his vitamin B and D levels. These allegedly showed borderline diabetes and insufficiency of vitamins B and D, respectively. Supplements!

Thus a growing list of disorders was generated, written as such in his specialists' reports: 1)...2)...3)...etc.

One of the neurologist's printed pages for patients to fill in was interesting. At the top of the page it was written, thrice: UPDATE!!! And underneath was the heading CLAUSTROPHOBIC QUESTIONNAIRE. This was followed by a list of questions including one with the splendid greengrocer's apostrophe: WHAT TRIGGERS YOUR PHOBIA'S?

These questions may be relevant for patients for whom scans have been ordered, since some people do feel anxious when confined in a scanner. But what about grammar? What about punctuation? What about using some thought before you commit yourself in writing? Or are people no longer embarrassed by, or even aware of, such schoolboy howlers?

Apart from that, were all these tests really necessary? Did they help in treating the patient? Or had they done more harm than good?

The Bible has got it right

The idea of investigating and treating people with no overt disease is a curious feature of modern life. Even if one feels perfectly well doctors are encouraged to seek out and offer treatment for risk factors for diseases that may never happen, apparently having forgotten that 'They that be whole need not a physician, but they that are sick.' (Matthew 9:12)

Ideally, we should discuss with patients the hoped-for benefits and possible harms of any proposed preventive treatment using a decision-making aid. One such is a diagram with one hundred manikins, most of which are coloured green and a few coloured red. If the pills are taken, there are slightly more green manikins and correspondingly fewer red ones. So patients, and doctors, are put in a dilemma.

The fact that the doctor raises the matter at all implies a leaning in favour of the treatment. But suppose the patient says, 'I don't know doctor, what would you advise?' or—no getting away from it now—'If you were in my position, doctor, what would you do?'

And what did I do under these circumstances? I never promoted or encouraged routine blood tests for symptomless people unless they had some special reason for having them such as a family history of cancer or premature death from heart disease. As a result, I did not become as rich as I might have done. On the other hand, not infrequently healthy people would request routine check-ups. If appropriate, I would always discuss relevant matters such as their weight, exercise or the lack of it, diet, smoking, and alcohol intake, and I would not disappoint them by refusing to do expected blood tests. But what would I do with the result if, for example, a slightly raised cholesterol was found? I would explain that in my view the theoretical benefit from treating it, such as with a statin, was small and if I were in their position I would not take it.

Turning healthy people into patients

We have moved very far from the Biblical injunction in the current mania—at least as one finds in Japan—for check-ups.

These days a considerable amount of medical activity is targeted at healthy people, or at least at those without any overt signs or symptoms of disease. The rationale for this is reflected in a humorous, if slightly cynical saying among doctors, which I do not believe, that a normal person is one who has been under-investigated. The purpose of check-ups is to detect disease at an earlier, treatable stage, and surely, prevention is better than cure. But it's not so simple as that.

In Japan everyone of working age—in other words the healthiest sector of the population—is expected to undergo an annual check-up. It's said to be mandatory but there doesn't seem to be any penalty if you avoid it. This means that every year tens of millions of people are required to absent themselves from work for a half-day or longer to attend a clinic or hospital where these check-ups are performed. The process is referred to in Japanese as *ningen dock* (human dock) which suggests, falsely, that

70

the human body is like a ship that needs to be put into dry dock from time to time to be checked over.

Medical check-ups in Japan are big business. Indeed, there are clinics which do nothing else. They are run like production-lines, and staff are employed to carry out the various procedures: blood tests, urinalysis, X-rays, scans, endoscopies, etc. You will get your blood pressure taken, they will measure your height and weight, and your hearing and vision will be checked. You will also need to enter details of your personal and family history, and whether you smoke and/or drink, etc., on a computer terminal, and there may be an interview with a doctor.

Some clinics and hospitals offer you a choice of different types of check-up. They are often presented in terms such as standard, superior, and executive, with the implication that 'more is better'. But is it? The choices may include tests for the early detection of cancer, playing on fear: you may be developing cancer and not know it but if you have high tech scans, blood tests for 'cancer markers', mammograms, etc., they may save your life.

Then there is the really high-end type of check-up available at a well-known clinic in central Tokyo and at many other places. They offer 'Premium Health Screening for Executives' for those with deep pockets. The problem with this is that it tends to blind people with science. How is one to know what, if anything, is relevant and useful to safeguard one's health apart from a few simple tests any doctor could carry out? For example, for women they offer female hormone status tests to measure five types of sex hormones, a cancer marker called CA125 with vaginal ultrasonography to detect ovarian cancer. The trouble with this is that no medical organisation anywhere in the world recommends any test or tests for the early detection of ovarian cancer—there is none.

These sorts of check-ups may produce false positive results, though as far as I am aware this is seldom if ever mentioned.

This can lead to over-diagnosis and over-treatment—a particular concern in screening for breast cancer by mammography and prostate cancer by the PSA test. In these cases, a false positive result could mean someone undergoes life-changing treatment for a disease which, if it had not been detected, would never have caused symptoms in the person's lifetime. Or it may be unclear whether some results are normal or not. This can lead to further testing, involving more inconvenience, loss of time, expense, and worry.

Furthermore, in Japan the results of these company check-ups are presented rather a like a school report, with grades A to F. An A means everything is fine, but if you get an E you may think something is seriously wrong, and if you get an F you had better go and see the Headmaster! This is patronising and can be misleading. One may be marked down because the results of certain tests may be deemed too high or too low. There may be little or no attempt at interpretation of the results. A result may be above or below the so-called reference range, but *is it significant? Does it matter for the patient?* You may merely be offered advice to 'be careful' and come back the following year to have the tests repeated. And if you get one of the lower grades, say E or F, you may be advised to have the matter of concern checked at a hospital, and to make the arrangements for this yourself.

On the other hand, routine check-ups can produce a false sense of security. It is possible to undergo the superior executive type of check-up, with all the results being reported as normal, and then step outside the building and drop dead from a heart attack.

In addition, in Japan the results of these company check-ups are not confidential. They are usually sent to the company's HR department and this sometimes can lead to an awkward conversation with one's boss, or it may have negative consequences for the employee's promotion prospects.

What is beyond dispute is that the Human Dock system

in its present form generates enormous costs in manpower, laboratory tests, imaging procedures, and follow-up which are paid for by the government via taxation. But are statistics kept, and published, of significant abnormalities discovered in these check-ups? It seems to me that unless it can be shown that this exercise is cost-effective it should be re-thought, or even abandoned.

Perhaps the main disadvantage of routine check-ups is that they can undermine someone's confidence in their own state of good health. In general, if you feel well, you *are* well, and you don't need high tech tests to prove it. It is sometimes forgotten that it is normal to be healthy.

A few routine tests may be recommended, such as occasional blood pressure checks and cervical cytology screening for women of the appropriate age. But in so far as it's in our own hands to stay healthy, the advice is simple: don't smoke, drink moderately if at all, avoid being overweight, exercise regularly, and eat a healthy diet.

CHAPTER ELEVEN
Smoking and Drinking

WHEN I WAS in my first year of medical school I made new friends and enjoyed doing things which previously I had been unable to do, such as drinking—there was a Wine Society and I would have occasional drinks in the students' bar—and, yes, smoking. I had the idea, which now seems ridiculous, that smoking would help me concentrate on my studies. But to my mild disappointment it didn't seem to help, and having my desk cluttered with a pack of cigarettes, matches, and an ashtray, and with the smoke getting up my nose and into my eyes, and with the ash falling onto my work, it was more a hindrance than anything else. Nonetheless, I persevered and was soon puffing away every evening while I pored over my textbooks and lecture notes.

Then, a few months into the course it was announced we would be taken in small groups on a visit to the hospital. We were all looking forward to learning on real patients in due course, but we had stiff examinations to pass first. Thus, a visit to the hospital at this early stage was exciting. I didn't know what was in store.

It was the men's chest ward. The senior doctor who led us into the ward stopped at the first bed and we gathered round a pale thin man in his sixties who had an oxygen cylinder beside him. You could see he was breathless even sitting up in bed. The doctor conducting the 'round' said, 'Good afternoon Mr …, please tell these young doctors what your trouble is.' (We were only students but they called us young doctors.) And he said, speaking with a weak voice and some difficulty on account of his breathlessness, what I will never forget, 'Oh dear, I've got emphysema[12]…I know it's all due to smoking, and *I wish I'd never*

---

[12] A disease in which the lungs are progressively destroyed, resulting in severe breathlessness and eventually death from respiratory failure. It is now usually referred to as COPD (chronic obstructive pulmonary disease).

started!' After a brief discussion with the demonstrating doctor we moved to the next bed, and this patient similarly was politely asked to tell us what was wrong with him. 'I've got lung cancer; it's because of smoking…' There were two or three others who all said the same thing, in slightly different words. This made a profound impression on me. I thanked my lucky stars that I had the privilege of being a medical student, and went back to my room thinking I didn't want to commit suicide. So I collected all my smoking paraphernalia and chucked the lot into the dustbin (trashcan). From that day on I have never smoked again.

This experience, however, aroused my interest in helping patients to stop smoking. It was frustrating. Pointing out the obvious that the smoker might get lung cancer and therefore should quit didn't make much of an impression. Scare tactics worked for me but I was at an impressionable age. What do you say to a middle-aged person who's been smoking a pack-a-day for two or three decades? He or she is well aware of the risks but it doesn't make any difference. Then there's the orthodox approach which uses so-called nicotine replacement therapy or prescription drugs combined with counselling. I find it illogical to treat nicotine addiction with nicotine. As for prescription drugs, the smoker is already in enough of a drugged state with nicotine, and I would hesitate to cause a further chemical imbalance in the brain—which is what such drugs (varenicline and bupropion) are designed to do—with the ever-present risk of side-effects including suicidal thoughts! There had to be a better way.

So I started talking with my smoker patients and listening to what they told me. This was a rich source of information that I couldn't find in any textbook or medical journal. Unlike the usual kind of research where population samples are questioned using box-ticking methods, I asked open-ended questions: 'Why do you smoke? What does it do for you? What do you get out of it? What happens when you don't smoke? What do you actually feel when you wish to have a cigarette but can't smoke for some reason?' The answers, or sometimes the lack of an answer, were revealing. Gradually I developed a simple method of smoking cessation based on helping smokers to *demonstrate to themselves* two things: why they *really* smoke, as opposed to why they think they smoke, and why quitting *seems* so hard.

I have now used this approach with hundreds of smokers, treating them in the course of my ordinary work as a GP, with about a 90 per cent success rate.

Alcoholism

Whereas with smoking, virtually everyone who smokes is by definition a nicotine addict, alcohol is different. Most people who drink can 'take it or leave it' and it will never become a problem. I have to admit that on rare occasions I have drunk too much. You wake in the middle of the night with a headache, dizziness, and nausea. Only time brings relief. And you feel such a fool because you have brought it upon yourself! While you're recovering from this excess the last thing you want is another drink.

Contrast this with an actual or potential alcoholic: he has a high tolerance for alcohol but doesn't get drunk—he may drink till he falls asleep. The next day he awakes depressed and anxious, his one thought being that he needs another drink. And in a sense he does—the 'hair of the dog'. Then he feels better but the cycle is repeated and eventually he may collapse and need hospital admission. It's a terrible situation because at risk is the alcoholic's job, marriage, health, and even his life.

Alcoholics seem to metabolise alcohol differently from other people, a characteristic which is often inherited. Understanding this should help to remove the stigma: in no sense is alcoholism a moral failing—it's a physical disorder. Nonetheless, such a person need not suffer from it as long as he or she refrains completely and permanently from drinking.

When I had discovered how to cure smokers of their addiction I thought, 'Right, this should work for any substance addiction!' The next commonest problem was alcoholism and I would invite patients in the grip of this affliction to come and see me for treatment. However, it soon became apparent that alcohol addiction is much more difficult to deal with than smoking.

The thinking and logic behind my approach went like this: once someone had not drunk for a week or more, they were no longer suffering from acute alcohol poisoning. Then, by judicious questioning and a non-judgemental discussion, the patient would realise that if she drank she would become ill. Maybe it wouldn't happen immediately, but sooner or later—more likely sooner—she would 'fall off the wagon' and be unable to stop drinking until, two or three days later, she would be in a stuporous state under the table. Therefore, she needed to see alcohol as poison for her, which indeed it is. She could visualise a label round the neck of the bottle with the word 'Poison' on it.

It is true that there would be a small sacrifice if someone could never drink again: the enjoyment of a nice cold lager on a hot summer's day, or a glass of wine with a meal. But surely these are minor sacrifices in order to avoid the awful situation of one's drinking getting out of control.

That sterling organisation, Alcoholic Anonymous (AA), says: 'Remember, you are powerless over alcohol'. This is true, but you are not powerless, once you have been dry for a week or more, over the decision whether to have another drink—or not.

One patient told me he had no interest in social drinking. Two or three times a week (I suspect it was more) after returning home from work, while sitting in front of the TV playing a DVD, he would proceed over the next two or three hours to consume a whole bottle of vodka. It was his way of trying to deal with the problems in his life.

Another alcoholic, who no longer drank, told me he never

used to drink as a means of escape. Why did he do it then? It was illogical and he couldn't say why, except that the urge to drink used to be overpowering. He was now 'an alcoholic who didn't drink'. What saved him were a supportive wife and the fellowship of AA. He hasn't touched a drop in ten years, feels no desire to do so, and can stay by himself at hotels on business trips and never even look at the mini-bar. But he still regularly attends AA meetings, partly to encourage others, but also to remind himself that being a non-drinking alcoholic is something one should never be complacent about.

Yet another alcoholic, Jonathan, showed how this addiction led him on a steadily downward and eventually irrecoverable path. Incidentally, his father had died from alcoholism.

He drank, he told me, to blot out life, to escape for a few hours. On the surface his life was a success: a married man with a son, he worked at a good company, and he was a fine amateur musician. There were, however, indications of problems brewing over ten years or more. He would give music lessons to a few students and but sometimes he would not turn up. His wife would call the student and make an excuse that he was unwell. Indeed he was unwell—from alcohol poisoning. Then his health gradually went downhill and he had an epileptic fit. No cause was found but almost certainly it was due to the drink. The next problem was when he started coming in late for work. They knew what was going on and suspended him while he had treatment, and he was lucky to be reinstated. This put a terrible strain on his marriage and eventually his wife divorced him. I can't say I blame her—living with an alcoholic would try the patience of a saint. She divorced him rather suddenly and moved most of the furniture and goods out of their rented house while Jonathan was in hospital with another bout of alcohol poisoning. So he came back to an empty, cold house, and he was suspended from his job. What was he do to all day? I supported him as much as I could, but alcohol is easy to obtain in Tokyo—the convenience store down the road kept him supplied with bottles of cheap whisky. Soon it became clear he wasn't coping and I managed to arrange for him to be admitted to a rehabilitation hospital on the coast. I even took him there in my car and collected him three weeks later when he was pronounced cured. He lasted three days. I then visited him almost daily—he lent me a spare key. I said to him, 'Jonathan, you absolutely must stop drinking. I don't want to turn up one day and find you dead!'

Sadly, this is exactly what did happen. It was just after Christmas. There was no response to my ringing the doorbell. That wasn't such a surprise because I would often find him sprawled on the sofa in a drunken stupor. So I let myself in. Then I saw his legs sticking out of the door of the downstairs toilet. He was fully dressed and slumped between the toilet bowl and the wall, obviously dead. I have seen quite a few dead people in my career but this was really upsetting, especially because he was a friend as well as a patient.

I called the police. They came immediately. I pronounced him dead and they took him away. An autopsy was inconclusive but clearly alcoholism was a contributory factor.

His poor mother turned up for the funeral. She seemed less upset than I would have expected but maybe she had seen this coming. Her comment was, 'He wanted to die.' Alas.

What I learnt from this sad episode is that curing someone of alcoholism isn't difficult—it's impossible.

CHAPTER TWELVE
Scientific Psychiatry

WHAT IS THE cause of depression? This sounds like a question a medical student might have to answer in an examination: state the causes of (for example) gastric ulcer, hypertension, or grand mal epilepsy. But if we ask, instead, 'What causes depression?' the answer is obvious. In most cases it's adverse life events such as abusive parents, bereavement, financial loss, exam failure, disappointment in love, etc. The question then becomes, when does ordinary depression, or normal human misery, become a mental illness, assuming there is such a thing? Where do you draw the line?

The highly esteemed *New Oxford Textbook of Psychiatry*, in the current (second) edition, 2009, considers depression under the heading of 'mood disorders' and approaches the matter cautiously:

> Depressive symptoms in the community are common, and defining both the symptom count and duration at which depressive symptoms count as part of a clinical disorder is arbitrary.

(It would have been better written without using the word 'count' in two different senses in the same sentence.)

This statement is part of a critique of the definition of depression in the DSM-IV (the so-called bible of psychiatry, the *Diagnostic and Statistical Manual*, 4th edition, of the American Psychiatric Association, now superseded by the 5th edition), in which two American writers are quoted as saying:

> ...they could find no empirical support for the DSM-IV requirement of duration of two weeks, five symptoms or

clinically significant impairment [whatever that means] and that this definition may be no more than a diagnostic convention.

Being unable to define, let alone state the cause(s) of depression, the *Textbook* then goes on to discuss risk factors. These include genetics, gender (it's twice as common in women), childhood experiences (lack of parental care, not surprisingly, is associated with increased rates), personality (it's associated with neuroticism, however you define that), social environment (for example, depression is commoner in single than in married men), and physical illness (not surprisingly).

The relevance of some of these risk factors is summed up in a reference to another paper which speculates:

> ...genetic factors influence the risk of onset of depression, in part, by increasing the sensitivity of the individual to the depression-inducing effects of stressful life events.

So if your genes have made you sensitive to developing depression, then stressful life events may cause you to become depressed. That's useful to know, I suppose.

Next, we learn that the writer hopes to integrate psychiatry into clinical medicine:

> ...success in depression would parallel that seen in moving the management of heart disease from the acute episode of infarction [heart attack] to the treatment of metabolic risk factors.

How can you compare diseases of the heart, a physical organ, with disorders affecting the mind? Such disorders, assuming they exist, by definition are difficult to grasp. Whereas in cardiology we have sophisticated machines to examine the heart (electrocardiographs, ultrasonography, CT scans) the way mental disorders are assessed is entirely subjective: it consists of the mind of the doctor observing the mind of the patient. But what is mind, or consciousness, anyway? Where does it reside? In the brain, no doubt, but in which part or parts, and how does the brain function to produce it? In other words, what are the neural correlates of consciousness? It has been said that our current understanding of how the mind works can be compared to the situation in which, hearing a symphony on the radio, we look inside the box to see where the musicians are. In other words, what we currently know in this area is *almost nothing*.

Then, as would be expected in a scientific textbook, they examine what they call the neurobiology of mood disorders. Here the writer, a Professor of psychiatry at a prestigious British university, expounds on key vulnerability factors, which seem to be more or less the same as some of the previously mentioned risk factors: genetics ('There has been a terrific (*sic*) proliferation of possible genetic effects'); temperament (this is with reference to animal studies, the relevance of which to human psychiatry eludes me); neuroticism (which is, apparently, biologically founded in negative biases in attention, processing, and memory for emotional material); and early adverse experience.

The last-mentioned factor is derived from cruel experiments in rats, though with the proviso: 'Whether separation or stress paradigms in rodents can be taken as precise models of the mechanisms underlying the risk of mood disorder...cannot yet be decided, but their general relevance to the human case seems obvious.'

Gentle reader, keep the last sentence in mind while I quote from the Preface to this noble two-volume tome:

> This new edition, like the first, aims to present a comprehensive account of clinical psychiatry with reference to its *scientific basis* and to the ill person's perspective. (Emphasis added.)

What they are saying is that it cannot be decided whether cruelly induced stress in rats is a model for the risk of mood disorder in humans 'but [its] general relevance seems obvious'.

In science it's not good enough that something seems obvious: it must be proved to be so. In any case, if these entirely predictable results seem obvious, why bother to do the experiments in the first place? After all that, we come to the bottom line:

> It remains true to say that no biological changes have ever been found that distinguish between depressed patients and controls better than does clinical assessment of the patients.

Nothing daunted, we can now move on to attempt to assess directly the functioning of the human brain. I shall not weary the reader with technical details of exciting recent developments in imaging: PET, SPET, and SPECT scans, as they are known. What do they tell us? That certain areas of the brain can be seen to be active in patients with certain symptoms. All very interesting no doubt, but in the practical matters of diagnosis and treatment of patients with psychiatric symptoms, of what use are they? Such techniques have been likened to a modern form of phrenology, where instead of assessing someone's personality and mental faculties from the shape of his or her skull, one attempts to assess brain function on a computer screen.

Hitting the telly[13] when it's on the blink

In the days before flat screen TVs, there were cathode ray tubes— bulky boxes on the front of which the transmitted images could be seen; they had nothing like the clarity of modern screens or computer monitors. Those old-fashioned TVs not uncommonly suffered from distortion of the picture. Sometimes one could

---

[13] British slang for television.

cure it by judicious manipulation of the controls, the vertical and horizontal holds, as they were called. If this didn't work one could resort to giving a firm blow with the bottom of one's fist on the top of the box. This manoeuvre, though risky, sometimes worked, for a while anyway.

Recently, the sobering fact has been mentioned in the medical and lay media that no new treatments for depression have emerged in the last fifty years. But now, a ray of hope. Two experimental drugs have been proposed to treat what is called treatment-resistant depression. These are a psychedelic drug known as psilocybin, and a general anaesthetic called ketamine, with a variant, esketamine. No one knows how these drugs work—it's empirical. That is to say, some seriously depressed patients to whom these drugs have been administered have appeared to make a dramatic improvement, for a while anyway.

This situation should give one pause for thought. It seems researchers regard depression as a brain disease and have been looking for a cure in the same way that a cure for some bacterial infections was found by the discovery of penicillin. Try this, try that, and if we go on long enough we may find the cure. This simplistic thinking is like hitting the telly.

Depression is a symptom, not a diagnosis. That is not to say that depressed people don't experience real suffering, and I have seen patients in hospital so overwhelmed by depression they were unable to do anything for themselves, even get out of bed. But these are extreme cases.

Chemical imbalance theory

Although antidepressants do seem to help some people, and I occasionally prescribe them myself, the oft-stated notion that depression is due to a chemical imbalance in the brain is nothing more than a theory. It's impossible to measure levels of serotonin, dopamine, or other neurotransmitters in the living human brain, and any changes in the levels of these chemicals, if they occur, could be the result, rather than the cause, of the symptoms.

If you take an antidepressant you feel something—commonly dizziness, weakness, or drowsiness. These are due to side effects of the drug; they may be mild and will usually diminish as patients get used to them. Many patients find these symptoms are a small price to pay for feeling less depressed. Could it be a placebo effect? You can tell the drug is doing something and you hope and expect to feel better, so you do. But even if we accept that depression is associated with some kind of imbalance of neurotransmitter chemicals, is it desirable or safe to compound this with an additional disturbance of brain chemistry by the use of drugs? It should be kept in mind that the way antidepressants work (if they do) and produce side effects is through causing a *drugged state*.

This being so, how much more cautious should we be about using drugs that are well known to cause major disturbances in the brain and which can and do result in psychoses. I am referring to hallucinogenics—LSD, mescaline, psilocybin, and the like. Yet this is what is actually being proposed by the well-named Professor David Nutt, who was dismissed in 2009 as chair of the UK government's Advisory Council on the Misuse of Drugs for saying that ecstasy, cannabis, and LSD are less dangerous than alcohol and tobacco. He was recently back in the news after having treated a small number of patients with treatment-resistant depression with psilocybin, and he now wants to carry out a larger trial using this dangerous drug. This is reminiscent of the era of drastic—even heroic—physical treatments for mental illnesses: insulin coma therapy, electro-convulsive therapy (ECT), and lobotomy. These are now rightly discredited except for ECT which is still occasionally used for severe depression.

As for ketamine and esketamine, these are experimental drugs which appear to relieve depression in the short term. They have many potentially serious side-effects including psychosis, dissociation (detachment from reality), increased blood pressure, and bladder inflammation.

Incidentally, Professor Nutt works in collaboration with Amanda Feilding, whom I've met, who in 1970 drilled a hole through her skull (trepanation) in an attempt to enhance her level of consciousness.

How do you make a rat depressed?

Before drugs are used in people they are usually developed through what is called an animal model. This curious concept means artificially inducing a disease in an animal, often a mouse or rat, and then treating it with a drug. If the drug works or appears to work in the animal it's assumed it may be effective for treating the naturally occurring condition in humans. But what is the scientific basis for believing that the results of animal experiments are applicable to humans? There is none.

How do you make a rat depressed? You do cruel things to it and then find its behaviour is altered, which is hardly surprising, but then by fanciful anthropomorphic thinking the rat is said to be depressed. It might well be disturbed, terrified, or distraught as a result of being so treated, but it is impossible to gauge the mood of a rat—does it even have moods?—and to say it is depressed is a preposterous assumption.

Readers of a sensitive disposition may wish to skip the next two paragraphs.

For example, you put the hapless creature in a vertical tube filled with water from which it cannot escape. It swims for its life and after a while gives up and floats until it is rescued (or drowns). Or you give electric shocks to a rat and find it gives up struggling in the water sooner than before. Next, you give the nearly drowned or electrically shocked rat a drug, and if it struggles in the water for longer than before, behold—an antidepressant!

Another way in which attempts have been made to create a rat model of depression, is by an experiment of obscene cruelty in which the rat's olfactory bulb is removed. This is the part of the animal's brain that processes the sense of smell. Rats relate to the world largely through smell, and if this sense is eradicated one can only imagine it is something like deliberately rendering a human both blind and deaf.

It has been said that the rat (or mouse) is an animal which, when injected, produces a paper. There are innumerable papers on experiments using these and other animals in psychiatric research, but the only result is that there will be yet another publication listed on the experimenter's CV—an example of the 'publish or perish' belief. In all likelihood these results will not be of the slightest value for understanding psychiatric problems in humans, and the papers in which they are described will merely gather dust in an ever-increasing mountain of discarded research.

It is no wonder that such experiments have been called crude, cruel, and useless.

The disappearing Jung

Can you imagine a history of Europe without mention of Napoleon? Well, the learned editors of the above-mentioned *Textbook* have done something similar in the current edition compared with the first edition (2000).

In the above-mentioned Preface it also says, 'textbooks are still needed to provide the comprehensive account of established knowledge'. Indeed. But right here we have a difficulty. To talk of established knowledge in psychiatry is an assumption bordering on hubris. How is one to decide what is established knowledge and what isn't? Even in physics, for example when considering Newton's laws of motion or the periodic table of the elements, such knowledge is only considered as established until disproved by later developments. Throughout the *Textbook* a much more modest approach is evident in the various sections where the provisional and speculative nature of many psychiatric diagnoses and treatments and their theoretical underpinnings are acknowledged.

In the current edition there is a whole section on Sigmund

Freud, but while there was a chapter by Anthony Storr on the famous Swiss psychiatrist, C G Jung, in the first edition, there is not a word about him (apart from brief mention in two footnotes) in the second edition, and his name is absent from the index.

I wrote to all four editors of the *Textbook* about this surprising omission and received replies from two of them. One said: 'We thought long and hard about Jung: Anthony Storr's chapter in the first edition was excellent but he died before we prepared the second. We therefore took—and followed—expert advice.' Unfortunately, he wouldn't tell me who these experts were nor their reasons for advising that Jung be excluded.

Anthony Storr died in 2001, so there should have been plenty of time to find someone else to write a new chapter on Jung if that was what they wanted to do. For one, there is Dr Anthony Stevens, an eminent psychiatrist who has written extensively on Jung. Or they could have simply reprinted Storr's chapter—the chapter on Freud is reproduced virtually unaltered. I also wrote to the publisher, Oxford University Press, and was told they wanted to keep the book to a reasonable size. Since the new edition is 110 pages shorter than the old one (2021 v 2131 pages), I found this unconvincing.

Why, then, when Freud and others in the psychoanalytical movement are mentioned, with Freud rightly having a chapter to himself, has Jung been excluded? Even if the editors disagreed with Jung, why didn't they say so in a section offering a critical assessment of his work? The contribution of Freud to psychoanalysis can hardly be over-estimated, but Jung built upon Freud's theories and developed them much further. The two men met in 1907 and until 1912 enjoyed a close and fruitful relationship. Jung was nineteen years younger, and at first Freud looked to him as his heir. But Jung's independent spirit and need to stick to his own path led to their inevitable falling out—a breach that took a heavy toll on both of them.

The main reason for this was that Jung could not accept

Freud's theories that the unconscious is merely the repository of repressed and forgotten memories, and that the sex drive is at the root of virtually all human motivation. Jung's concepts include the collective unconscious and the archetypes—two of the most important twentieth-century contributions to psychiatry. He also developed the theory of psychological types, including introversion and extraversion (note the spelling).

An example of the importance of Jung today can be seen in the twentieth congress of the International Association for Analytical Psychology, held over five days in Kyoto in 2016, where I was one of nearly 700 attendees from all over the world.

I am, therefore, left to speculate as to the reason for this glaring omission from the *Textbook*, and can only conclude it is because Jung was perceived as not being 'scientific' enough. This criticism he often had to deal with in his lifetime, especially, as he ruefully observed, when it was made by people who had not read his books, let alone understood them. Jung was at pains to emphasize that he was an empiricist; he dealt with observable facts. For example, if someone believed in God, that was a psychological fact. Whether God actually exists, being a question of theology, he was not in a position to say. Jung was even accused of being a mystic, but it will be obvious to anyone who takes the trouble to study his works that he was nothing of the kind.

Jung said: 'People sometimes call me a religious leader. I am not that. I have no message, no mission; I attempt only to understand.'

Talk therapy

From reading websites on non-drug treatment for mental symptoms, one may get the impression that what is offered in talk therapy—I prefer to say psychotherapy—are techniques with scientific-sounding, if slightly scary, names such as cognitive behavioural therapy, psychodynamic psychotherapy, cognitive analytic therapy, etc. There have been attempts to classify and subject these various types of 'intervention' to scientific assessment to see if there is evidence that supports their use for particular disorders. And this means that patients first need to be assigned to diagnostic categories such as major depressive disorder, generalized anxiety disorder, panic disorder, bi-polar disorder, attention deficit hyperactivity disorder, etc. So many disorders!

Then, a potential patient—I prefer the word patient to client or mental health service-user—might get the impression he or she will have to undergo a 'process' or submit to a kind of psychological excavation to delve into the past and dig up disturbing events from childhood. Some people may find such a prospect off-putting and be deterred from seeking this kind of help.

In regard to techniques, what does 'cognitive' mean? The Shorter Oxford English Dictionary defines cognition (cognitive is the adjective) as 'the action or faculty of knowing, now specifically including perceiving, conceiving, etc., as opposed to emotion and volition; the acquisition and possession of empirical factual knowledge.' So now you know! The currently popular cognitive behavioural therapy (defined as 'a type of psychotherapy in which negative patterns of thought about the self and the world are challenged in order to alter behaviour or mood) does seem to help some people, and as it is usually time-limited, can be applied in a health service setting.

Teaching these ways of coping with distressing symptoms, useful as they may be, do not, however, get to the root of the problem. The kind of therapy I have found most useful for this, and which I practice myself, is eclectic, though it's based on Jung's analytical psychology (if we are to put a name to it).

As Jung pointed out, for the therapist it doesn't matter so much *what you do* (what techniques you offer), but what matters greatly is *who you are*. That is to say, rather than techniques (and patients can hardly be expected to know in advance what will suit them), what is most important is the relationship which develops, if it does, between the patient and therapist.

I find it best to approach each new patient with a completely open mind. There is no process, much less a syllabus (!), which is followed to delve into this or that from their past life. On the contrary, when given the undivided attention of a supportive and non-judgemental therapist, patients usually have *plenty* to say about their concerns, worries, and fears. Certainly, the pace and nature of the material revealed are entirely in the hands of the patient and no attempt is made to get them to talk about things they would prefer not to mention. It has to be said, however, that not everyone is suited to this kind of therapy and in such cases the above-mentioned techniques may be useful.

The role of the therapist, above all, is to listen. This of itself can have a healing effect. In addition, when appropriate, observations and interpretations may be offered and the therapist can act as a kind of mirror or sounding-board. The object is always to help patients find their own solutions to their problems or at least to come to terms with them.

In this connection, dream analysis can often be of the greatest value, particularly if a patient feels 'stuck' in a situation or difficulty. Dreams can represent 'another view'—one that comes from deep within, from the unconscious. They are not necessarily to be taken as forgone conclusions, but more as suggestions or possibilities. Dreams, however, can be complicated to interpret, because they often speak symbolically and indirectly, though occasionally they can be blunt to the point of tactlessness. In Jungian psychology, dreams are regarded as having a balancing or compensatory function between one's conscious and unconscious attitudes.

Freud famously said, 'Dreams are the Royal Road to the unconscious.' And so they are—if one only takes the trouble to work with and understand them.

CHAPTER THIRTEEN

Dr James Cyriax

WHEN I STARTED working in general practice it soon became clear that hardly a day would go by when I didn't see at least one patient, and often there were several, who had pain arising from the muscles, tendons, or joints: stiff neck, shoulder pain, backache, sciatica, tennis elbow, etc. These disorders are ubiquitous and cause much suffering.

Also, it was only too obvious that the orthodox approach to these problems has little to offer. An X-ray of the affected part or blood tests might be ordered, though these would seldom shed light on the matter. As for treatment, the available options were limited to trying pain-killers or anti-inflammatory drugs or, if spontaneous recovery did not occur after a reasonable time, sending the patient for physiotherapy. I have the greatest respect for physiotherapists, and they do their best for patients who are often referred to them with neither a diagnosis nor a suggested prescription: 'Re Mrs Jones with shoulder pain: please see and treat.'

But if physiotherapy doesn't work, after a further delay the patient might be referred to a specialist, typically an orthopaedic surgeon. Referral to a surgeon implies a decision to treat accordingly, that is, by an operation. But why are there no specialists in disorders of the moving parts of the body who can treat them by non-operative means?

Then by chance I came across Dr James Cyriax. He was an English orthopaedic physician of impeccable medical credentials who had recently retired from his consultant post at the renowned St Thomas's Hospital on the south bank of the River Thames in London. After his retirement he continued working in the NHS by holding clinics at St Andrew's Hospital in London's east end. He also ran training courses there for interested doctors and physiotherapists. I enrolled in one of these week-long courses in 1975.

It was a revelation. Here at last was a system—based entirely on established principles of applied anatomy and physical examination—whereby one could reach a clinical diagnosis in the majority of patients with aches and pains in the muscles and joints. Having done that, one could then treat the part at fault using orthodox, logical, non-surgical methods. These include steroid (cortisone) and local anaesthetic injections, spinal manipulation, and deep friction massage. When these techniques are applied in the correct manner to suitable patients, they result in many cases in the rapid relief of symptoms— much to the gratification of the patient, and, indeed, of the doctor. I have continued to this day to use Dr Cyriax's diagnostic and treatment methods with regularly good results.

After the course had finished I learnt as much as I could about this work, sitting in with other observers at his clinics at St Andrew's hospital, and later, when I had gained proficiency in Dr Cyriax's methods, for a time working with him at his private practice in Wimpole Street in London's west end.

Of the many patients who were referred to him at St Andrew's Hospital whom I observed, two were of particular interest. One was a woman with long-continuing low back pain. She said to him, 'You're my last hope, Dr Cyriax, and if you can't help me I shall jump in the river!' He quietly replied, 'I've been the last hope for thousands of people.' Then he carried out his standard physical examination and determined that she had a disorder that was suitable for treatment by spinal manipulation. This was performed there and then by his attending physiotherapist and the patient was rapidly relieved of her symptoms. (The physiotherapist worked with him in his private practice and had been trained in his manipulation techniques.)

Another patient, a middle-aged man, came in wearing a supportive neck collar. He complained of pain at both his upper arms. The collar had been provided by another practitioner because an X-ray of his neck showed what was called degenerative disc disease, and on this basis it had been assumed that the arm pain was due to a disorder in his neck.

We observed the meticulous systematic way that Dr Cyriax took the history and then examined this patient. He started with the neck: all the movements were of full range and painless, and there was no disorder of the muscles. Then he proceeded to examine on both sides the movements (active, passive, and against resistance) of the patient's shoulder blade, shoulder joint, elbow, wrist, and hand. When the patient pressed his hand up against the doctor's resistance, this reproduced his pain. It was clear, therefore, that he was suffering from tennis elbow on both sides. This is a common disorder, not confined to tennis players, and is due to a strain of the tendon at the elbow of the muscle that raises the hand at the wrist. Dr Cyriax gave a steroid injection to the appropriate place at both elbows, and the collar was abandoned. At follow-up a week later the patient was pain free.

When I first tried using these methods on my own patients, as you can imagine I was slightly apprehensive. Would I be able to make the correct diagnosis and properly administer the appropriate treatment?

It was not long before a lady turned up with a very painful shoulder that had come on quickly a few days previously for no obvious reason such as an injury. She was hardly able lift her right arm away from her side and was almost in tears with the pain. After examining her in the way I had learnt, I diagnosed acute subdeltoid bursitis. (The subdeltoid bursa is the space just underneath the bone at the top of the outer aspect of the shoulder; it can become spontaneously inflamed.) Then I loaded a syringe with a steroid suspension and local anaesthetic and, while she gritted her teeth, did my best at injecting her right subdeltoid bursa. I asked her to come back five days later. This was to see how she was as well as for my educational benefit. She came in with a smile on her face and exclaimed, 'I could have kissed you!' The pain had subsided rapidly after the injection and did not return.

Frozen shoulder

One of Cyriax's most important discoveries was in the treatment of frozen shoulder. This is a common disorder of unknown cause in which a middle-aged person develops pain and stiffness in one or other shoulder joint. The Japanese call it *gojuu kata*, fifty (year old) shoulder. Untreated, the condition worsens over about six months, remains painful to the point of disturbing sleep for another six months, and then gradually recovers over a further year.

Frozen shoulder responds well to an injection into the joint of a steroid suspension called triamcinolone. Of course it must be done for the right reason, with the correct technique, and with proper sterile precautions. Usually the pain is relieved from the first injection, but since one injection will produce only temporary benefit, it must be repeated a number of times at gradually increasing intervals. A typical patient with frozen shoulder may need five or six injections spread out over about three months. The pain and inflammation can thereby be safely aborted and the process of recovery compressed into this short time, without pain. I have treated hundreds of patients with frozen shoulder in this way and have never seen any complications.

Nonetheless, it's a sound principle that a doctor shouldn't do to a patient anything he wouldn't be prepared to have done to himself. I use the masculine pronoun deliberately here, because the reader may be amused to learn that I have suffered from a frozen shoulder myself. I got my nurse to inject me and was soon cured. I was privileged because I knew what was wrong and had the facilities at hand to deal with it. For many patients with frozen shoulder, however, what usually happens is as shown in the following account of a middle-aged Swiss gentleman whom I know, called Alex, who was on a short visit to Tokyo. (This case is described with his permission.)

He complained of the typical gradually increasing pain and stiffness at his right shoulder. His sleep was disturbed and he was in quite a miserable state. After diagnosing Alex with frozen shoulder I gave the first of what I recommended to be a series of triamcinolone injections to the joint. But as he needed to return to Switzerland soon there was only time for one injection. He was already under the care of his general practitioner and an orthopaedic surgeon in Zurich, but they had been unable to help him except with painkillers. So I wrote a letter to the orthopaedic surgeon, with a copy to the GP, setting out my findings, diagnosis, and description of the treatment, and requested that he continue the injections as I recommended. I even took the trouble, or perhaps I should say the liberty, of copying the relevant pages of Dr Cyriax's textbook and enclosing it with the letter.

If there's one thing guaranteed to get a doctor's back up it's another doctor telling him or her uninvited what to do. My letter was as polite and tactful as I could make it, but I was not favoured with the courtesy of a reply. More importantly, it was disappointing, if predictable, that Alex just had to put up with non-treatment in his own country, and after a long uncomfortable interval he recovered.

Back pain and sciatica
Back pain and sciatica (pain felt in the leg from pressure on a nerve in the lower back by a displaced disc) are also very common symptoms. Except in rare cases they are not due to any serious disease but can cause much pain and disability. Many people with these symptoms will recover in time (weeks to months) but not a few develop persisting pain. This is a big problem and, if physiotherapy is unavailing, these patients may

end up consulting an orthopaedic surgeon for consideration for an operation. I can imagine orthopaedic surgeons, on seeing yet another patient with backache for whom they have little to offer, will regard such patients with a sinking heart.

Dr Cyriax made it clear he didn't have a cure for backache, and neither do I. But there is a lot that can be done through his systematic approach to make a working diagnosis, thereby enabling one to offer logical treatment. For example, if the history and examination indicate a displaced (slipped) disc between two vertebrae at the lower back, then spinal manipulation may be effective in reducing (correcting) the displacement and relieving the pain. Or, if the patient is unsuitable for manipulation, other measures can be offered, in particular with what is known as an epidural injection.

This is administered through the small opening at the lowest part of the sacrum (the triangular-shaped bone at the lower end of the spinal column) that nature has thoughtfully provided in case a person needs one of these injections. If done in the right way and for the right reason, it is remarkably safe—the injection does not go near the spine itself—and is a most useful treatment in many cases of sciatica as well as for acute severe low back pain. For example, it is not uncommon for someone to be immobilised with sudden severe pain at the lower back ('lumbago'). The usual treatment is to recommend rest and painkillers and await spontaneous recovery. But if an epidural injection is given the duration of pain may be shortened to a few days. I have found this a valuable treatment to carry out there and then, on the examination couch in my consulting room, or if a patient is unable to get out of bed due to pain, to perform in the patient's home or hotel room.

I should stress that this kind of treatment is not something clever or difficult; it consists of applying basic knowledge that any interested doctor can acquire. There should be at least one person with orthopaedic medical expertise in the group practices that GPs work in these days. As well as being convenient for patients, it would avoid the cost of many hospital referrals.

A Prophet is not without honour...

So why haven't Dr Cyriax's methods been widely taken up? He provided the answer, with some irony, himself: 'You're not allowed to cure the patients the wrong way!' In other words, a prophet is not without honour except in his own country, for his approach has been recognised more in the USA and parts of Europe than in Britain. Although he had a dedicated following among many individual general practitioners and physiotherapists, he wasn't popular with everyone. Maybe he wasn't the most tactful person, and certainly in his old age did seem to become slightly paranoid and he quarrelled with some of the doctors who worked with him.

One of Dr Cyriax's main ambitions was to obtain the recognition of his work that he felt it deserved. To this end, in the 1970s he established, with my help, the Institute of Orthopaedic Medicine, one purpose of which was to provide year-round teaching of his methods. However, for various reasons including the fact that I was planning to immigrate to Japan, I resigned from the Institute but it continued under a different name, the Society of Orthopaedic Medicine. Subsequently, the name was changed again to the Society of Musculoskeletal Medicine (SOMM).

What is the aim of SOMM? Their website it is not entirely clear:

> The SOMM approach is based on the seminal work of Dr James Cyriax...The Society was formed in 1979 to continue to develop and integrate the approach into musculoskeletal practice through its educational courses...

From this it seems that what SOMM does is only *based* on the work of Dr Cyriax and that this is in the process of being 'developed and integrated' into something else, what they call musculoskeletal practice. But what is musculoskeletal practice (better called orthopaedic medicine) if not that which rests on the foundation of Dr Cyriax's diagnostic physical examination methods? The failure of SOMM to respond to some of the nonsense which is published from time to time in mainstream medical journals in the field of orthopaedic medicine is perhaps explained by their apparent departure from Dr Cyriax's seminal work.

For example, there was in 2016 an article on the current state of treatment for frozen shoulder published in the BMJ. It is almost a counsel of despair. Cortisone injections are mentioned only to be dismissed as ineffective. I had a letter[14] published about this lamentable state of affairs; it went unheeded. But where, oh where, was the voice of SOMM?

After some perseverance in contacting the honourable Society, I was eventually put in touch with a nice woman, a physiotherapist, who is one of the organisers. We had an interesting and wide-ranging discussion but I didn't get very far. For a start, SOMM appears to be run by physiotherapists, and although I was told there are five GPs on the council and in the teaching team, on their website only three are mentioned, and there appears to be little medical input.

To the points I raised I eventually received a composite answer from a number of people in the Society, in which, among other remarks, they said it appears that my 'views and practice are much the same as when I worked with Dr Cyriax in the 1970s,' and that the Society's clinical approach, although inspired by Dr Cyriax, is 'firmly based in modern research and best available clinical evidence.'

This is the whole point. If modern research and best available

[14] BMJ 2016;354:i4162

clinical evidence result in the kind of article on shoulder pain mentioned above, it is because Dr Cyriax's teachings have been diluted to the point where they are in danger of being lost. This is shown in the Society's approach to frozen shoulder: it is disappointing that they say, 'There is no standard agreed treatment for frozen shoulder.' Cyriax's approach is mentioned, though it is inaccurately described, and is not given the prominence it deserves. I wanted to discuss this situation and related matters directly with one of the GP advisors; they all declined.

Another problem is that the courses run by SOMM are open to non-medically qualified people, to wit, osteopaths and chiropractors. One of Dr Cyriax's ambitions was that orthopaedic medical expertise should be widely available *within the medical sphere*. Thus, if a patient needed, say, spinal manipulation, it would be performed by a trained doctor or physiotherapist, and lay manipulators would become superfluous.

Otherwise, this is what can happen. It was recently reported by the BBC[15] that an 80 year old man in the City of York in England went to see a chiropractor for pain in his back and legs. During his third treatment a manoeuvre was performed as a result of which his neck was broken and he died the next day. The BBC report shows a photo of the chiropractor's premises on the outside of which a quotation from Hippocrates is proudly displayed: 'Look well to the spine for the cause of disease.' Hippocrates died nearly 2,400 years ago and medical science has moved on a bit since then.

Dr Cyriax, who died in 1985, must be turning in his grave.

---

[15] https://www.bbc.com/news/uk-england-york-north-yorkshire-50380928

CHAPTER FOURTEEN
Treating Neck and Low Back Pain

FAMILIARITY WITH DR Cyriax's methods of examination and treatment enabled me to be much more effective than I would otherwise have been in treating people with disorders of the moving parts of the body. A few examples are described below.

A 51 year old American man came to see me with an eighteen month history of pain in the region of his right shoulder blade. The pain was made worse by bending his neck forwards and to the left. After examination I concluded his condition was suitable for manipulation of his neck. This I carried out with the simple techniques I had learnt. They were accompanied by the elicitation of a number of satisfying clicks and immediately afterward the pain was much diminished. I asked him to return in a few days if he had any residual symptoms. He sent a fax five days later saying his condition was markedly improved and it was the first time in a very long time that he had been pain-free. If only they were all that easy!

This satisfactory result and his complimentary message led me to reflect that many such case are straightforward to treat, and it is regrettable that the simple techniques I used are not generally available.

Then there was a fit-looking 34 year old American who came to see me with a complaint of a constant pain at the right side of the back of his head since the previous month. It had come on while weight training and was bad enough to distract him at work. The pain was aggravated by moving his neck. Examination revealed the pattern of painful movements that indicated a diagnosis of a displaced disc in his neck. I carried out a simple rotatory manipulation; there was a click and the pain disappeared.

This was another common situation where if this patient had gone elsewhere they likely would have taken an X-ray and given him pain-killers. This would have been of little help and probably resulted in a considerably larger bill than mine. Thus, a more knowledgeable or skilled doctor may take a smaller fee than a less competent one, even though the patient is helped more.

Another patient was a typical example of how low back pain is so often mishandled by doctors. She was an American aged 29 who had developed low back pain three months previously. It was almost constant and she had observed that the pain was worse if she bent her head forwards or if she pulled her foot up with her leg straight out in front of her—these are classical signs of pressure on a nerve root in the lower back. She had been to another clinic where the doctor was unclear whether the pain was arising from the muscles or bones and had subjected her to expensive X-rays. Then anti-inflammatory medicine and a muscle relaxant were prescribed. Not being satisfied with this, she sought the opinion of a doctor in Hong Kong where she used to live, who also appeared uncertain as to whether it was a muscle or bone pain, mentioning a possible hair-line fracture. He had wanted to repeat the X-rays but she gave up at that point and a friend recommended her to me.

Examination showed she had a small displacement of a disc in her lower back (slipped disc). I manipulated her lumbar spine and achieved a full range of painless movements. This was simple to do with the right approach, but her problem had been completely misunderstood and mishandled by two other doctors.

On another occasion I saw a 25 year old man with a history of pain at the left side of his neck that had started two weeks previously. Then, a week after the onset the pain had spread down his left arm and he had tingling and numbness at the middle three fingers and palm of the hand. Understandably, he was very worried about what these symptoms meant. He had asked his girlfriend, a nurse, about this and all sorts of terrible things had been mentioned, from multiple sclerosis to an impending stroke. Examination showed the typical pattern that some of his neck movements increased the discomfort at his neck and tingling in the arm. He had no weakness of his muscles and there were no neurological abnormalities in his arms or legs. The clinical diagnosis was, therefore, compression of the left seventh cervical root from a slipped disc in his neck.

If this common disorder is recognised one can be confident in reassuring the patient that it will recover spontaneously within three months of the onset of the pain in the arm. The treatment, therefore, is reassurance and the prescription of pain-killers to be taken if needed, especially for pain at night. Scans and X-rays are unnecessary unless one has reason to suspect a serious disorder is present.

Not all cases of back pain are easy to deal with, especially when there is a psychological component. An example of this situation was an American patient suffering from low back pain who had called to inquire if I could provide the same medication he had been prescribed in the US. I said I would need to see him first. He arrived forty-five minutes early and had to wait thirty minutes before I was free. When I collected him from the waiting area he evinced pain on arising from sitting, then enquired, 'How are you today, doc?' and commented pleasantly on my British accent.

The first problem, significant in itself, was that he couldn't give a simple answer to a simple question. I asked him to tell me his age: 'Well, let's see now, I was born in 1955 so that makes me...,' and when I asked how long he had had the pain, he said, 'It started because my neck was in a pushed-forward position, and my neurosurgeon told me I would definitely get back pain, maybe in a year, maybe in five years or ten years.'

He was a tall thin man with one glass eye and a suntan who

was temporarily in Tokyo working as a caddy for a visiting professional golfer. When invited to give the history of the problem, he spoke non-stop for about ten minutes. In brief, three years ago he was involved in a car accident, sustaining fractures of the three lowest vertebrae in his neck. This was treated by fusion (fixing together) of the affected bones which had left him with his neck slightly protruding forwards, and, true to prediction, two years later he developed chronic low back pain. It was only relieved by an opiate-type pain-killer, though he had tried epidural injections at a pain clinic, with little benefit.

On examination, he had a long scar at the back of his neck. All his neck movements were markedly limited and apparently very painful. Even testing unrelated movements, such as pushing his arms away from his sides against the resistance of my hand, were allegedly painful. His lower back movements, likewise, were restricted and painful, though he could bend forwards nearly to 90° when encouraged to do so. All the movements of his hips appeared painful and straight-leg raising was only 20° (it is normally painless and of 80° or 90°). At this point I stopped examining him, and he remarked that I had given him a really good work-out!

I thought he was a man who was living the role of a chronic pain patient. He agreed that treatment in a pain clinic was the most helpful and he would visit one when he returned to the US. I gave him a moderately strong non-narcotic pain-killer, but agreed to prescribe codeine if this didn't work. (He had come without a supply his usual medication for fear of breaching Japanese law— one can get into trouble for attempting to import narcotic drugs, even if prescribed by a doctor in another country.) This situation illustrates an all-too-common situation. No attempt had been made to diagnose his low back pain to see if it could be treated directly, such as by manipulation; and he had been given an opioid pain-killer to which he had probably become addicted and would therefore be likely to continue taking indefinitely.

Then there was a call on a Sunday morning from a patient for a home visit. I'd seen the family a few times so they knew what services I offered. The husband had severe back pain and they had called their physician in the States who had recommended muscle relaxants. I was requested to obtain this medication, and a house call would be welcome if I brought it with me. I explained that I didn't normally prescribe muscle relaxants for back pain, so they agreed that 'I was the doctor' and the treatment was up to me. I said I would be there after about ninety minutes. The wife seemed concerned I couldn't go sooner, but agreed to wait. A short time later she rang again to cancel the visit, saying they would wait and see. I suspect this meant that they had found someone else to provide muscle relaxants. I thought it was extraordinary that even a family who know me apparently had more confidence in their physician in the US than in me, and it's always slightly annoying if someone uses me merely to provide the treatment that a doctor in another country has advised. On the other hand, although I lost the fee I was glad I didn't have to disrupt my Sunday.

What's wrong with muscle relaxants, so called, for back pain? As always, one needs to make a diagnosis before deciding on treatment. With back pain the disorder does not lie in the muscles, though the pain is felt there. One has to treat the cause, for example, a slipped disc, by manipulation or epidural local anaesthesia. Muscle relaxants have an appeal for patients, but they do little good and are likely to upset the stomach. I have never used them.

State of the art
The ongoing scandal of lack of provision of effective treatment for low back pain was highlighted by a recent article in BMJ.[16] This was a systematic review (a study of other studies) of what

---

[16] doi: https://doi.org/10.1136/bmj.l689 (Published 13 March 2019)

they called 'spinal manipulative therapy in chronic low back pain'. The authors looked at forty-seven randomised controlled trials which included 9,211 patients. The conclusion, disappointingly if predictably, was that spinal manipulation produced similar effects to 'other recommended therapies'.

What are these other recommended therapies? It almost makes you want to cry—like the patients who may already be crying with their pain. Here they are, according to NICE:

• Provide people with advice and information
• Consider a group exercise programme
• Consider psychological therapies using a cognitive behavioural approach

In other words, do nothing.

Advice and information? 'Don't worry, most back pain gets better by itself, so just take some painkillers if you have to, and wait.' Group exercises and psychological therapies are merely ways of passing the time; they are almost insulting to a sufferer from back pain. How can you exercise if your back is hurting? And back pain is not a psychological disorder.

Spinal manipulative therapy in this paper was taken to mean 'any hands-on treatment of the spine'. So any and all types of hands-on treatment were lumped together as if they are a single treatment. It gets worse. What do they mean by low back pain? This a symptom, not a diagnosis. Nonetheless, they looked at trials of treatment of any sort of manipulation for patients with undiagnosed pain at the lower back. (Of course, rare serious causes of back pain like cancer or infections were excluded.) How can you expect to get meaningful results from any kind of investigation under these circumstances?

There was a letter published in the BMJ in response to this paper from a GP who is also an osteopath, that is to say, he had been to the trouble of acquiring a qualification from the

London College of Osteopathic Medicine. He said he has treated thousands of patients with osteopathic spinal manipulation and that it's very effective. Intrigued, I wrote and asked him to tell me what criteria he uses to select those patients with low back pain who are suitable for manipulation from those who are not. He replied that he uses it for musculo-skeletal pain where he can diagnose or elicit 'somatic dysfunction' as the cause. I suspect he meant he uses it for virtually all patients with back pain. So I wrote to him again asking what he meant by somatic dysfunction. He didn't have a clear answer but offered his opinion:

> During the course of a movement, there is a dynamic mismatch between the proprioceptive input from muscles versus arthrodial proprioceptors (perhaps a jerky, stilted or changed movement, especially if subject to loading). The spinal reflexes respond to the mismatched input by a clasp reflex, which seeks to stabilise/immobilise the originating segment of the mismatch. The aberrant reflex can sustain over weeks, months or years, but no doubt many don't. The locked segment's proprioceptors presumably recalibrate to their new, locked, position, thereby stabilising the segment in its irregular position.

Dear reader, if you have difficulty understanding this, so do I.

The question the authors of the above-mentioned paper should have asked is: 'What type of low back pain is suitable for manipulation?' This leads to the heart of the problem: low back pain commonly seems to be regarded as a disease entity in which no attempt is made at differentiation. And the reason for this extraordinary and highly unsatisfactory state of affairs is that *most doctors don't know how to examine a patient complaining of low back pain.*

Yet this deficiency can easily be remedied if a doctor takes the trouble to learn how. And I don't mean that he or she needs to acquire a qualification in osteopathy which, as we have seen, results in the ability to offer only one treatment, osteopathic manipulation, to virtually all comers with back pain.

If you see your GP with a complaint that might arise from a disorder of the heart, you will be examined in a standard way: feeling the pulse and measuring the blood pressure, listening to the heart and lungs with a stethoscope, and observing for enlargement of the liver and swelling of the feet. This is a basic skill that all medical students are taught. But what are they taught about examining the musculo-skeletal system? They learn how to recognise disorders such as gout, osteoarthritis ('wear and tear') of the hip or knee joint, or rheumatoid arthritis, but what about the ordinary aches and pains arising from the muscles or joints not due to gout, osteoarthritis, or rheumatic disorders? There is overlap with sports medicine to which medical students may be exposed, but this still leaves by far the largest group whose disorders are not acquired in the course of playing sports—what about them? Dr Cyriax wrote an article[17] in the BMJ as long ago as 1972 lamenting the void in the teaching to medical students of effective methods of diagnosis and treatment in musculo-skeletal disorders. The situation is the same today. More than thirty years after Dr Cyriax's death there is still no department of orthopaedic medicine in any NHS hospital in Britain.

---

[17] https://www.bmj.com/content/4/5835/292

PART THREE

Medical Practice in Tokyo

CHAPTER FIFTEEN
Acquiring a Japanese Medical License

HAVING BEEN OFFERED a post at a large private clinic in Tokyo serving the expatriate community, I first had to obtain a special Japanese medical licence by passing an examination. This was administered through a scheme known as the Anglo-Japanese Agreement on Medical Licensing. It is a reciprocal arrangement under which doctors from Britain[18] can work in Japan, and vice versa. However, when I came to Japan the licences granted to British doctors were restricted to five, but the number of Japanese doctors allowed to practice in Britain was unlimited. There were certain conditions in that my licence was limited to a clinic at a designated address, and I was only supposed to treat non-Japanese patients. The latter stipulation was something of a grey area, its apparent purpose being to prevent a foreign doctor competing in the Japanese Health Service—something I had no desire to do anyway.

The examination was based on the one that Japanese medical students take to qualify, though it was held in English. The subjects were medicine, surgery, gynaecology, and Japanese public health. It consisted of a multiple-choice written paper with sixty questions, and two vivas.

The application process for permission to take the examination was extensive and in this I received sterling assistance from the British Embassy in Tokyo. The Japanese authorities wanted to know how many hours I had spent studying anatomy, physiology, biochemistry, etc. Luckily, Bart's still had the records and I was able to provide the required figures. The then British Consul called it 'an exercise in paper collecting'.

I arrived in Japan a few days before the examination to

---

[18] The scheme has since been extended to the US, France, and Singapore.

recover from jet-lag. During this time I unexpectedly received what seemed like an informal invitation to visit a professor of anaesthesiology at a hospital somewhere on the outskirts of Tokyo. I knew enough of Japanese etiquette unquestioningly to accept this invitation and was taken to the place in a chauffeured car. The professor emerged from the operating theatre and took me to the staff common room where I was offered a cup of tea. Then he asked me, 'How is Mrs Thatcher?' and, 'What is the weather like in England?' and suchlike innocuous questions. After some ten minutes of pleasant small talk, the professor stood up, politely thanked me for coming and announced that he had to return to the operating theatre.

The next day I received a similar invitation to tea with a junior official in the Ministry of Health and Welfare. This took place in the staff canteen of one of the Ministry buildings. The official was a young man who similarly engaged me in polite conversation: 'How is Mrs Thatcher?' and, 'What is the weather like in England?'

I found the examination itself quite difficult. There were only a few of the multiple choice questions that I was confident I had answered correctly, and I believed I didn't shine in the vivas either. In these I was asked, among other things, to state the diagnoses shown on X-rays and CT scans. The latter were then relatively new and my knowledge of them I had to admit was sketchy. After the examinations I returned to London convinced that I had failed, but when the official result came, I had passed after all!

Later I realised—and I believe this is true though I could be mistaken—that the written examination and vivas were formalities, and what really mattered were these two interviews: they wanted to see if I was someone who would fit in, as a foreigner, in Japanese society.

Having cleared this hurdle, a few months later I moved to Japan and started work at the above-mentioned clinic. I ended up there as a salaried assistant for almost eight years. In the normal way, after a period of mutual assessment of around six months, this would have led to an invitation to join the partnership, or to my contract not being renewed if they thought I was unsuitable for them. It wasn't so simple, however. For one thing I baulked at the very large sum of money they wanted as 'goodwill' for the privilege—a kind of joining fee. Second, one of the three partners was a rather brutal Japanese surgeon, about whom more will be said later, and third, I found the standard of medical practice in that place overall was below that to which I aspired. Examples are described in the following chapter.

As I wished to stay in Japan I therefore sought an opportunity to set up a new, independent clinic, with the aim of offering a larger choice of medical facilities to the foreign community.

The main problem was to obtain permission from the Japanese Ministry of Health and Welfare to change the address of the premises where my licence was recognised to a new address in another part of Tokyo. What should have been a simple administrative procedure turned out to require a major diplomatic effort, taking some years of dedicated work by the British Embassy. It involved *notes verbales* going from the British Embassy to the Japanese Foreign Ministry to the Ministry of Health and Welfare, and back again. In the end permission was granted, for which those involved at the British Embassy have my lasting gratitude.

Tokyo British Clinic

The practice I eventually set up, the Tokyo British Clinic, was the realisation of a dream: an ideal practice, or as near to it as it was possible to achieve. I was lucky to be in the right place at the right time.

I found pleasant and spacious premises of a new office building in the trendy Daikanyama area of Tokyo. There I organised a fully equipped and staffed clinic with two English-speaking receptionists and a full-time nurse. I also set up X-ray and laboratory facilities, and a pharmacy. The Clinic was officially opened on 19th July 1992 by the then British Ambassador to Japan, Sir John Boyd.

The clinic aimed to provide comprehensive medical services to the foreign community. As far as possible everything was done in-house. I learnt, with the assistance of a friendly radiographer, how to take X-rays. It was not difficult once you got the hang of it. Of course, precautions were taken to protect the patients and staff from radiation exposure—the room was lead-lined and we used a special apron to cover the lower part of the body when taking a chest X-ray. My nurse learnt how to set the patient up in front of the film cassette and put in the correct exposure, but only I, being medically qualified, was allowed to 'press the red button' and actually take the picture. We started with a mechanical developing system where the exposed film was passed through a chemical bath in a darkroom, but when it became available we switched to a digital machine. This was extremely useful because if there was a film which I was unclear how to interpret, I could send it over the internet for expert an opinion by arrangement with a hospital-based radiologist. In day-to-day practice, if a patient came who I suspected was suffering from pneumonia or a bone fracture, I could take the X-ray myself on the spot. Likewise, part of the nurse's room was devoted to basic laboratory tests. Thus, in the case of, say, a urethral or vaginal discharge, I could examine a specimen myself under the microscope—my nurse was expert in making a Gram stain[19]—to have an answer within minutes while the patient waited. Blood specimens were examined in a commercial laboratory; for this a delivery man would call twice a day, once to take specimens away and again to bring the results of tests from the previous day. Being a dispensing practice was very convenient for patients.

---

[19] A commonly used technique for staining microscopy specimens developed by the Danish bacteriologist Hans Christian Gram in 1884.

If medicines were needed they were provided at the end of the consultation, and it brought in useful additional income. I was very lucky with my nurse who, in addition to ordinary nursing duties, acted as a radiographer (except for 'pressing the button'), phlebotomist (taking blood), laboratory technician, pharmacist, and occasionally as a receptionist too. She was with me for twenty years and I owe her an inestimable debt of gratitude.

Applying the art of medicine

At last, in my own clinic I could organise everything as I wanted. I could see patients in an unhurried atmosphere and apply the skills I had learnt or taught myself through experience.

I would always greet patients in the waiting area myself, and then invite them to follow me into my consulting room. One could learn a lot from observing patients in this way. They might be restless and pacing about, or someone might even be lying down if they were feeling really ill. (I would usually be alerted by my staff in such a case.) Shaking hands with everyone was also informative: a hot and dry hand might be due to a fever, or it might be cold and clammy (the 'wet fish' handshake) in anxiety. Tell-tale signs of nicotine-stained fingers with the smell of tobacco on their person would give away a smoker; and watching someone's gait could be useful—they might have a limp or other walking difficulty, such as in Parkinson's disease.

Something that is not done by doctors as often as it should be, is to take a dietary history, that is, ask patients in whom it is relevant, to describe what they eat and drink in a typical day. This might reveal a clue to the cause of gastric troubles. For example, one elderly lady came to me complaining of wind (gas). It emerged that she would drink a whole bottle of tonic water every day, believing this would benefit her as a 'tonic'. I advised her to desist and she was soon cured. Then, some people with their 'hectic' life-styles eat a diet which contributes to or actually causes stomach or intestinal disorders. They get up too late for breakfast and grab a sandwich made of white bread from a convenience store on their way to work; they drink three or four (or more) cups of coffee throughout the day, each sweetened with two (or more) spoonfuls of sugar; lunch may consist of a hamburger and chips (French fries) washed down with Coca-Cola; and dinner might be taken at a cheap restaurant including a sweet desert and be accompanied by several alcoholic drinks; fruit and vegetables are notable by their absence. Dietary advice would often be very helpful in such cases.

CHAPTER SIXTEEN
Tokyo Medical Misadventures

SUDDENLY, AGONISED SCREAMS rent the air. I could hear them through two closed doors. What in God's name was going on?

The clinic in which I worked on my arrival in Tokyo in 1984 offered me a position as a salaried assistant on a two year contract, renewable by mutual agreement. It was run by three partners including a Japanese surgeon who had trained in America. The clinic was very well equipped and included a small operating theatre.

The screams were due to a baby boy having part of his penis cut off! This outrage masquerading as a formal surgical procedure was being perpetrated by the Japanese surgeon (I'll call him Dr Suzuki) whose nickname among the patients, deservedly, was 'the Butcher'. The screams continued for about forty-five minutes.

Gentle reader, I could not stand it. I had to leave the building to wander around outside until it was over. When I later questioned this doctor about what he had done, he seemed almost proud of the fact that he used no anaesthetic; nor was he about to change his practice over this, let alone give it up. I then I spoke to the head of the clinic. His lame response was, 'It's a service to the community.' I thought it was more a service to the clinic's bank balance. The other partner with whom I also raised the matter merely shrugged, commenting, 'Yes, it's noisy.' I imagine it generally is when someone is being tortured. This, and other matters, led eventually to my shaking off the dust from my feet of that place to set up my own practice.

It wasn't just I who was upset by Dr Suzuki's over-enthusiastic use of the scalpel in this way. A mother who had subjected her son to this procedure also complained to him, though from a different perspective. With hindsight, it wasn't unexpected that I should receive a notice from this woman whose son I had been seeing for routine immunisations, saying she wouldn't attend the clinic anymore. The reason was because she was unhappy with Dr Suzuki who had cut off her newborn boy's foreskin but hadn't done it to her satisfaction. She wrote a letter to him setting out her grievances and enclosed a copy to me.

The letter is extraordinary in that the mother seems more concerned about herself than the poor baby. She mentions *her* very unhappy experience, that *she* suffered mentally until she found a doctor who could re-do the operation to her satisfaction, that *she* will have a lifetime scar and that *she* cried tears of fear, anger, and frustration. She added that when the scar heals all will look normal and the boy won't even notice.

As is so often the case where part of a baby's penis has been cut off without medical need, his sufferings are regarded as non-existent or of no importance. One might ask, what about the *baby's* very unhappy experience, *his* mental and physical suffering, the irreparable damage from cutting off his foreskin that will affect him for the rest of his life, and that he will notice all too readily when he is older what was done to him without his consent?

This dreadful practice is discussed further in Chapter 22.

Putting his foot in it

When I was a student we were taught, 'If you don't put your finger in you'll put your foot in it.' This was to encourage trainee doctors not to hesitate to carry out a rectal examination if it was clinically indicated (needed to be done to seek important information). However, in the case of Dr Suzuki, an occasion arose in which he put his foot in it in a potentially serious way because he *did* put his finger in!

At the time when I was working in this establishment we were contracted to carry out pre-employment medical checks for a well known European airline. Almost all the applicants were fit young people, mainly women. These examinations, though important, were a formality: we already had their medical histories and usually no more was required than to examine their ears (because of the pressure changes they would be subjected to in frequent take-offs and landings) and measure their blood pressure.

One day the head of the clinic received a letter from the chief medical officer of said airline: some of the stewardess applicants had complained that they felt upset and humiliated by having a digital rectal examination performed on them as part of their routine medical assessment. The letter concluded with a demand that this practice must cease immediately if we were to continue doing the work. The perpetrator was clearly Dr Suzuki. I'll give him the benefit of the doubt and put it down to an excess of thoroughness rather than any improper motive.

An avoidable tragedy?

An experience I had in my London locum days was revisited upon me in 1990 when I was still working in that clinic. One day a distressed English couple turned up. They were the actor Sir Alan Bates and his wife, Victoria, who were seeking answers in connection with the then recent tragic death of their 19 year old son, Tristan[20], one of twins. Although I had never seen the poor boy, the delicate task of talking to the bereaved parents was delegated to me on the grounds that I was also English. In other words, the senior doctor and head of the clinic didn't have the guts to fulfil this responsibility himself.

The story was a series of disasters. Tristan Bates was working for a modelling agency in Tokyo and had been planning a holiday in Thailand. Believing, incorrectly, that cholera immunisation was advisable for this trip, he turned up at the clinic. In those

---

[20] As this story is in the public domain the patient's and his parents' real names are used.

days patients seeking immunisations could go direct to the nurse who would give the injections on the spot without reference to a doctor. This was indefensible. Tristan turns up and requests a cholera shot. Please role up you sleeve. Injection given. See the cashier on your way out. Next please!

Unfortunately, early the following morning he was found dead in a nearby public toilet, wedged upright between two urinals. An autopsy was carried out with inconclusive results, but it was thought he had died of an asthma attack. A press report questioned whether it was a drug overdose—unlikely since drugs are tightly controlled in Japan and addiction is relatively rare. All one can say is that Tristan received a cholera immunisation and died within a day thereafter. Were the two events connected? It is impossible to say with certainty but he could have had a reaction to some component of the vaccine. But the vaccine should never have been given in the first place. It is not recommended for ordinary travellers, though one would consider it for an aid worker in an epidemic area.

Well, Muggins, rather than the head of the clinic, had to deal with the inconsolable grief of the parents. What could I have offered them other than platitudes? 'I'm sorry your son died, and I would like to say it was probably nothing to do with the unnecessary cholera shot we gave him.'

They changed the policy after that. Thenceforth all comers for direct nurse-administered treatments had to fill in a questionnaire about untoward reactions to previous injections, allergies, etc.

That wasn't the only problem. I noticed the nurses were giving immunisations with the patients standing up. This is not a good idea—you may have someone crashing to the floor in a faint.

There was another doctor working there, a relative newcomer who had had no general practice training. His previous experience included working for a pharmaceutical company where he had been involved in animal experiments. When I mentioned to him that it was inadvisable to give injections with patients standing up, he merely laughed and said, 'Ha ha, just like pigs—they faint sometimes when you given them injections.'

Back in Budleigh Salterton

There were further problems with this doctor who found it amusing when pigs fainted. I was working in the clinic one day when a woman was sent in to me who had seen him the previous day. The record showed she had been given antibiotic drops for a sore eye. She said to me, 'I saw Dr — yesterday about my eye, but *he didn't give me anything for the pain.*' Immediately this set alarm bells ringing. I was back in Budleigh Salterton. Severe eye pain likely means a serious disorder. One glance at the eye confirmed my suspicion. The pupil was opaque, fixed and dilated in a vertically oval shape—the classic appearance of acute glaucoma, an ophthalmological emergency. It is due to high pressure developing at the front part of the eye. Acute glaucoma is a diagnosis doctors should be aware of even though they may never see a case. I arranged immediate referral to an eye specialist. Delay may result in blindness.

Another of this doctor's peculiarities was as follows. All medical students are taught that patients should be examined from their right side. There are good reasons for this. It helps for consistency when remembering which side of the patient one is concerned in, and, since most people are right handed, it is easier when examining, say, the abdomen, to feel with the edge of the index finger of your right hand if the liver or spleen is enlarged. Even the disposition of a doctor's room should not force one to examine patients from their left—you would simply put the pillow at the other end of the couch or turn it around if the head part lifts up. One might make an exception for a left handed doctor if they had difficulty using their right hand in the standard position. Also, in general practice, when visiting patients at home, I found it almost invariable that they would be lying in their bed in such a way that I was obliged to approach them from the left. This is one of the many skills a GP needs to acquire: you either use your right hand from the left side of the bed, which is awkward, or you learn to be ambidextrous. It is a giveaway in films with medical scenes that professional advice has not been obtained, when an actor playing a doctor positions himself at the patient's left.

The doctor in question, who was right handed, had the couch in his room arranged so that he examined patients from the wrong side. Once I asked him about it; he was unconcerned. That was the trouble!

'If you don't go the patient will die!'

While working in this clinic one day I was on duty when I received an urgent request for a home visit to a pregnant woman who had developed abdominal pain. When I arrived at her luxury apartment in a fashionable area of Tokyo I took one look at her and knew I had an emergency on my hands. She was as pale as a sheet, as the saying goes; there had been major internal bleeding, most likely from a ruptured ectopic pregnancy. (A pregnancy developing in one of the Fallopian tubes instead of in the womb, and the tube had burst with sudden heavy bleeding.) The only thing to do was to call the emergency number for an ambulance. This I did, an ambulance soon turned up, and the patient was carried down to it on a stretcher. I followed to learn which hospital they were going to take her to. But then the ambulance just sat there. The ambulance men were calling a number of hospitals to find one that would accept her. Apparently they couldn't just turn up at the nearest hospital with an emergency department; they had to find somewhere with an available bed. After about twenty minutes of waiting the patient's husband came rushing home. Quickly apprised of the situation he wanted to take his wife in his own car to a hospital and demand treatment. This was the point at which I told the two ambulance men that if they didn't take her to a hospital *now* the patient would die. Fortunately, they had just received word that the nearby Jikei University Hospital (where I trained in paediatrics in 1967) would receive her. At last the ambulance set off with the patient and her husband on board. I followed in my car. But a few minutes later the ambulance stopped. I rushed over to the driver. Now what? Apparently some further complication had arisen. I was incensed, opened the back of the ambulance, and with the husband's help picked up the poor woman bodily and put her into my car, intending to drive to the hospital ourselves. At this the ambulance men came to their senses, or rather I think it was a matter of not wanting to lose face, and they promised to take her to the hospital immediately. As they could make faster progress with their siren and flashing red lights she was transferred back into the ambulance.

On arrival at the hospital she was promptly admitted, resuscitated, and operated upon. She survived and made a full recovery, though it was inevitable the pregnancy was lost.

That wasn't the end of this outrageous affair. The husband, a senior executive of a major foreign bank, was understandably furious over the ambulance fiasco and potentially fatal result. Soon after his wife's recovery he wrote letters to *The Japan Times* (a widely read English-language newspaper), the ambulance service, and to the governor of Tokyo as well. As a result, the system was supposed to have been reformed—but why should it have taken a near-tragedy to bring about an obvious and essential change to the emergency ambulance service?

A few years later when I was working in my own clinic, the same thing happened, though it was not such a serious case. I'll relate it here.

I was called one evening to a hotel to see a member of an a Middle Eastern airline flight crew who had apparently been involved in a car accident, and the crew captain was uncertain whether the man should go to hospital. When I arrived the room was dark with the only source of light being a bedside lamp, as is often the case in hotel rooms. I had to inspect the patient with the aid of a torch. The captain, another man, and three stewardesses crowded into the room. The patient was breathing heavily but orientated and alert. He had severe peri-orbital haematomas (bruising around the eyes) and much swelling at his upper lip. There was also a cut at his left eyebrow and a puncture wound at his left lower leg. I thought it was more likely he had been in a fight or had been attacked by someone rather than being hit by a car. I wasn't happy about leaving him in the hotel room on his own all night, especially as I had to accept his version of how he came by his injuries. (If he had been in a car accident, unless it was a hit-and-run affair, the police would have been involved.) So I asked the manager of the hotel to call an ambulance. The ambulance duly arrived, and the patient and two colleagues boarded it. But then—again!—the ambulance just sat there while they tried to find a hospital which would accept him. Eventually I left, assuming the ambulance would sooner or later find somewhere. I thought it was absurd that the system was still so disorganised that an ambulance cannot go directly to the nearest government hospital which would be obliged to take him. But at least it wasn't a life-and-death emergency as in the previous case.

The next day I called the hotel and spoke to the manager. He was most grateful I had attended last night. The patient was seen at hospital where he had skull X-rays taken which showed no fractures, and his injuries were dressed. Later the captain called to confirm everything was taken care of and the patient had improved; he asked me to send a certificate saying he was fit to travel.

CHAPTER SEVENTEEN
Hotel Medical Visits

I LIKED DOING hotel visits in Tokyo—they would frequently enliven my evenings. There was a routine for these. I would park my car in the hotel's garage or leave the keys with the valet to park it for me. Then I would head for the duty manager's desk where he would be expecting me, and naturally I was given the red carpet treatment. He would call the guest's room and escort me there. When the consultation was concluded I would go back to the reception area and write out my bill for the visit. Payment was in cash, the fee being added to the guest's bill, though sometimes I was paid by a patient's insurance company.

Visiting hotel guests occasionally brought me into contact with celebrities in the entertainment world. It was interesting to see their human side as ordinary patients rather than as their stage personae. Sometimes these visits resulted in offers of free tickets to classical musical concerts, ballets, operas, and the circus. The pop concert ones I gave to my staff which they accepted with delight. One distinguished classical pianist whom I visited made the interesting remark that in the particular five-star establishment where he stayed when on concert tours, they always complied with his request to turn off the piped music in the public areas. This was because, his head being full of the wonderful music he was due to play, he didn't want to be distracted by noise coming out of the loudspeakers. I thought, wistfully, that they wouldn't do that for me!

There were interesting social aspects as well. Once I was called to see a boy aged 10, a member of the royal family of a far eastern country. He was in Japan for the purpose of visiting the then newly opened Disneyland. The family occupied the whole floor of a five-star hotel. When I had negotiated the complex security arrangements I met the lad and his nurse—the mother was unavailable. He had a sore throat of the sort that I was as sure as I could be that it was due to a viral infection which would recover on its own in a few days. But under the circumstances it felt difficult to decline giving him an antibiotic. It had been assumed from the start that this would be the result of my visit and was their reason for calling me. Afterwards I reflected that it was unfortunate, just because someone came from a high social level and belonged to a fabulously wealthy family, they should receive worse treatment than an ordinary patient.

On another occasion I was summonsed to see a princess from another far eastern country who was staying at a hotel near Tokyo Disneyland. She was an intelligent, educated lady who had developed a stiff neck as a result sitting in an awkward position in the private jet on which she had flown here. Reassurance and the provision of simple pain-killers did not satisfy her; she wanted an MRI scan. In vain did I point out, as tactfully as I could, that a scan was not of the slightest practical value, and as it was a Sunday all the scanning facilities I knew were closed anyway, so I thought she would let it go at that. Not a bit of it. I heard later that her poor secretary/interpreter had spent hours on the phone and had eventually located a clinic that would perform the scan straight away, no doubt for a large fee. And the result? Normal. Evidently this lady needed the reassurance of a normal scan before she could relax about the matter. Are royalty more anxious than ordinary people?

Airline crew

There was one particular hotel where the crew of a major far eastern airline would stay on their stopover in Tokyo, and I was fortunate to be the doctor who was routinely called—probably because I would nearly always be available, even in the middle of the night. On arrival the duty manager would greet me effusively, with much bowing and sucking in of air through his teeth. 'Thank you for coming, Dr Symonds, we are so grateful to you for helping our guests', etc. It was a ritual, but it always seemed genuine, and even if it wasn't genuine it was a very *nice* ritual.

In this hotel I gained something of a reputation among the stewardesses, because if one of them requested a visit, then often three or four others would take advantage of the opportunity to have some minor ailment attended to, or to get another opinion about a condition for which they had seen a doctor in their home country. I didn't mind this because I charged the normal visiting fee for each person seen on the one visit. Most of the problems with which I was presented were minor, but as always one needed to be alert for more serious problems. For example, once in the middle of the night I had to attend a woman with a severe allergic reaction—she was coming out in hives all over her body. I ended up giving her a couple of adrenaline injections. One has to be careful with this as it can set the heart racing and cause other side-effects. This greatly improved the condition, and I left a supply of prednisolone (a strong anti-inflammatory drug) for her to take till she got back home.

I continued to be asked to do this work for something like ten years, and I made a small fortune from the fees. Not only that, but on each occasion of an evening visit, I would be invited to a complementary meal at their excellent buffet and be given a selection of delicious cakes from the hotel's bakery for my staff. Then suddenly the requests for visits stopped. Not a word from the hotel. No explanation. No thanks for my long service. Just silence. Out of curiosity I went to the hotel and enquired what had happened. It was simple. The airline's bean counters decided it was costing them too much, so arrangement were made for the staff, in case of medical need, to be treated at a nearby Japanese clinic or to attend hospital if the clinic was closed. It's true that my arrangement was an informal one; there was no contract with the hotel or the airline. Nonetheless, it was disappointing that they just cut me off, but that was always the way in the kind of private practice I was engaged in. On the other hand I found that if one regular source of patients dried up, another would appear.

Groupies

I was called to visit a young man at a luxurious hotel in the northern part of Tokyo. He was with a pop group playing gigs on a tour of Japan. Following the usual procedure I parked at the front of the hotel, my arrival being expected by the doorman, and entered the lobby. On the way in I noticed a queue of a dozen or so people—they seemed to be all young women—who I presumed were waiting for the bus.

I was taken by the manager to the guest's room. The patient, a young man of courteous manner, was suffering from a minor complaint which necessitated that I examined his abdomen. He was in a suite with a separate bedroom which was open to the living room area where I took his medical history. When I indicated that I wished him to lie down on the bed, he first of all went to the bedroom, which was in darkness, and I noticed a naked female form arise from the bed and go into the bathroom. I thought the coast was then clear and we could proceed with the examination. But no. A second naked female then discretely arose from the bed, also to wait in the bathroom. Finally I could examine the patient and give my diagnosis and advice. (It was not a serious problem.)

Having collected my fee (which naturally took into account the extra travelling involved) from the manager, I walked back to my car. On the way I again noticed the bus queue—it appeared slightly shorter than before—and then I realised: they were the groupies, awaiting their turn!

Pop singers

On another occasion I was called late in the evening by a woman from an agency which arranged musical events to see a member of an English pop group staying at a hotel in a fashionable area of central Tokyo. The patient had something wrong with his knee. I arrived about 10.30 pm. There were a number of heavily made-up young women hanging around who I thought, similarly, were some of the groupies. I observed one of them who kept going up and down in the lift, clutching a pack of cigarettes on top of her handbag. Then the patient, a young man with long hair, soon arrived limping, assisted by another member of the group, a tough-looking hulk with several earrings in his ears, tattoos, open leather waistcoat, gold chains, and bovver boots. Apart from the fucking this and the fucking that, uttered several times, they were polite and respectful—'Oh, sorry doctor!' when the vulgarity slipped out. They all reeked of tobacco. We went up in the lift with the friend, who appeared to be drunk, to the patient's room. It was in disarray with clothes and recording equipment all over the floor. The friend kept on trying to tell me what was wrong with the patient and how his injury had come about, which rather annoyed him—he wanted to tell me himself—but his description of a twisting strain at the right knee (similar to the footballer's injury) which he suffered while prancing about on stage the previous night, was probably accurate. He had pain at the inner side of the knee with no swelling of the joint itself, but there was some limitation of both straightening and bending, with marked tenderness at one spot in the painful area. Recalling what I had learnt from Dr Cyriax, it was clear to me that the young musician had strained his right medial collateral ligament.

The annoying friend left us alone, first going into the bathroom after announcing that he wanted to fart, and then finally departing.

I gave a steroid infiltration to the tender part of the ligament. It would likely have recovered in its own time, but he had another performance the following night before returning to England. I also left him some pain-killers. The friend returned and a discussion ensued about the condition and prognosis. I thought that, apart from his intimidating appearance and coarse manner, he was not unintelligent. Finally I got my fee paid by a more reasonable human being who seemed to be one of the group's managers. Apparently they had been on the road for four months and had given about eighty concerts.

Studying medicine for seventeen years

Once I was asked make a hotel visit to see a well-known film actor. He was with his entourage in the best suite in the hotel. I wasn't sure who he was from the name but immediately recognised him from seeing him on the television. He was in Tokyo to make a film. We sat on the bed in the bedroom and he immediately told me, 'I've been studying medicine for seventeen years.' I didn't know whether this was to put me in my place by impressing on me that he knew a thing or two about medicine himself, or whether he was just making conversation. Around the bed were a large number of bottles containing herbal remedies, vitamins, etc. He was worried that he couldn't work properly with a stuffy nose, a not unreasonable concern under the circumstances. He wanted an injection of a mega-dose of vitamin C, which he thought would cure the problem. I told him I didn't think this would help, and recommended a decongestant for symptomatic relief, which I supplied. He immediately went into the bathroom to swallow one of these tablets with a drink of water, and I was shown out.

A different sort of hotel visit

The mutually cooperative relationship I had in those days with the British Embassy meant that I was always ready to help them with medical matters affecting distressed British nationals. On one such occasion I went with a consular official to see an inmate of one of the main prisons in Japan, in Fuchuu, just outside Tokyo.

He was a young Englishman who had been sentenced to two years for drug smuggling, and was very depressed because his mother had died while he was incarcerated. He had been treated with high doses of tranquillisers and antidepressants, though he had recently stopped all these on his own initiative. The place wasn't so forbidding as the remand centre at Kosuge in the northeast of Tokyo where I once went to see another prisoner awaiting trial for alleged drug offences. At the Fuchuu prison we met the chief warder who gave the impression of being tough but fair. I think the young man felt better for meeting me. He had no complaints about his physical health, but was so depressed and tearful that he couldn't work in the prison factory so he was put in solitary confinement, which made him even more depressed. I tried to get them to agree to allow him to mix with other English-speaking prisoners and to have a meeting with his brother who was also in the prison for the same offence. (The rules forbade mixing of family members imprisoned together.) He seemed in reasonable physical shape, though his hands were cold due to the lack of heating in the prison. We sat across a desk in a small interviewing room with an interpreter and prison officer sitting at the back. Our conversation was translated by the interpreter who also took notes, but they probably couldn't hear much. Japan is a country that has zero tolerance for illicit drug dealing or possession, and the penalty on conviction is usually a prison term, followed by deportation in the case of a foreigner.

CHAPTER EIGHTEEN

More Medical Visits

IN JULY 1994 I was asked to do a home visit for middle-aged Englishwoman whom I'll call Angela—an affable, overweight, long-term resident of Tokyo. I had known her for many years but recently had not been so well disposed towards her because of difficulty in getting paid for consultations for her family and employees. She ran a language school and brought young men and women teachers out from England on short-term contracts. Her lifestyle was what used to be called Bohemian.

On the day in question she had severe abdominal pain with vomiting and diarrhoea. I found my way to a two-storey house in a pleasant residential area of Tokyo. It was in the process of being renovated, or 'reformed', as the Japanese say, and carpentry work was being done to the veranda, so the place was in chaos. Angela used the house as a family home, office, and dormitory for her employees. On the ground floor there were some half-dozen cats and kittens lying on tables and chairs, as well as several Japanese secretarial staff who were working at typewriters and smoking. A handsome young man, who introduced himself as David, greeted me and invited me to enter. It was unnecessary to have taken off my shoes in accordance with the Japanese custom, but once in a really filthy place I didn't take them off and was then asked to do so! I was shown up to the second floor[21] where Angela was lying on a divan, in obvious pain. She was somewhat dehydrated, but without fever and was no longer vomiting. After examining her I concluded she didn't have a serious disorder but was probably suffering from gastroenteritis, likely due to a viral infection. I gave her a strong pain-killer by injection and left some anti-spasmodic tablets.

---

[21] In Japan the ground floor is called the first floor.

The next day I phoned to ask about her condition. She had not passed urine since yesterday and the pain was just as bad, so I arranged for her to be admitted to hospital. Later I heard that the hospital concurred with my diagnosis of severe gastroenteritis and dehydration, and she was responding to treatment.

Angela called me when she had been discharged from the hospital. She wanted to thank me for sending her to such a good place—the Jikei University Hospital. She said they looked after her marvellously and she felt like a new woman, having lost 14kg and was now completely well. The doctors and nurses went to much trouble and were very kind. This was good news, and I hoped she would then pay my bill promptly!

About two years after this event I was called by the British Consul who was concerned about a distressed 30 year old British woman, Miss M—. She was said to be exhibiting disturbed behaviour and he didn't know what to do. I said I had better see her, but in general people in such a situation need to go back to their home country as soon as practicable. In the meantime she was being helped by another British woman. The problem was compounded by the fact that Miss M— didn't want to see a doctor or even an Embassy official, but the Consul said he was going to meet her anyway.

Soon after, the patient turned up at my clinic with the British Consul and the woman friend who, to my surprise, was none other than Angela! (She defaulted on my bill for the home visit described above. I ended up writing to her and saying I thought she was dishonest, which she was, and threatened to sue her, which I didn't.) Angela wanted to talk to me first, so I invited her into my consulting room, and she said that Miss M— was camping on her floor and had no money. Angela also wanted to tell me that she too had no money, having lost her business, but would pay her outstanding bill when she could. (She never did.)

Miss M— looked disheveled and smelt as if she hadn't had a bath in a long time. Her manner was superficially cheerful; she denied that anything was wrong except inability to sleep, and she couldn't understand what all the fuss was about, adding that she just wanted to go back home to Britain. She appeared to have no means of support and was dependent on friends. As I expected, she needed to be repatriated as soon as possible. The Embassy was going to try to arrange this through her relatives in Britain and with the cooperation of a sympathetic airline. I prescribed a small quantity of diazepam (a tranquilliser) to be kept by Angela and administered to the patient as required. The question of payment for my services and medicines was not raised, and it was obviously pointless expecting Angela to pay. The only thing to do was to regard this as a charity case and waive the fee.

Service to the community
Being available for home visits was an important part of the service I offered, since sometimes it was difficult for patients to come to my clinic.

I was on my way home one evening when I got a call from a tearful patient, Elfrida, whom I knew well, requesting a visit. She had recently given birth at home, since when she had had intermittent abdominal pain with night sweats and chills. The pain was much worse today and she had fainted and cut her head. She was a charming and pleasant lady, married to a Japanese man, and was keen on 'natural living' and vegetarianism and didn't believe in immunisation. Although she hardly ever came to see me, she not infrequently called for advice over the phone.

When I arrived she was in obvious pain, pale and groaning, lying on the sofa in their living room where her husband, two older children, and a maid were going about their normal activities and not taking much notice of her. The room was rather dark but I could see she had a nasty gash at her right eyebrow. Apart from that her symptoms were pain in the lower abdomen with urinary frequency and burning; this might have been because she had been catheterized by the midwife during the birth. She had a temperature of 37.4° and lower abdominal tenderness but examination was otherwise unremarkable. I thought she probably had a urinary infection. She complained of feeling chilly and thirsty, so she was given water to drink and blankets were piled on.

I was able to close the skin wound at her eyebrow without stiches using 'Steri-Strip' tape, and gave an antibiotic for the presumed urinary infection. The next day I returned with my nurse and we took a urine specimen back to the clinic. A subsequent bacterial culture test produced no growth. The other possibility was a uterine infection for which the antibiotic would likely have been effective.

A few days later I re-visited with my nurse. Elfrida was much better; the pain had almost gone. I also took a blood sample for haemoglobin estimation, since she looked very pale, but it was normal. Anyway, she was recovering with a little medical help.

Hernia problem
On another home visit I saw a 63 year old man, the father of one of my patients, who was on holiday and staying with his family in Japan. He had a large groin hernia since several years and this morning it had become painful. However, when I arrived he had recovered and the hernia could easily be reduced (gently pushed back into the abdomen) so it was not a strangulated hernia, which is an emergency. I asked if he had seen a doctor about it, and he said that he had not, but recently had attended his GP's surgery in England at the instigation of the practice, for a health-check. This had been performed by a nurse, and included blood pressure measurement and a urine test. He was also sent to the hospital for blood tests. He told the nurse about the hernia, and she said he should not to wait too long if it gets worse, or gave some similar vague advice. Thus, the only matter that really did need attention did not get it. (One would normally recommend an operation for a hernia.) So much for check-ups conducted

by non-medically qualified people. It seems in general practice in England these days you have a whole healthcare team to look after you, so that the busy doctors have more time to attend to the patients who are *really* ill. It reminded me of a cartoon in an edition of *Private Eye* from a few years back of a doctor's waiting room where there was a large notice saying, 'THANK YOU FOR NOT BEING TOO ILL'.

Was he a drug addict?

I received a call from an Englishman staying at an expensive hotel in Tokyo asking for my urgent help as he had a kidney stone. He was able to come to the clinic and gave his name as Dr White. When I asked if he was a medical doctor he said that he was. A balding middle-aged man in a pin-stripe suit soon arrived, clutching his crotch and apparently in some pain.

He said he was working in public health and was here to give lectures at a number of universities and other institutions. He said that diclofenac suppositories (a non-narcotic standard treatment for kidney stones) did not help. His history was of recurrent stones and the passage of gravel which had been investigated in England and treated two years previously with lithotripsy (a technique to break up kidney stones with high-frequency sound waves). After I had examined him I gave 100mg of pethidine intramuscularly. He then declared that he felt much better and went off in a taxi which we called for him. As he was a colleague I only charged for the medicine.

However, later the same day I was at dinner with a friend when Dr White called from his hotel saying he was in considerable pain again. So, conscientious doctor that I was, after finishing dinner I went round to the hotel. He showed me a glass containing wine-coloured liquid which he said was his urine, but I could not confirm it was blood without the necessary equipment. Then, in the way of small talk, I asked him which medical school he had graduated from, but he was unable to answer because just at that moment he was overcome by a severe spasm, and I didn't pursue the matter. I told him I would like to communicate with his GP, but he couldn't remember the name or phone number. Doubts were beginning to add up, but under the circumstances I felt I could only give him the benefit of them. I gave him an injection of pentazocine (a strong non-narcotic pain-killer) and left four more ampoules of this drug with syringes and needles in case he should need further pain relief during the night, and told him that if this didn't suffice he would need to be admitted to hospital. I had a nagging feeling that I might have been taken for a ride.

Eight months later, out of the blue I received another phone call from this man. He was back in Japan on business and, strange to say, was having another episode of severe pain with passage of gravel. Once again I felt I had to give him the benefit of the doubt and visited him at his hotel. I found he was either suffering a genuine attack of ureteric colic (an extremely painful condition) or was putting on a convincing act. Anyway, once again I gave him an injection of pentazocine and left him with a supply of two more ampoules with syringes and needles.

But that wasn't the end of the story. A few days later I heard from my above-mentioned friend that he was having dinner with an English doctor whom I knew who works at another clinic, on the day before my last meeting with Dr White. Their dinner, likewise, had been disturbed by a phone call from this same patient. The other doctor had also visited him at his hotel in the afternoon of that day, and had given him an injection for severe pain due to a kidney stone. In the evening the pain had returned and he wanted a re-visit. But this other doctor, taking a more robust attitude than I did, refused to interrupt his evening and told the patient that he couldn't sit with him all night and if he was in such a bad way he needed to call an ambulance and get himself seen at hospital!

I understood that the refusal to re-visit had nothing to do

with any suspicions about illicit drug use but was because he couldn't be bothered. If this was true it didn't reflect well on him. Having seen a patient once you have a responsibility for dealing with any follow-up treatment that may be needed; at the very least he should have offered himself to arrange hospital admission and call an ambulance for the patient. So I wondered why the patient hadn't called me in the first place if he was having a genuine recurrence—maybe it was because he wanted to keep me in reserve.

I still couldn't make up my mind whether he was genuine, but I thought that if comes to Tokyo again and calls me, I shall ask him a few questions, such as 'What are the names of the bones of the forearm?' and 'How many cranial nerves are there?' Even a doctor who has been out of clinical medicine for many years would know the correct answers.

Middle-of-the-night call
Being available for domiciliary consultations means one must be prepared to get out of bed.

One night a call came at 3.00 am from the head of a large international bank. He had had fairly severe spasmodic abdominal pain for several hours. He was very apologetic about calling me, and seemed reluctant for me to visit when I suggested it, but as he was in considerable pain I went to his home. This was in an area of Tokyo called Roppongi, an entertainment district popular with young people, and I was surprised to see how crowded with traffic it was at that time of night. The patient lived in a spacious apartment on two floors, and he came to the door himself—with two enormous Alsatian dogs. As he said, they had no security problems!

When I examined him I found he was markedly tender over the gall-bladder area. I thought the diagnosis was gall-bladder colic due to a stone. At such an hour on a home visit one needs to decide on the spot what to do: send him to hospital or treat him myself. I opted for the latter and gave an injection of pethidine.

Later in the day he called to say he had slept very well after the injection, was pain-free and had gone to work—and was most impressed with my prompt and efficient service.

Girl in the bed

I was asked to visit a young man at a five-star hotel near my clinic. He had had pain for several days at the back of his chest, at the lower right aspect, but was otherwise well. This is the kind of case where, in a hotel setting, clinical judgement is all-important. It seemed to me the pain was arising from the joints of the spinal column at the back of his chest. It was interesting that he had had similar symptoms before which responded to chiropractic manipulations. He wanted a muscle relaxants and pain-killers but I only had pain-killers so I provided some for him.

But the interesting aspect of this patient was that he could only be described as morbidly obese, about twice as broad as a normal man. In addition, he seemed to be on his honeymoon, because the room was full of flowers, and there was a slim young blonde woman lying asleep in the bed.

A difficult decision

I made a home visit to see Wally, a 3 year old English boy. He was one of four delightful young brothers, all with round faces, fair hair, and blue eyes. For the past three days he had had a high fever, with drowsiness and vomiting since that morning. When I arrived he was lying in a brightly-lit room in a yellow bed which was like a car. It was concerning that he kept saying the back of his head hurt and he was lying with his head bent back but otherwise he didn't look too bad.

I found his temperature was normal, but this might have been because he had been given paracetamol an hour previously. Examination showed no abnormalities except that his neck was so stiff one could easily lift him up with a hand placed under his head. However, he didn't seem ill enough to have meningitis—a diagnosis one must not miss—and I discussed this possibility with the mother. She was not at all keen on taking him to hospital for a lumbar puncture, so we decided to wait and see. Two hours later she called as I had requested, to say he had got up and wanted to join in their Sunday lunch, but after that had become drowsy again and his temperature was rising. Once more I suggested it might be a sensible precaution to have lumbar puncture performed, but she still wanted to wait, mentioning this time that her husband had told her Wally had fallen off a see-saw in the park yesterday and hit the back of his head. So maybe that was why he had neck stiffness.

The next day I called the home and Wally himself answered the phone; he had recovered. I think this sensible mother made the important decision herself, after discussing the matter with me. The conflict in this kind of situation is deciding where the responsibility lies. If she declined hospital admission and he did turn out to have meningitis, it would have been her decision rather than mine. On the other hand, if I had taken the physical sign of neck stiffness at its face value and insisted he should go to hospital (with a lot of trouble and upset for both mother and child) then I would have covered myself. Better to be safe than sorry! But I wondered if it had been a different mother, especially if she had looked up meningitis on the internet, she might have been pressing for a lumbar puncture anyway. In this case, I supported the mother in what she wanted to do, as there was no clear reason for hospital admission, and her instinct, as so often is the case, turned out to be right.

Bedside manners
One Sunday morning I was called by Mr Chowdhury, a 31 year old striking-looking man with long black hair, dark skin, and blue eyes. He was originally from Pakistan but had lived in

Scotland and spoke with a perfect Scottish accent. He had fairly severe abdominal pain since a few hours and had vomited three or four times, but when I arrived his temperature was normal and there was no abdominal tenderness. It was unclear whether he had appendicitis or a viral gastroenteritis, so I decided to wait and see. Four hours later I called him but he was no better, so I visited again. The condition had progressed; he was very tender at the lower right part of his abdomen—a classic sign of appendicitis.

He lived right in the middle of the Harajuku district of Tokyo, where in the afternoon in the street outside there was a large crowd of young people parading up and down in fantastic costumes as if they were going to a fancy-dress party. Considering the difficulty an ambulance would have finding his apartment and getting through the crowd, I felt the only reasonable thing to do was to take him to hospital in my own car (with a bucket just in case), having first arranged with the Jikei University Hospital that they would receive him.

I managed to get him into the emergency department where he was quickly attended to most efficiently and courteously by several nurses who took his blood pressure, temperature, etc. There was some form-filling, but at least he was not sitting outside in the waiting area. He must have been in quite bad pain.

Suddenly, a young man in a white coat with a stethoscope around his neck—I think he was a hospital intern but it could have been a medical student—made for the patient without so much as a 'by your leave' or even greeting. He started prodding vigorously upon the lower right part of Mr Chowdhury's abdomen, I suppose to see if he could elicit the physical sign of known as rebound tenderness. All that happened was the patient winced in pain and I hoped the doctor (if he was a doctor) was satisfied. I was appalled, but wasn't quick enough to object to this behaviour.

It reminded me of when I was a student during a session of

bedside teaching, one of our number was invited to examine a patient with a hernia. In his embarrassment at having to perform in front of everybody, he rushed in and drew back the bedclothes to examine the patient's groin area, when he was stopped and admonished by the tutor: 'Just a minute, just a minute! Do you usually behave in that way with someone you don't know? What's the first thing you say to a patient?' The student in his embarrassment couldn't think of the answer, but was soon put right by the amused onlookers. It is, of course, 'Good morning,' or 'Good afternoon,' as the case may be.

I thought the above-mentioned emergency room doctor, as I shall assume he was, failed on three counts: socially—inept to the point of rudeness and totally lacking in bedside manners; medically—incompetent, in that he didn't take the history first; and ignorant—of the proper method of examining the abdomen. I quote from a well known textbook, Bailey and Love's *Short Practice of Surgery*, 23rd edition, with emphasis added: '*Gentle* superficial palpation of the abdomen…will detect muscle guarding…Asking the patient to cough or *gentle* percussion over the site of maximum tenderness will elicit rebound tenderness [in the diagnosis of appendicitis].' Some surgeons say that rebound tenderness is of little value anyway; all it does is cause additional pain. I thought it was lucky the patient didn't clock him one!

Mr Chowdhury was operated upon that evening and a gangrenous appendix removed. His post-operative course was uneventful.

Over-treatment of a cold

A Frenchwoman called me in a panic over her 13 week old baby girl. The mother's behaviour was *extraordinaire*, and the same word could be applied to the treatment given by the hospital involved if it were not so common as to be almost routine in Japan.

I had not seen the baby before but she had been admitted

to a major Tokyo hospital on that day. The reason was that the mother, instead of calling me, had gone direct to the hospital to see a strange doctor with whom she could not communicate. The baby had had a cough and runny nose since that morning and was taking about half her usual amount of formula feed. In other words, the baby had a cold. It was not as though the mother was inexperienced—she had older twin girls.

The person who was inexperienced, however, was the young doctor on duty who, for reasons that are unclear, admitted the baby for observation. Did he not have to get a more senior doctor to confirm the need for admission? Apparently not. Maybe this was something to do with the fact that Japanese hospitals seem to be run like hotels: they want high bed occupancy. This results in many unnecessary or needlessly prolonged admissions and is why it is often difficult to get a patient admitted when urgently needed: no beds are available.

A chest X-ray of the baby was taken; it was normal. Then blood tests were done which showed only a raised CRP (a nonspecific marker of inflammation of no practical relevance) and she was given an intravenous drip—it seemed to be another standard procedure. The mother was not happy with all this and wanted to take her baby home. I went to the hospital straightaway. The baby was lying in her bed, alert, smiling, and with no fever. Her breathing was a bit noisy from transmitted sounds due to mucus in the nose and throat, but her lungs were clear (normal) on listening with a stethoscope, and her breathing rate was not increased.

In my opinion she had a viral upper respiratory tract infection (a cold) and there was no good reason for her to be in hospital. I said I would take responsibility for the mother taking the baby home. Upon hearing this, the young doctor in charge wanted to prescribe a medicine called Mucodyne. This drug is supposed to help liquefy secretions and make them easier to cough up. I told the doctor it should not be prescribed for babies and is of little value anyway.

I arranged to see the child for follow-up at my clinic two days later. But that very morning the mother had first been to a local paediatrician, and she wanted me to advise on the medicines which *this* doctor had prescribed! These were, inevitably, an antibiotic, and several other drugs. I was tempted to tell the mother I couldn't be involved while the baby was under the care of someone else, but decided for the baby's sake to go along with her request. Since the baby's condition was fine except for a mild cold, I advised stopping all the medicines and, as they were planning shortly to travel to France, pronounced her fit to travel.

Déjà vu

I had a feeling of *déjà vu* soon after the previous case when a 5 month old baby boy, Jamie, was brought by his mother because he had had a cough which disturbed sleep since a few days. Apart from a mild fever, he was alert and lively and everything was normal on examination—a very common scenario. I diagnosed a viral respiratory infection and prescribed a sedative antihistamine to be taken at night. However, the cough became worse, but instead of contacting me again they took Jamie to a hospital where he was treated as an out-patient. This involved giving an intravenous drip (of course) which upset him (naturally) but then he was allowed home with several medicines for treating his condition which the hospital doctor misdiagnosed as asthma. The next day they went back for reassessment and admission was advised. The hospital doctor did, however, offer the alternative of not being admitted and using a bronchodilator for asthma in the form of skin patches—a useless treatment. The father wanted my opinion whether the child needed admission or whether the hospital was over-reacting. I said I couldn't advise without seeing the child and they must decide under whose care they wished to be. Then the following conversation ensued:

'It sounds as if you are annoyed because we went to the hospital without telling you.'

'Not at all, you are perfectly entitled to go anywhere you wish.'

'Look, all we want is for Jamie to get well, and we would appreciate your general views on Japanese hospitals.'

'It's no good giving general views. What you are asking me, presumably, is whether Jamie needs admission. I cannot say without seeing him.'

'But what can you do if you do see him?'

And so on.

I found it difficult to understand why this English family should behave in such a way. Perhaps it was because the baby became worse after seeing me and they lost confidence in my ability to handle the matter, or perhaps they blamed me for not anticipating he would get worse. So they go somewhere else, which is fine, but when the somewhere else is not up to their expectations and they find themselves in a muddle, they come back and expect me to sort it out! (This happened not infrequently with other patients.)

The father called again an hour later saying they had decided to take Jamie home, and would I please do a home visit that afternoon. I did so, and found the baby was alert, had no fever, was coughing occasionally and going red in the face, but otherwise he was well and smiling. His respiratory rate was slightly above normal and he had an intermittent wheeze. I thought he had a viral respiratory infection. The hospital had given him, in addition to the skin patch, an antihistamine, another type of bronchodilator by mouth, and, inevitably, Mucodyne! All this was pointless. I recommended a bronchodilator called salbutamol to be given by mouth and left a supply of the syrup. I did not raise the issue of why they went to the hospital; it was clearly due to anxiety. But, predictably, they were made *more* anxious by the hospital visit, and quite alarmed by the advice that he should be admitted. I called the next morning and learnt he had had a good night and was on the mend.

Pneumonia in a child

A child of mixed British and Japanese parentage, aged 10, was brought by his mother because of two days fever, cough with scanty blood-tinged phlegm, vomiting, and pain at the back of his chest on the right side. The presumptive diagnosis was pneumonia and this was confirmed on a chest X-ray—very useful to be able to do this in my clinic on the spot. He was breathless with a fever and a rapid pulse, and slightly dehydrated. I arranged admission forthwith to a well-known children's hospital called the National Center for Child Health and Development.

I like to visit all my patients who are admitted to hospital, and went to see him three days later. The hospital was impressive: child-friendly with lots of space, play areas, and bright colours, being designed to make it look like a playground rather than an operating theatre. I found the young patient in good spirits, relaxed in his nice hotel-like single room with his mother on a narrow bed next to his hospital bed. He wasn't in any hurry to go home as no doubt he liked having his mother all to himself. He had just polished off a good lunch, but still had the intravenous catheter in his arm for administration of the antibiotic.

The treating doctor, a pleasant Japanese-American, pointed out there is a difference in the way patients are treated in the Japan and the US or Britain, but for foreigners they would compromise and allow him out earlier than they would a Japanese patient. They wanted to observe him for a few more days after changing to the oral route for the antibiotic. I negotiated discharge from the hospital after only one more day and arranged to follow him up with an X-ray at my clinic to ensure the pneumonia had resolved.

'In sickness and in health…'

A 28 year old western man, working as an English teacher and married to a Japanese woman, suffered a very bad stroke. He received good treatment in a Japanese hospital in the initial stages and was at least kept alive, but he remained unconscious and had to be fed through a gastrostomy (an opening made into his stomach). Then the question arose about what to do in the long term. It seemed best for him to return to his own country where his parents would care for him with the assistance of the local medical services. But how to get him there? It was heartening that when someone was in such serious trouble how people came to his aid without any question of payment. An airline arranged to fly him home. He needed to be accompanied by a nurse to give his feeds and medicines, and a doctor to keep an eye on his condition. The latter role I volunteered to take on. When all was ready we went by ambulance to Narita Airport, entering by a special security gate, and then the patient on his stretcher was lifted on a hoist to enter the aircraft by a rear door. Although he was screened off, other passengers of course noticed that we were carrying a very sick person, and there was a sense of sympathy and concern from them as well as from the airline staff. The journey was accomplished without incident and his parents and an ambulance were waiting at the destination.

After some months I heard he had regained consciousness and was gradually starting to recover. But what about his wife? As soon as she learnt of his serious condition she started divorce proceedings. I wondered how she would have felt if it had been the other way around—if *she* was the one to have been struck with a major illness.

CHAPTER NINETEEN
Eccentric and Unfortunate People

A LADY CAME to see me who was visiting Tokyo from America. Her appearance was slightly scary. She had white hair, was hard of hearing, and walked with a cane. This wasn't surprising since she was aged 83. But there was something wrong with her face: it had no wrinkles! Two weeks previously she had had a face-lift—her third, she told me—and needed to have the stitches removed from the back of her neck. This simple procedure I performed and she went on her way. I was then left to ponder, what is wrong with looking your age?

Cultural and communication difficulties

In my clinic most of the patients were British, American, or European, but I would see people who had come from all over the world. This would sometimes stretch my communication skills and occasionally I would find myself in a position that reminded me of the Irish joke:

Patient: Oh doctor, I've got a terrible pain!
Doctor: In which part of your body is the pain?
Patient: Oh doctor, if only I knew dat!

This kind of thing really did happen, as in the following situation.

A patient from the Indian subcontinent came and when invited to state what was troubling him, told me, 'Too much pain, doctor, too much pain.' On being asked to show me where he felt the pain he indicated with his open hand the whole of his abdomen, and when asked how long he has had it, after a moment's thought, replied, 'Five years.'

In other words, he was telling me what he thought I wanted to hear and exaggerated it in order to impress on me the seriousness of his condition, presumably in the hope that I would give him what he wanted. It was difficult to understand what this was. If I had tried to approach the problem in the same way as with a western patient we would have got nowhere. As it turned out, he was suffering from erectile dysfunction but was too embarrassed to say so. On top of all this there was a language problem which was not helped by the 'interpreter' who accompanied him, since he had even less English than the patient. After satisfying myself there was no obvious physical cause for the problem, such as diabetes, I concluded it was psychogenic. But apart from reassurance there little I could do for him because Viagra was not then available in Japan.

Professional hypochondriac

An old patient, a Frenchman aged 53, Mr Hulot, came to see me with various minor symptoms about which he wanted reassurance. He was a man who seldom smiled, though did have a self-depreciatory sense of humour, and he frequently complained how ignorant other doctors were and how their treatment caused him to suffer side-effects.

One of his many hypochondriacal concerns was the accumulation of toxins in body fat from when he used to work in the ship building industry, for which reason he had wanted an apronectomy (removal of abdominal fat); another was over his risk of a heart attack or stroke. To protect himself from these possibilities he regularly took unphysiological doses of vitamins C and E as anti-oxidants against the dreaded free radicles. He was an avid reader of medical articles and had a touching faith in their relevance for his many symptoms. It was sometimes difficult to convince him that just because a treatment is claimed to be effective in a clinical trial published in a medical journal, it does not necessarily follow that it will be beneficial in a way that matters to patients. He brought to mind the famous saying of

Alexander Pope: 'A little learning is a dangerous thing.'

On one occasion he turned up and announced he had suffered a retinal haemorrhage because he had cloudiness of vision of his left eye. I could find nothing wrong with his eyes, and a general medical examination including blood pressure and urine was normal. So I tried to reassure him that there was no sign of any eye disease. But he wasn't convinced.

Then I made a tactical error. An optometrist, Dr Sato, about whom I shall have more to say later, happened to be in the clinic when Mr Hulot came, so I thought I would ask him to take photos of the patient's retina (the back part of the eye) in order to reassure him fully. Although not a medical doctor, Dr Sato knew a lot about eye disorders and was expert at fitting glasses and contact lenses, but in retrospect it wasn't a good idea to refer Mr Hulot to him. If I needed the opinion of an ophthalmologist (a doctor specialising in eye disorders) then I should have referred him to one. My optometry friend did a very thorough eye examination and found nothing amiss. But then *he* wanted to refer the patient to an ophthalmologist!

This is the problem with lay practitioners. They may know a lot about their particular fields, but may not be able to interpret their findings in relation to the patient's situation as a whole: it needs wide experience in medicine to be able to do this. Dr Sato should have just told me his opinion and left it up to me to take further action if I thought fit. The result of him suggesting this referral, therefore, was merely to increase the patient's anxiety. All this was unnecessary because when I called the patient a week later, he said his symptoms were resolving, so nothing more needed to be done.

Mr Hulot's next visit was three years later when he came with a written list of problems. He had put on a lot of weight and said he felt the need to shed some money by coming to see me, and I replied that he would then feel much better! On a recent trip to South Africa he had developed diarrhoea and parasitic worm eggs had been found in his stool. I prescribed pyrantel (an anti-worm medicine) for him and his family. In view of the weight gain he wanted to have blood sugar, insulin-resistance factor, and urinalysis performed to detect diabetes. I told him that measuring his blood sugar alone would suffice. He also wanted to have the second of a course of Japanese encephalitis immunisations since he lived near a mosquito-infested area outside Tokyo, and this I gave him. In addition, he had pain at his left arm which he was concerned might be a symptom of heart disease: it was due to a mild degree of tennis elbow which didn't need treatment. Finally, he placed in front me a sheet of paper in which he had written a list of complaints, including that I had a contemptuous and dismissive attitude to his problems. I assured him that I always took his symptoms with the utmost seriousness, and said I thought this was a bit unfair. He did, however, still come to see me. On one occasion it was to request a visit to his mother-in-law who was seriously ill in hospital. This is described in Chapter 29.

Loyalty, or the lack of it

Another patient illustrated how people appear to have no particular loyalty to one doctor. She was a pale thin Scottish woman with two children. The younger, a boy then aged 4½ years, had some developmental delay especially with his speech, and he was rather clumsy. The mother had brought him to me a year previously at which time I found nothing basically wrong: there were no neurological signs, he was of normal intelligence, and I thought his speech development was within the normal variation. However, she wasn't satisfied and took him to an American specialist who produced a verbose report, impressive in its detail, but the thrust of it was that he did have motor coordination problems. There was a critical reference to me as the general practitioner whom the mother had consulted initially.

Subsequently, she took him to a paediatrician at a hospital

in Glasgow who produced a very thorough and well written report which she showed me today. It was reassuring, saying the child had no neurological signs but was clumsy and had slight developmental delay, but he was very optimistic about his likely progress and included sensible advice on giving him practical help. This assessment had been born out by his recent improvement, just as I had originally predicted. I think the mother in retrospect appreciated that I had been right and the other specialist in Tokyo had only made her more anxious.

This lady also had recently been to see a doctor at another clinic on account of palpitations. An ECG had been done which was pronounced as normal, but the doctor had then proceeded to undermine his reassurance by making the meaningless comment that the tracing showed 'a lot of electrical activity'—I should jolly well hope so, or she would really be in trouble! I think in the end she come back to me having done the rounds and found I wasn't so bad after all.

Doctor shopping

A new patient wanted to talk to me before coming. She had already seen four doctors in the last two months but none had been able to help her. She related how she had been treated in Canada with various courses of antibiotics for a cough and phlegm, without benefit, and didn't just want to see me to get another course of antibiotics. I could only say that I would do my best to help her, and I put her through to the receptionist to make an appointment. But there was something about her manner which made me say to the receptionist, 'Make sure you tell her the consultation fee.' She didn't want to come when she heard it. Patients who are straightforward—the vast majority— just make an appointment, but I find if they start telling you all their problems and how badly they have been treated by other doctors before one actually meets them, then they are usually neurotic and it is best not to get involved.

Another person I had not met before wanted to speak to me before making an appointment. A middle class Englishwoman's voice on the other end of the phone. She has a 3 year old daughter with autism and wants to find a specialist in Tokyo who can supervise this condition, since she is under the care of her GP and a specialist in Britain. I suggest she comes to see me with her daughter so I can gain an understanding of the situation at first hand, and then I would try to arrange specialist referral if appropriate. Visions of endless phone calls, but it's all part of the job. So far, so good—I'm responsive and trying to be helpful. But then she goes off on the wrong foot:

'Do you have experience in dealing with autism?'

'To be honest, no. I haven't seen many children with autism since it's not all that common.'

This seemed to be taken as a challenge by the mother who immediately contradicted me saying that it was actually quite common. The prevalence of autism in Europe, Asia, and the United States ranges from 2 to 25 per 1000—not exactly what I would call common.

'Well, would you like to make an appointment?'

'No, I want to call other paediatricians on my list first.'

'Fine, but I doubt you'll get very far. Of course, you're welcome to come and see me anytime if you wish.'

It can't be easy bringing up an autistic child, but it seemed to me the mother was going about finding help the wrong way. She should have come with the child to see me, if possible bringing full medical and social services reports from Britain, so I could find out exactly what help she had in mind, and then I would have done my best to assist her.

Another example of the situations one has to deal with in private practice was shown in a call from a patient I had seen once for an insurance medical examination. He asked if I could recommend a neurologist for his son. It emerged that his son, aged 5 years, was suffering from headaches and had been seen at another general practice where a CT scan had been done. This apparently showed a tumour of the meninges (the membranes covering the brain). That clinic did have an attending neurologist but he was not available for the next two weeks. Thus the father called me to see if I could arrange an earlier referral.

I felt this was rather a cheek. He goes somewhere else, but when he is not satisfied with the arrangements made there, he calls me and expects me to run around for him—no mention of paying for this. I told him I would need to see the child first. He replied that he would confer with the mother and 'get back to me'. He didn't.

Two shocking cases

The following is from my clinical notes:

> Husband and wife from Malaysia, both aged 30, came together. Two daughters by Caesarian section and now 14 weeks pregnant. They wanted to know if this was an appropriate time to determine the foetal sex by ultrasound: if the baby was female they would want to abort it. The stated reason was that she believed she would need another Caesarian section and probably this would be the end of her child-bearing days, so it was their last chance to have a son.

I told them that what they proposed was in my opinion unethical and I would have no part in it. I mentioned a recent article on the demographic problems resulting from female infanticide in *Newsweek* which the husband said he had read. Even so, he wanted to go ahead. I added that in some parts of the world they murdered baby girls because girls were valued less than boys, but in civilised countries this was illegal as well as immoral. I urged them to reconsider and the husband said he would. No charge was made.

About a year later I was confronted with the same situation.

An Indian couple in their early thirties came for the first time. I thought the wife looked rather unhappy and the husband did all the talking. The woman was pregnant and they wanted an ultrasound scan. Immediately alarm bells started ringing. Why did they want a scan? They wanted to know the sex of the child. And what would they do with this information? He came straight out with it: if the baby was a girl they would want to abort it. I was incensed. I said something about their and my morals being different, and showed them the door.

Reflecting afterwards, I wondered if I might have been able to persuade them to accept the baby whatever its sex, but on further consideration this would have been unlikely—an ultrasound scan is easy obtainable in Tokyo. I understand ultrasonography for determining the sex of the foetus is illegal in India, though many clinics flout the law.

Unrealistic expectations

A young Englishwoman called me from a town some distance from Tokyo and said she was scheduled to have surgery for a cartilage in her knee in five days' time. She was taking the oral contraceptive pill but the doctor didn't seem to understand that this could increase her risk of blood clots. Apart from stopping the pill, she wondered if she should be given heparin (a drug which may prevent blood clots during surgery on the knee, though it has its own risks) according to the advice she had heard from a friend in England. She wanted me to call or send a fax to the surgeon advising him that she was on the pill, and suggest appropriate preventative measures for her increased risk of developing a blood clot. Similarly to the patient mentioned above, I thought it was rather a cheek for a stranger to request me to do this over the phone. She made no mention of paying for this service, and even if she had it wouldn't have been proper for me to intervene in this way. She didn't even know whether she was going to have a local or general anaesthetic. I told her I cannot take responsibility for advising someone without seeing them, so I merely said she needed to tell the surgeon that she was taking the pill and be guided by him, and if she didn't have confidence in him she should seek another opinion. She seemed disappointed to hear this, thanked me rather formally for taking up my time, and rang off.

Another call was from a young-sounding man who said he had a urethral stricture for which he regularly catheterized himself, and he needed to have a sound passed; could I do this at my clinic? I said I wouldn't do it myself but would refer him to a urologist if it needed to be done. He insisted that it *did* need to be done, and asked if he could by-pass coming to see me first. I told him that I couldn't refer him to a specialist without seeing him and making my own assessment. He seemed a bit put out at this, saying it was urgent and asking how long it would take to see the urologist. I replied that I couldn't give an exact time, but would endeavour to refer him to a suitable specialist expeditiously, and added that if he didn't want to come to see me first he could go directly to a hospital. He replied that he had already tried that and he thought 'Japanese doctors were a bunch of incompetents'. Why did he, a complete stranger, assume I didn't have a high regard for Japanese doctors and might be offended by this gratuitous remark? In the event, he couldn't come to see me until five days later, because that was when he got paid. (He made an appointment but later cancelled it.)

On occasions I've even had strangers calling who say straight out they can't afford to come and see me, being on the Japanese national health insurance scheme, and they just want a free opinion. I don't give medical opinions or advice to strangers on the phone.

Problems of love

An pleasantly eccentric 46 year old man came to see me. When I went to fetch him from the waiting room he was in the process of chatting up a young Japanese woman who also had an appointment, and he asked me to wait while he wrote down his phone number for her!

An American by accident of birth, as he put it, he sported a week's growth of beard and reeked of tobacco. His manner, however, was pleasant and courteous, and he started by saying he was pleased to have found me as he admired and respected British doctors much more than American doctors, who he said were very judgemental. He was thinking of giving up his American citizenship: 'Who needs it?' he asked rhetorically.

Then he told me his medical problems. The main one was that he suffered from genital herpes and had been taking an anti-viral drug called acyclovir continuously since twelve years. It worked well but as soon as he stopped it he would get recurrent attacks. He obtained this drug from the US where it was much cheaper than in Japan. He also had a cough with green sputum (not surprising in view of his smoking) and a urethral discharge. The latter was related to a recent sexual contact. 'It was casual for her, not for me,' he said. She was described as a very beautiful Japanese girl whom he went out with twice, and who then indicated that she was busy for the rest of her life.

I diagnosed bronchitis and thought it likely he had a chlamydial urethritis (the commonest type of sexually transmitted infection) even though no discharge was present at the time.

As he had come a long way, I gave treatment to cover both conditions, an antibiotic called clarithromycin. I also asked if he would be interested in my smoking cessation method.

'But if I gave up smoking I wouldn't have anything left to make myself feel bad about,' he said. 'There's usually no difficulty for people to find things to feel bad about,' I replied. He agreed, but added that if he stopped smoking he would have to go out with even more Japanese girls and he had difficulty finding condoms big enough to fit him in Japan. This was a tasteless attempt at humour, and I thought it was inappropriate to trivialise the serious matter of smoking. He added that the only way for him to survive here was to be determined not to get emotionally involved with Japanese women: 'When I first came I fell in love every five minutes, now it is every five weeks; and when it is only every five months I know I will be cured.'

A Biblical disease
Part of my work consisted in doing medical examinations for US visa applicants. One such applicant came with a very interesting history. He was a Russian man, born in Japan in 1928, and had suffered from Hansen's disease. (It used to be known as leprosy, but this name is obsolete.) His symptoms started in 1940 and he was admitted to a sanatorium in 1946. In those days in Japan people with this disease were kept as virtual prisoners and it was only in 1996 that the discriminatory law was repealed.

Repeated skin tests in this patient showed the disease had been non-infectious for many years. He was a charming and interesting man in spite of his appearance, and had been invited by a religious brotherhood in US to go and live there. After completing the examination I called the US Consular office to try to expedite his application. I made no charge for the examination or for the immunisations which he also needed as part of the application process.

Contrasts
A young man came for follow-up of urethritis. He put a plastic bottle of coffee on my desk and drank out of it right in front of me as I was preparing the bill on my computer.

Another patient, an African American (he was as mystified as I that such an expression is used to describe his race: why is he not just called an American?) who appeared rather intimidating because of his large build, but who was very polite, came with his daughter for paternity testing for US residency purposes, so he was naturally anxious and wanted me to be well disposed towards him. He had a baseball cap but took it off as soon as he entered the clinic. Not only did he not wear the cap in front of me, as so many people do, but he put it on the floor beside his chair. I picked it up and put it on the desk. He said he didn't put it on my desk as he thought it might indicate disrespect!

I thought I had seen everything in thoughtless and disrespectful behaviour by patients but there was one egregious example. It was the American husband of a Japanese woman who came for a US visa medical examination. It was a very hot day and he was sitting in the waiting area stripped to the waist. He was a rather overweight man in his sixties so it wasn't a pretty sight, not that this made any difference. I went over and politely asked him to put his shirt on. He did so, complaining about the heat. I suggested he sat a bit nearer the air-conditioner. People often come dressed as if they were going to the beach, but I thought this behaviour just about took the biscuit!

Muslims

Then there was a woman from Pakistan, a doctor she said, working under a special arrangement in the anaesthetic department of the Jikei University Hospital, who came with her face hidden in traditional Islamic dress except for her eyes. I found it rather disconcerting talking to someone like that, and I was tempted to ask her to remove her veil, but thought her husband, who accompanied her, might misconstrue this request. She was suffering from an anxiety state because she believed that her husband was planning to take another wife. This he denied, but she didn't believe him. Under the circumstances I thought it best to refer her to female counsellor.

A doctor is not obliged to treat someone if it is against his conscience to do so, provided a reasonable alternative exists. Tokyo is a big place, and the Tokyo British Clinic is not the only source of medical help. The clinic, however, was near what was known as the Libyan People's Bureau (Embassy). This situation put me in a dilemma.

In 1984 a woman police constable, Yvonne Fletcher, was murdered by gunfire from the Libyan Embassy in London. As a result of this atrocity diplomatic relations between Britain and Libya were broken off. Since I did not wish unknowingly to treat the murderer of this poor woman—he might have been posted to Tokyo after escaping from London—I instructed my staff not to accept appointments from the so-called Libyan People's Bureau. However, if it was an emergency or a sick child, of course they would be seen.

This arrangement seemed to work and no Libyan Embassy personnel turned up at the Clinic. But on an occasion when I employed a part-time woman doctor, the burka-clad wife of one of the Bureau's staff slipped through the net and had a consultation with her. As they were leaving I intervened to say that the Tokyo British Clinic could not see the staff of the Bureau in future (emergencies and children excepted), and I refused to accept the fee. This resulted in a confrontation later that day with two officials from the Bureau. They affected incredulity about my policy, and a somewhat awkward discussion followed. They insisted that I accepted the fee for the earlier consultation, and, bearing in mind that the then Libyan dictator, Colonel Gaddafi, had a habit of murdering his critics, I agreed to this. But I seemed to have made my point because no more staff from that establishment darkened my door again. As for the fee, I donated it to the UK Police Memorial Trust.

Mercury poisoning?

A long-term foreign resident of Tokyo, a man aged 59, came to see me because of concern about mercury or other heavy metal poisoning. A tooth crown had recently come off, and in replacing it the dentist had remarked that the tooth underneath looked black, which could have been due to the use of a mercury amalgam filling. The patient then had developed a belief—almost an obsession—that this was the cause of various long-standing symptoms (tiredness, aching in the joints, skin septic eruptions) which no one had been able to diagnose even though he had had extensive testing. He didn't want me to go into his symptoms but to treat him empirically for assumed mercury poisoning. He looked well apart from a few infected areas on his thinning scalp, and certainly didn't present the appearance of a poisoned patient. He was somewhat dramatic in the way he gave an account of his problem, leaning towards and asking in a hushed voice, 'Is this absolutely confidential?' When I confirmed that it was, he stood up and came closer round my desk, saying that when he had suggested the possibility of mercury poisoning to another dentist, he could smell his fear (!), and from that time on he knew it was true.

In such cases it is important to go along with the patient's wishes, as far as is reasonable, because one is never going to convince them otherwise. So we settled for measuring his blood levels of cadmium, lead, chromium, and mercury, together with the routine blood tests one might do in a general check-up. All the results were normal.

CHAPTER TWENTY
Difficult Colleagues

IT'S NOT JUST patients but sometime colleagues as well who show curious behaviour.

A young Brazilian orthopaedic surgeon who was studying arthroscopy and other techniques at a university hospital in Tokyo came to see me for an HIV antibody test. This had been insisted upon by his Japanese girlfriend—maybe she thought all foreigners were high risks for HIV infection and should be checked before one sleeps with them. I suggested that *he* might want *her* to have the test for the same reason. Feeling sympathetic to him as a colleague, I discounted my fee, although I normally charged doctors who come as patients—they usually have insurance anyway. What made me regret not charging this man the full fee, however, was that as he was leaving he took it upon himself to offer a gratuitous critical comment on a letter I had had published in the BMJ a few months previously in response to an article on shoulder pain. He said, 'I completely disagree with you!' So much for tact or gratitude to me for assisting him.

A few days later he returned to find out the result of the HIV antibody test—it was negative, as expected—and to collect the laboratory report to show his girlfriend. No doubt much relieved in his mind he thanked me most courteously for my assistance.

Then there was a British doctor who was the wife of a man who had been posted to Tokyo for three years for his work. She had passed the special medical licensing examination and was working part-time as a GP at another clinic serving the foreign community. Before she started there, very properly she came to my clinic to pay her respects.

Shortly after that she called me on the phone; this was because she wanted something. She wished to know how I obtained *Haemophilus influezae type b* (HIB) vaccine, as there was a demand for it among her patients. (At that time HIB vaccine was unavailable in Japan but I received supplies by post from a helpful chemist I knew in London.) Rather than give away a trade secret, so to speak, I suggested that she might refer these patients to me. She didn't want to do that, and showed her disappointment over my stance by commenting, 'I thought you believed in doing your best for the patients.' So I do, for *my* patients, but not for those who decide to go to elsewhere; that's their choice and they have to take other clinics as they find them.

There was also the case of a young Canadian doctor working as an obstetrician and gynaecologist on a three year contract at one of the American military bases in Japan, who came to see me for career advice. He spoke Japanese fluently and had qualified in the US, after which he had worked in London for a while at a large teaching hospital. Thus he was in the position of a consultant or specialist and was considering making his career in Japan. I thought that a young doctor in his speciality, if he was keen enough, could have a most interesting and rewarding professional life in Tokyo. He was married to a Japanese-Korean and was thinking about studying for the Japanese medical license, although he was not too taken with the Japanese hospital system where you have to see thirty patients an hour!

He seemed a pleasant enough young man and I quite took to him, but I noticed that he was a bit casual, sitting with one knee bent up and resting on the edge of my desk. I asked his age (32), which was relevant for me to know, but it wasn't appropriate for him to ask my age. And although I outlined a potential brilliant career for him here, his reaction was, 'I'm afraid that I will be so successful that if I'm on call twenty-four hours a day, 365 days a week, then it will be too demanding and exhausting, so I will have no family life.'

What I also found disappointing about him was that he felt he could not refuse cut off part of a newborn boy's penis if requested to do so by the parents, even though he said he hated doing it, because he was subject to military discipline. I thought this was spineless, because a medical officer in the US military is of fairly high rank, and surely can refuse on medical grounds to carry out a procedure which in his opinion is unnecessary and harmful. And if it came to a showdown over such an important matter of conscience, then have a showdown!

Sometimes it can be difficult with patients who are doctors. One such situation was an Indian paediatrician. She had two small children, one of whom, in the way that children do, suffered recurrent colds, and when another cold developed the mother pulled rank to request an antibiotic in case the child became worse on a forthcoming trip. I reluctantly complied.

A while later she phoned to say that a friend of hers had a 7 year old son who was having adjustment problems since moving to Japan, and she wanted the name of a child psychologist. I told her that I dealt with such problems myself and in any case I would need to see the patient before I could make a referral.

'You can't just give me the name of a child psychologist?' she persisted.

'No, I need to see the child in order to decide the most appropriate referral, if that is needed.'

'But I'm a paediatrician and I have experience in these matters.'

'I know, but I deal with those problems myself, and in any case I need to see the child first.'

'I see. Thank you. Goodbye.'

It is not that I had reason to doubt her expertise as a paediatrician—in fact I welcomed it—but I wondered why she appeared to doubt mine. I can't make a referral without seeing the patient, and in any case, if this was a problem beyond my scope, to whom would I refer the child? English-speaking child psychologists are not easily to be found here. I would have expected another doctor to be aware of the protocol for referrals—it would have been quite wrong just to give out a name even if I had one.

Ill-considered onward referral

It is unfortunate how some Japanese doctors behave over the matter of referrals, even those who are familiar enough with western ways to know better.

A staff member of a western embassy whom I knew well came to see me about the sudden onset of bad headaches, recurring several times a day. He was a 49 year old overweight unfit man, a pipe smoker who enjoyed wine and cocktails every evening. His blood pressure was raised at 160/110, but it was unclear whether the high blood pressure was the cause of the headaches. So I sent him to a neurologist who was able promptly to arrange a brain CT scan: it was normal. But instead of so informing me and leaving it at that, he changed the treatment which I had just started, added a pain-killer for relief of the headaches, and prescribed a tranquilliser for good measure. He also arranged follow-up for a week later.

My patient felt things were getting a bit too involved with the hospital, and he wasn't happy with being treated there. But why did my otherwise excellent neurology colleague take over the whole management of this patient when I only wanted his opinion and a CT scan? In order to avoid upsetting him I didn't say anything—Japanese doctors can be defensive over anything they perceive as criticism—but I had to advise the patient how to extricate himself from the hospital so that he could continue under my care.

Grasping radiologist

Then there was the surprisingly behaviour of a professor of radiology whom I had known for about ten years. After I set up my own clinic, about three times in the preceding few months I had gone, by appointment, to the hospital where he was working to show him X-rays for which I needed his opinion. It would take him about thirty seconds to look at the film and give me a brief verbal report. I appreciated that he was doing me a favour, but it was as part of a collegial relationship.

About three weeks after my last visit to his hospital, I called to arrange to show him another X-ray, and the following conversation ensued:

'Dr Symonds, I think you should pay me.'

'Oh, all right.'

'How much would be reasonable for you?'

'Just tell me your usual fee.'

'Well, then, ¥15,000 (£115, $150) per case, in cash.'

'All right.'

'I can see you today, or tomorrow,' he said with some eagerness.

'I'll have to check my schedule and I'll get back to you,' I lied.

After this pleasant little exchange I realised I would have to rely more on my own judgement, or if necessary I could ask someone else for an expert opinion.

Such an occasion arose a little while later. I went to meet a radiologist whom I knew at another hospital. It was a case of an asymptomatic patient whose chest X-ray showed what is called miliary mottling; it is sometimes found in advanced tuberculosis. We had an interesting discussion about the differential diagnosis of this X-ray's appearance. His opinion was that the patient probably had sarcoidosis, an inflammatory disease of unknown cause which can affect the lungs, but no treatment was warranted at the present time. I asked him if I might occasionally show him further X-rays and he readily agreed, being glad to assist a younger colleague. I felt that if I had raised any question of payment he would have been offended. In any case, there is the charming Japanese custom of *Oseibo* (winter gift-giving) whereby I unfailingly showed my appreciation of colleagues' support. One can easily arrange for this to be done through department stores. There is a similar custom of *Ochugen* (summer gift-giving) but the former is regarded as the more important.

Give an inch…

The Tokyo British Clinic had a spare consulting room. This was useful when I employed other doctors or if a patient needed to lie down, but most of the time it was unused. Therefore, when Dr Sato, whom we met in the previous chapter, approached me about using this room part-time, I was interested. But I made it clear, or thought I had, that the room might need to be used by other people when he wasn't there, and hinted that he should start modestly so we could see how we got on together.

But on the day he moved his equipment in, a Sunday, there were delivery people coming and going over several hours. The spare consulting room was filled up with some half-dozen bulky items—slit-lamp, computer, corneal topography machine, retinal camera, etc. That was bad enough, but then the next day when the clinic was open he started throwing his weight around. He asked one of my receptionists to be a guinea-pig for testing one of the machines. I intervened and told him that I would be a guinea-pig if he needed one, and he shouldn't ask my staff. He also used the telephone and copying machine without asking permission and had had his old slit-lamp put in the nurse's room as a kind of favour to me, I suppose, without asking. (He didn't want me touching his expensive new one!) In addition, he wanted to have his computer hooked up to my printer. It was as if he was taking over the place. I was rather overwhelmed by all this and didn't say much, but on reflection, it was outrageous. Somehow we managed a compromise and he moved some of his equipment into the staff room and got rid of the old slit-lamp.

A few months later when Dr Sato was in the Clinic, I asked him if I could use his splendid new slit-lamp in case I needed it to examine a patient's eyes when he wasn't there. At first he seemed reluctant, but then agreed and showed me how to operate it. Little did he know how close he came at that point to being kicked out of the clinic!

Storm in a teacup
It is usually not difficult to strike the right balance between being over-confident on the one hand and being over-cautious on the other; but some doctors, due to inexperience or ignorance can get into a muddle.

A younger colleague working at another clinic catering to the foreign community wanted my advice. Or maybe he just wanted to unburden himself. This was the story.

A guest in a five-star hotel was recommended to consult my colleague since his clinic was nearby. The guest was suffering from influenza, as was obvious from his symptoms of fever, runny nose, mild cough, and aches and pains. The treatment is that of the symptoms, with reassurance and an invitation to get in touch again in case of any concerns. Now, for obvious reasons, hotels don't like guests with infectious diseases, and it's not unreasonable for hotel managers to ask—and they usually do—what a staying guest's diagnosis is. One should not, however, say that the diagnosis is influenza: this will only cause unnecessary alarm. I would merely say *Kaze desu* (it's a cold) and everyone will be happy.

So what does my friend do? He takes an unnecessary nasal swab to prove the obvious, that the patient has influenza, and then he puts his foot in it. He asks the patient to sign a release form for him (the doctor) to inform the hotel that he (the patient) has got influenza which might get worse and develop into pneumonia! Patient is alarmed and not happy that his medical details are not confidential, and he complains to the hotel. Hotel manager is not happy because guest complains. Manager complains to the doctor; they won't send him anymore guests. A storm in a teacup, perhaps, but easily avoidable by exercising a bit of common sense.

Students
Occasionally Japanese medical students would contact me

wanting to sit in at my clinic to learn about general practice. I would welcome this—it keeps one on one's toes—and I found it enjoyable to contribute to teaching the next generation of doctors. Incidentally, in Japan general practice is not recognised as a speciality, and in the days before internet advertising I used to notify the public about my clinic, among other ways, by the Yellow Pages telephone directory. Their rules, however, prevented me saying 'general practice' so I had to make a list of the specialities I covered, and this was probably more eye-catching.

All the students, except one, who sat in with me were as keen as mustard to learn; it was a privilege having them. But the one, a young woman whom I accepted at the request of her mother (the mother was one of the specialists to whom I would sometimes refer patients) was different.

She arrived on the first day twenty minutes late. There didn't seem to be a good reason for this lapse of courtesy and I wondered how serious she was. As the session went on I also wondered if she regarded her attendance at my clinic as a kind of amusement rather than study. Then I found she wasn't advanced enough in her course to benefit from sitting in with me.

It soon became clear she hadn't much idea of how of to lay her hands on a patient. Her reaction when faced with something unusual or, from her point of view, embarrassing, was to giggle. She came encumbered with a pile of dictionaries and an electronic translator (though she spoke English reasonably well) and made notes on a clip-board all the time instead of paying close attention to the patients in front of us. When I gently pointed this out to her she became slightly upset.

A medical student needs to become familiar with both men's and women's bodies and to learn how to do appropriate physical examinations. Or at least she could have observed me examining patients, with their permission. One patient was a man with bumps on his penis. These were mollusca contagiosa—in spite of the name they are a harmless type of wart, though they can be sexually transmitted. Incidentally he did have a rather splendid *membrum virile*. The patient was lying on the couch, screened by curtains, naked from the waist down. I wanted to show her these lesions (bumps). She turned away in embarrassment. I thought for her to *refuse to look at a patient* was perhaps a sign that she was not suitable to become a doctor. So I made some excuse to her mother about her English language ability and she did not come again.

Then there was a person who booked himself in to see me in the normal way as if he was a patient. However, he only revealed his true purpose in coming when he was sitting in front of me. He was a 29 year old medical student from Australia, but he didn't want a consultation: he wanted career advice, particularly about the possibilities of working as a doctor in Japan. I should have shown him the door for misrepresenting himself, but as he was there we did have a brief chat. I got the impression he wasn't serious about entering the medical profession—he talked of taking two years off to travel immediately after qualifying. I gave him some advice about finding his way in life and on the importance of establishing himself in a career. He obviously didn't know how to behave: if he had straightforwardly told me in advance why he wanted to meet me, we could have had proper chat over a cup of coffee.

CHAPTER TWENTY-ONE
Poor Treatment and Other Problems

A WOMAN AGED 35 came who had injured her thumb two weeks previously. This happened while she was trying to remove the stone from an Avocado pear with a sharp kitchen knife! She had a deep cut at the flexor aspect (front) of the interphalangeal joint of the thumb, and the skin had been sutured at a local hospital. Since then she had been unable to bend the end of the thumb. Although the hospital doctor had commented on this, he had done nothing about it—a negligent omission. She clearly had severed her flexor pollicis longus tendon, and I referred her to a hand surgeon.

Two days later she called to let me know that she had been operated on the same day that she saw the hand specialist. He re-joined the ends of the cut tendon and had sutured a severed nerve as well, under regional anaesthesia. She was very happy with this treatment and grateful to me for referring her. There are good specialists in Japan but one has to know who they are—this is an important part of my job!

Unlucky encounter

I was involved in an unfolding saga of a foreigner in a Japanese hospital. Late one night I got a call from Australia, from a mother worried about her 18 year old daughter who had been admitted to a hospital in Tokyo with abdominal pain. The parents had been given my name by the Australian Embassy. I said I would contact the hospital the next day and asked the parents to call me again later. My nurse called the hospital and managed to speak to the young woman who was still in the casualty department.

The story was that she had fallen and banged her head the previous day, and by the evening was feeling dizzy and unwell so had gone direct to the hospital. They had X-rayed her head and neck and found nothing wrong, but she had a fever and abdominal pain as well. For this they were giving her an intravenous infusion and were planning to admit her for a week. She had been given a list of possible diagnoses including pancreatitis, urinary infection, or a pelvic infection. It sounded like an over-reaction to what was probably a simple problem (most likely a urinary infection), going down a list of causes of abdominal pain and doing tests to exclude them. I wondered why the hospital doctors couldn't use their clinical judgement, if they had any, instead of frightening the patient with unlikely possibilities like pancreatitis.

The father of the young lady called later from Australia and I did my best to reassure him that there was probably nothing seriously wrong with her. This indeed turned out to be the case when the patient herself called me later to say they had determined she had urinary infection but were admitting her for intravenous antibiotic therapy. I invited her to keep in touch if she felt unhappy with the hospital treatment.

After a four day hospital admission she came to see me. She had been treated with intravenous and intramuscular antibiotics to be followed by oral treatment for ten days in all. I thought this treatment was excessive; probably a week's course of oral antibiotics without hospital admission would have sufficed. But there was more to her condition than a urinary infection. When I saw her she had a raised temperature with tender enlarged glands at her left groin, vulval soreness, and discharge. Examining the discharge under the microscope I found no evidence of monilia (yeasts), trichomonas, gonorrhoea, or Gardnerella vaginalis (a common bacterial infection of the vagina which may produce a fishy smell). This was the great advantage of having a microscope on the premises: I could examine a vaginal discharge on the spot, rather than having to send specimens to a laboratory. In those days I couldn't do a chlamydia test in my clinic, so for this infection I had to send it out: it was negative.

This young woman had a moderately severe vulvitis with multiple shallow ulcers—typical of herpes. Herpes will recover on its own, though it will probably be quicker with anti-viral medicine. However, she didn't want this treatment because of the expense. She told me she was working part-time in a hostess club and had succumbed to the occupational hazard of smoking. That was bad enough, but it was a great pity she had got herself infected with herpes which is likely to recur during the rest of her life.

Hazards of blood tests

An Englishman aged 36 came to ask my advice about the following situation. He had been required to undergo a medical examination as part of his application for a job with a Japanese company, and had then been informed by phone that they would not consider him further because the blood tests showed he had liver disease. Just that. No explanation. No advice about further investigations or treatment. So he was concerned on two counts: that he might have something wrong with him, and that he failed to get the job he wanted. He was a fit-looking man who practised Judo and did regular weight-training. There was no history of liver disorders, he had not taken any drugs, and physical examination was normal. I repeated the blood tests and these showed that in the liver function tests some of the figures were slightly above the quoted upper levels of the reference ranges—a common situation of no significance. In other words, he did not have liver disease and I provided a report to that effect.

This illustrates how important it is not to do blood tests in isolation; the results should always be interpreted in relation to the patient's health situation as a whole. In any case, it is unethical to do tests and then abandon the patient if a possible abnormality is found.

Over-treatment getting out of hand

An overweight American woman aged 49 came to see me because she was worried about osteoporosis (thinning of the bones). She had had a prophylactic hysterectomy with removal of both ovaries when aged 45 because her mother and grandmother had had uterine cancer. Now she was taking hormone replacement therapy, calcium, atenolol (for high blood pressure found on a routine check-up two years previously), and aspirin (to prevent heart attacks because these had occurred on her father's side of the family). She told me that she still attended her gynaecologist for an annual check-up—an odd situation, because since all her internal gynaecological organs had been removed, by definition she no longer needed the attention of a gynaecologist. Her worry about osteoporosis was based on the beginning of a 'dowager's hump' and mild discomfort on certain movements at her neck and lower back. The result of her involvement with doctors was that she had been persuaded through fear to submit to a major operation to prevent a disease that would probably never happen, and now she was on long-term treatment with four drugs.

Around the same time a 46 year old Canadian lady came to see me with a mild infection of an abdominal surgical wound. I took a swab for culture and gave her materials for dressings. The history of the surgery was interesting. Two years earlier in Canada she had had a hysterectomy with removal of both tubes and her left ovary because of infection. But on a routine follow-up this year, cysts were found in her remaining ovary and she was persuaded to have it removed too because it might be cancerous. It wasn't. Unfortunately, the operation was complicated by puncture of the bowel which required removal of the damaged part, and this was followed by a persisting wound infection. I could not understand why she needed to have her remaining ovary removed. Routine ultrasonography is not recognised as a screening test for ovarian cancer and the serious complications would not have arisen if she had not had the operation.

More over-treatment

An American man aged 44 whom I had seen a year ago for low back pain, came for follow-up having recently had a 'complete physical' by his physician in the States. He was already taking two drugs for high cholesterol. After checking his blood pressure once and finding it to be 160/100, the doctor had given him fifty tablets of an anti-hypertensive drug and advised him to be followed up in Japan, since he only visited the US once a year.

The patient, a courteous pleasant man of large build, somewhat overweight, and with a thick head of hair, said he felt worse after visiting the doctor than he did before. He had had a full blood 'work up', urinalysis, chest X-ray, and electrocardiogram. As for the results, these were merely reported to him over the phone. What about a written report and a letter addressed to a doctor in Japan requesting follow-up for the suspected hypertension? At least he should have been given a copy of the results; after all, he had paid over $700 for the examination and tests. And why did the doctor think treatment was so urgent that he started it after only one blood pressure reading? We discussed all this and I advised him stop the anti-hypertensive and come again in two weeks. When I then re-checked his blood pressure it was 136/100, a level that I regarded as acceptable.

Blood pressure treatment should not be initiated after merely one reading (unless it is excessively high) since it may be raised due to anxiety. It should be checked several times over a few weeks, and treatment only started if it is thought it will do more good than harm. Otherwise, one may be condemning someone to decades of pill taking. A doctor should be prepared to justify any proposed treatment to the patient, and to himself.

Dangerous loss of blood

A woman who was a new patient turned up late and had to lie down as soon as she arrived because she was feeling faint. She looked extremely pale and had obviously lost a lot of blood.

She was aged 43 and taking the oral contraceptive pill. Her last period had come as expected but then heavy vaginal bleeding continued for a week. She had tried to see a gynaecologist at two others clinics patronised by foreigners, but was told none was available and the non-specialist doctors there had seemed unconcerned.

I immediately sent her to hospital by ambulance. Later I heard that on admission her haemoglobin was 4.3g/dl, representing a dangerous loss of blood. She had a blood transfusion and treatment to remove the cause: a fibroid just underneath the lining of the womb.

Tears of frustration and relief
An American woman in her thirties came to see me, and the first thing that happened when she sat down in front of me was that she started to cry—tears of frustration at her previous experience with the medical system here, and of relief at having found me! She had had painful urination and frequency with vulval burning for which she had sought an appointment with a gynaecologist at another clinic catering to foreigners. But being unwilling to wait for the next available gynaecological appointment she requested a urine culture test and settled for a new female doctor there—I'll call her **Dr Blackby**—who is promoted by that place as having gynaecological expertise, although she had to wait several days even to see her because she only worked part-time. The urine culture produced a growth of *Staphylococcus epidermidis* which the patient herself thought was a harmless bacterium found on the skin. Apparently Dr Blackby didn't agree as she prescribed an antibiotic called co-trimoxazole. The patient was happy neither with the diagnosis nor the proposed treatment, so she decided to come and see me.

A urine specimen which I examined on-site showed no evidence of infection, but I sent part of the specimen for bacteriological culture to make sure. I found no abnormalities on gynaecological examination except for a mild non-specific vulvitis for which I prescribed a steroid cream. She called three days later to hear the culture result: no bacterial growth. Her vulval soreness was much improved with the cream. So I had another grateful patient, but all I did was to carry out some basic procedures and give a simple treatment.

When to stop investigating?

An American woman aged 51 told me that for the last fifteen years she had had annual mammograms and six-monthly physical examinations of her breasts because of recurrent cysts and lumps. Sometimes she had discovered these herself and sometimes doctors had found them. She had had many aspirations (removal of fluid with a syringe and needle) of the cysts and several excision biopsies. Now she was worried about lumps under the nipples and said her breasts were painful.

These routine checks-ups always resulted in anxiety because no one would give her a definitive answer that everything was all right; she always had to come back for more tests. There was a keloid scar on one breast but otherwise I thought her breasts were normal. She was not at higher than average risk for cancer because there was no family history of breast disease and she had breastfed three children: this is protective against breast cancer. We discussed all this and I advised her not to have any more routine physical examinations or mammograms and not to examine her breasts herself because this just made her anxious. She was much relieved to hear me say this, thinking that she had some dreadful disorder called fibrocystic disease, and that she was prone to cancer.

Lumpy breasts

Another patient illustrated the same problem. An Englishwoman aged 47 came who was worried about her breasts. Also, one year ago she had had her right kidney removed for recurrent infections and ten years ago her gall bladder was taken out. She had been told she had lumpy breasts and should have a mammogram every year. How easy it is for an unfortunate choice of words to slip out and greatly upset patients! What is the expression 'lumpy breasts' supposed to mean? The normal texture of the female breast is described as being finely nodular, that is to say, lumpy, but women may greatly fear the word. Anyway, her breasts felt perfectly normal to me and I told her she did not need any more routine mammograms. She was very grateful to me for listening and giving her time to talk about her worries over the loss of a kidney and her doctor-induced fear of breast disease.

This patient reminded me of an anecdote reported in a medical journal of man who was in despair because he thought his wife was going to die of breast cancer. This was because he had been told that her breast lump, for which she had been investigated, was benign. Being a man of simple education he was unfamiliar with this word and thought it meant the opposite of what the surgeon intended to convey.

Heavy breasts

A Danish woman aged 60 came to see me with long-standing pain at the trapezius muscles, at the area between the sides of the neck and the shoulders. She was convinced this was due to her heavy breasts and wanted a reduction operation. She emphasised this was entirely for reasons of comfort and not for appearances. Her breasts didn't seem *that* large to me, but she asked me to stand behind her and lift her breasts up, saying, 'Feel how heavy they are!' I though this showed a charming degree of confidence and trust in my judgement, but how could I, as a man, feel what it's like to be woman and to have breasts? I could only take her word that the discomfort was instantly relieved by lifting up her breasts, and I arranged referral to a surgeon.

What men don't talk about

Here is another case of mismanagement by Japanese doctors, in which I was involved. An Englishman aged 43 told me he was under treatment at a hospital for benign prostatic hypertrophy (enlargement). His symptoms were a weak urine stream and dribbling after urination. Just that. The dribbling amounted to a few drops of urine which soiled his underclothes. Instead of reassuring him the doctor at the hospital arranged for what is known as a retrograde urethrogram to be performed and pronounced that the patient had an enlarged prostate gland with narrowing of the urine passage. The treatment was a prescription for two drugs which were meant to reverse the alleged enlargement and he was warned that an operation might be necessary to prevent kidney damage.

I gave him my opinion about all this: it was nonsense. He did not have any symptoms of prostatic hypertrophy. His symptoms were normal phenomena at his age and he should not worry about them. There was no reason to take medicine or to have any further investigations. The apparent narrowing seen on the urethrogram was likely an error of interpretation. In other words, a careful assessment of the patient's symptoms would have led to an understanding of the true nature of the problem.

These symptoms are not uncommon in men. I explain it is like the garden hose when you turn off the tap (faucet)—the hose is still full of water! The 'tap', the sphincter muscle of the bladder, is just below the prostate gland at the base of the bladder, which is about 15cm (6 in) from the urethral opening at the end of the penis. Therefore, it is a normal, if inconvenient, phenomenon that men may be aware of; it is not a symptom of disease that needs investigation or treatment. I've noticed that some Japanese specialists feel pressured to diagnose *something*, so they make the X-ray or scan findings fit a pre-conceived idea of a possible disorder; if they can find nothing wrong it's a kind of loss of face.

Misdiagnosis of rectal pain

An Englishwoman aged 35 came with a four day history of pain in the rectal area. There was no bleeding. She had a temperature of 37.4° and there was a tender hard swelling I could feel inside her rectum. On visual inspection with an instrument called a proctoscope everything looked normal and there were no internal haemorrhoids. I thought she had an abscess from which pus needed to be drained. Unfortunately I couldn't get hold of the surgeon I knew who would be able to take care of this problem, so I sent her to a well-known large hospital to see the duty surgeon. I spoke to him on the phone and gave the patient a letter in which I explained the situation as I saw it.

However, to my surprise the patient called later to say they had diagnosed internal haemorrhoids and had given her suppositories to use for two weeks. This clearly was a misdiagnosis: the cardinal sign of internal haemorrhoids is bleeding, which she did not have. Also, haemorrhoids are not painful unless there is some complication, and they do not cause fever. I thought that, especially as I had stated the diagnosis and suggested the appropriate treatment, it was inexcusable for the hospital doctor to make such a mess of it.

Later I did I manage to reach my surgical colleague and he came to see the patient the next day at my clinic. By then her temperature was 37.9° and the swelling was larger than before. Clearly, she had an abscess which needed to be drained under anaesthesia, and he arranged for her to be admitted immediately to his hospital to do this.

I thought I would have a word with the doctor who saw her at the first hospital. Predictably, it was a waste of time: he became defensive, tried to justify his opinion, and didn't want to listen to me. He said her mild fever was not significant, and he couldn't see an abscess on proctoscopy. He claimed he had advised the patient to return if she became worse, saying the diagnosis was either haemorrhoids or an abscess. He wasn't interested in learning from me the physical signs which differentiate these conditions.

It makes one wonder how Japanese doctors are trained. They often seem to jump to a conclusion and make the clinical features fit their first impression, as in the misdiagnosed prostate enlargement mentioned above. They don't seem to know how to think, use their judgement, consider other possibilities and weigh them up. The phone call ending with him saying, 'I'm sorry I couldn't do what you expected.' I wondered if he would then go to the library and learn about the surgical pathology of the anus and rectum so that the next patient who turns up with a problem in that area will be better served. I doubt that he did.

The next day my surgical colleague called to say he had incised the abscess and she had been admitted because of continuing fever. He was scathing of the misdiagnosis at the other hospital.

Appendicitis or not appendicitis?

An Indian gentleman aged 31 came to see me in a conflict over whether to have an operation. He was with his wife, and they requested another opinion urgently because he was on his way to hospital to have his appendix removed for 'impending appendicitis' that very afternoon.

The story was that one month previously he had developed a feeling of pressure at his upper abdomen on both sides. This would come on around midday and last three or four hours, but was somewhat relieved by pressing upon his abdomen; he would ask his young daughter to sit on his tummy. It was not a daily occurrence and did not disturb sleep. He had gone to another clinic where blood tests and ultrasonography had been done, and the question of appendicitis was raised. Then he saw the surgeon, Dr Suzuki, whom we met earlier, who arranged a repeat ultrasound and on the basis of that and in conjunction with an apparently raised white cell count, told the patient he should have his appendix removed without delay. However, when he came to see me he had no pain at all.

On examination I could find no abnormalities. In particular, his temperature and pulse were normal and I could elicit no tenderness in his abdomen. I told him that in my opinion he did not have appendicitis, impending or otherwise, his symptoms were benign, and he did not need an operation. They went outside for a private discussion and returned after an interval. Then they told me they had called Dr Suzuki to say they had decided against the operation, at which he apparently became quite annoyed. The patient asked me why he thought the operation was recommended. This was an invidious question to which I hesitated to reply, but then he supplied the answer himself: Dr Suzuki wanted the money.

Period trouble

The 48 year old wife of a diplomat in Tokyo came to see me about a problem with her periods. She had been bleeding for fifteen days, and the same thing had had happened the previous month. She was markedly pale, with a pulse rate of 138/minute and normal blood pressure. Her uterus was enlarged. Clearly, this was a sick woman suffering from major blood loss. I arranged for her to be admitted to hospital straightaway, mentioning in my referral letter that she needed an urgent blood transfusion and investigation.

Four days later I spoke to the gynaecologist who was in charge of her case. She thought the bleeding was due to fibroids and a hysterectomy was needed, but the patient wanted to have this done in in her own country where she was planning to return in a week's time. On admission her haemoglobin was only 4.4g/dl (normally it should be at least 12.0g/dl). I asked about a blood transfusion, and to my surprise she said they wanted to avoid transfusion because of the theoretical risk of passing on HIV or hepatitis B and C infections, so she was being treated with intravenous iron. If the haemoglobin was not increasing after a further week they planned to give a blood transfusion, but in the meantime they were not worried because her general condition was improved (lying in bed doing nothing) and the bleeding had stopped. I found this management incredible and wanted to discuss it with the gynaecologist. Therefore I arranged to meet her at the hospital, but she didn't turn up at the ward at the agreed time. So I went to see to the patient and her husband who was with her.

The patient was lying in bed and still looked the colour of the bed sheets. She told me that if she attempted to walk across the room she was breathless and her heart would race—not surprisingly. She was having an infusion of iron which looked like *mugicha* (Japanese tea, drunk cold in summer). The patient and her husband were wondering why she wasn't having a blood transfusion. I had to agree, and thought her treatment almost amounted to malpractice.

If someone needs a blood transfusion that's what they should get. Concern about passing on infections like HIV and hepatitis is unwarranted in Japan because blood donors are unpaid and are anyway routinely tested for HIV and hepatitis B and C. Treating her just with iron would take weeks before her haemoglobin reached a reasonable level, and intravenous iron has its own risks. In the meantime, she was feeling ill and was on the verge of heart failure. She was not only short of iron and red blood cells, but also of white blood cells and platelets so was prone to infection and bleeding.

I called the doctor in charge and emphasised that the patient needed an urgent blood transfusion. I had also briefed the patient and her husband to push for this themselves—this is sometimes what one has to do in a Japanese hospital.

Eventually I received a faxed discharge summary. The gist of it was that the patient received iron injections and a blood transfusion, and her haemoglobin recovered from 4.4g/dl to 8.2g/dl. I thought this was acceptable, but was concerned about the treatment she was given on leaving the hospital with a high-dose combined oral contraceptive. This was to prevent renewed bleeding from the womb, but with that kind of pill at her age, and because she had been lying in bed for a week, and because she was soon going on a long flight, there was a serious risk of a deep vein thrombosis (blood clot). But as I heard nothing further I presumed she arrived home safely.

Take your choice: under-investigation or over-investigation
A 30 year old Irishman came with the story that he had passed blood in his urine intermittently in the last three weeks. He had been to a Japanese clinic where he had been diagnosed with an infection and was given an antibiotic. When the problem persisted they wanted to give him a different antibiotic. At this point he sought my opinion.

The passage of blood in the urine requires investigation. I sent him to a urologist who found the patient had two bladder stones. These were treated by lithotripsy. It is surprising that the other clinic out of ignorance or laziness failed to assess his condition properly.

Then there was another case of a Japanese hospital over-reacting and causing unnecessary anxiety. A baby boy aged 2 months who had had a fever for one day was taken to a hospital where a doctor mentioned the possibility of meningitis and wanted to admit him. The parents weren't happy about this and took him home. They brought him to see me the next day. The baby had a temperature of 38.0° but nothing else wrong that I could find. He was breast-feeding normally. I thought he had a viral infection and advised observation. Two days later the parents called to say he had recovered

I wondered why the Japanese doctor didn't use his judgement as to whether admission was really needed. A fever in an otherwise well baby is very unlikely to be due to meningitis, and to mention this as a possibility merely caused the parents anxiety.

I think the main reason for this over-reaction is the lack of a general practitioner service in Japan. Babies and children who develop fevers are taken by worried parents to a *hospital*. There they will meet a doctor who has never seen them before and the patient will likely be investigated according to a protocol: blood and urine tests, chest X-ray, and even a lumbar puncture to exclude meningitis. Putting up an intravenous infusion is very common. I have seen in a hospital waiting area children with intravenous lines attached to their arms drinking juice and being fed snacks by their mothers. Even if no serious disorder is found, it is almost invariable that a prescription for several medicines will be issued.

Not what he expected
An Englishman aged 61 came to see me. He had sent a summary of his medical history and concerns in advance by fax. Two years previously he had gone on his own initiative (referral was not needed) to a dermatologist at a large hospital in Tokyo where a number of skin lesions on his face had been removed with a good cosmetic result. Then one year ago he developed an ulcerated area at the left side of his forehead. The diagnosis was a squamous cell carcinoma and it was treated at the same hospital by wide excision. This meant the removal of a 5cm circular area of skin and tissue down to the bone, followed by a skin graft. He was shocked when he awoke from the anaesthetic as he said he had not been warned about this. The cosmetic result was indeed shocking: there was a very obvious large ugly depression at the left side of his forehead. He should have been treated jointly by a dermatologist, plastic surgeon, and radiotherapist. The only thing to do was to seek the opinion of a cosmetic surgeon in England, to where he was due to travel shortly, but I doubted that much could be done.

Wrong specialist
This case is another illustration of the disadvantage of going direct to a specialist without referral by a GP. It means, in the

first instance, that the *patient* has to decide which specialist to consult. Then you take pot-luck whether the specialist is any good, especially in Japan where there are no post-graduate qualifications and any doctor can call himself a specialist in anything.

A 17 year old Japanese girl who had been living with her family in South America came for a medical examination for a US visa. She was very small and thin: her height was 149cm and she weighed only 30kg. She said the previous year her family had been had been affected by hurricane George in which there was severe flooding and devastation. As a result of this trauma she had lost 10kg. Not surprisingly her periods stopped, and on this account her mother had taken her to a Japanese gynaecologist. The treatment was a hormone injection followed by tablets 'to bring on her periods'. It should have been obvious that the cause of her secondary amenorrhoea was anorexia nervosa; she showed the typical stick-like limbs and fine soft body hair (lanugo) of this condition.

I advised the mother to stop giving hormone treatment and get her to a specialist in eating disorders. She should have weighed at least 40kg. It seemed the gynaecologist didn't look above her waist.

Misdiagnosis of epilepsy
Another example of how patients are ill-served by poorly-trained Japanese doctors. A woman aged 22 came for a routine medical examination for a Canadian visa. She was healthy but had been taking sodium valproate for the previous sixteen months for 'epilepsy'. This amounted to an episode of brief loss of consciousness when she was coming out of a hot bath. Her mother had heard her fall, rushed into the bathroom and in a panic called an ambulance. She probably had a simple faint but it was diagnosed as epilepsy by the hospital doctor. Apparently an initial EEG (brain-wave test) was abnormal

although a subsequent one was said to be normal. Nonetheless, she was given sodium valproate (an anti-epileptic drug) to prevent further fits. The diagnosis of epilepsy is a clinical one and cannot be made on the EEG alone.

Even if she had had an epileptic fit, she should not have been given anti-epileptic medication after a single episode: 50 per cent of such patients never have another fit. But the diagnosis has serious implications: she can't drive, ride a bicycle, or go swimming alone, and it could limit her career opportunities. I had to mention this on the application form for the visa, and as expected, the Canadian immigration authorities wanted a full report from a neurologist, so this held up her application.

It seems in Japanese hospitals these sorts of decisions are often made by junior doctors and there is no subsequent review by more experienced staff.

Getting in a sweat
A diplomat working at a European Embassy, aged 40, came to see me with a three year history of increasingly disabling sweating (hyperhidrosis).

This was especially problematic when he was under stress such as when giving a presentation or in face-to-face business meetings. It affected his head, face, and chest and was noticeable to others: the sweat would run down his face. It was getting to the point where he was afraid he would be unable to continue his work.

The extraordinary thing about this case was that for the past three years he had been under the care of a Japanese psychiatrist at another clinic popular with the expatriate community. He was prescribed an antidepressant in combination with an antipsychotic drug. Different doses of each were tried, and when no benefit resulted, the treatment was changed to a tranquilliser. This this didn't help either so, in near despair, he came to see me.

I could not understand why he had been referred to a

psychiatrist in the first place, since he clearly was not suffering from a mental illness. While it might have been reasonable to treat him with an anti-anxiety drug for a short while, I could see no possible justification for using an antidepressant or antipsychotic drug at all, let alone in combination. I thought he had grounds for a complaint against the other clinic for unsuitable treatment with the attendant risks of side-effects, and for his wasted time and money.

Hyperhidrosis is a difficult condition to treat and I did some research on how best to manage it. Fortunately, I came across a paper which reported success in a case of hereditary hyperhidrosis with a drug called diltiezem, commonly used to treat high blood pressure, and I prescribed it for him. Happily, it produced a very good effect: the excessive sweating was almost completely abolished.

A complicated approach to a simple problem

A patient came to see me with a small swelling on the back of his left hand. It was under the skin and attached to a tendon. This is a common, harmless but unsightly condition called a ganglion. It contains viscous fluid and sometimes one can make it disappear by sucking out the fluid with a syringe and needle. This I tried but it was unsuccessful. A traditional treatment is to hit it with the family Bible or other large heavy book, but I don't recommend trying this at home.

As the patient was keen to get rid of the swelling I referred him to an orthopaedic surgeon whom I'll call Dr Sakai.

After the traditional three hour wait, he had the traditional three minute consultation with Dr Sakai whose manner was reported to me later as arrogant. Then he was sent for X-rays. Why? The swelling clearly was not arising from the underlying bone. But this wasn't enough for Dr Sakai, who next wanted an MRI scan. I called him to ask why. He said he wanted more information about the nature of the swelling, because he didn't think it was a ganglion. What did he think it was then? 'A fibroma or a neurilemmoma.' These possibilities were very unlikely, but knowing how sensitive some Japanese doctors are to perceived criticism I was reluctant to argue. I thought an MRI would do no any harm and advised the patient to go ahead. Mistake. The scan involved being stripped to a loincloth and being incarcerated for twenty minutes in a kind of metal tube while the machine performed its gyrations to the accompaniment of a deafening noise. And the cost? A mere ¥60,000 (£340, $500). He didn't have this amount of cash on him. Would they take a credit card? No. The cashier stood in his way seeming to prevent him leaving. 'Try to stop me,' he said, and brushed past her.

After this little adventure I thought I had better call Dr Sakai to confirm that at the patient's next visit to the hospital he would finally remove the tumour. No, the next visit would be for a chest X-ray and liver function tests!

I said, 'You must be joking! Why does he need a chest X-ray and blood tests for a minor operation under a local anaesthetic?'

'The hospital rules.'

'Ah, now I understand: he needs all these tests because of the hospital rules!'

In response to my incredulity, Dr Sakai said,

'If he won't have these tests we cannot do the operation.'

'I see. In that case, goodbye!'

It seems these rules are designed to extract the maximum amount of money from the health service, or from the patient directly if he is not covered, by doing as many tests as they can think of whether they are needed or not, and to see patients many times instead of the minimum number necessary for proper treatment. This is because Japanese hospitals are paid on an item-of-service basis. The obvious reform is for hospitals to be given a budget by the central government. Then they would have to economise and justify all the tests and treatment, instead of the present system where the patients' needs take second place to the financial aims of the hospital.

Then I called a good general surgeon at the same hospital whom I knew personally, Dr Yamamoto, and asked him to intervene. He called me back, saying 'Dr Sakai was very angry'. (The Japanese often say 'angry' when they mean irritated or upset.) He mentioned that *he* would not have ordered an MRI. So I asked him to see the patient, even though it might have been a bit awkward since Dr Sakai was his friend and colleague, but nonetheless he agreed. Subsequently, the patient attended once more for an initial consultation with Dr Yamamoto (as well as some routine blood tests and no doubt with an HIV test thrown in), and soon thereafter the swelling was removed under a local anaesthetic. It took nearly an hour and the patient was able to watch the procedure in a mirror. And the diagnosis? A ganglion.

A fatal disease

As a doctor one is privileged to hear many sad stories about people's lives.

A middle-aged Englishman came because he was worried that he had started losing at tennis to a weaker opponent whom he usually had no difficulty defeating. He then realised the reason for this was that his muscle strength seemed to be less than usual. In addition he noticed frequent cramps in his arms and legs. There was nothing abnormal to find on physical examination nor in his blood tests except he had a markedly raised level of an enzyme called creatine phosphokinase, indicating the possibility of a muscle disorder. This combination was worrying so I referred him to a neurologist. Unfortunately, a diagnosis was reached of motor neurone disease, and this was confirmed by two more neurologists he sensibly saw for further opinions in Australia. Motor neurone disease is a terrible affliction of unknown cause in which the muscles become progressively weaker and death usually occurs within two years of the onset. (An exception was the famous physicist and cosmologist, Stephen Hawking, who survived with this disease for more than fifty years.)

This patient was resigned to his fate and held a farewell lunch at a local hotel for his friends and colleagues, to which I was also invited. In spite of his dire prognosis he presented a cheerful face and was philosophical about his condition. He had arranged to go back to England for what remained of his life— he survived for just under two years from the diagnosis—and courageously acknowledged that he had 'picked the short straw'.

CHAPTER TWENTY-TWO

How Much Do You Want Cut Off?

A tragedy in two scenes

Characters:
Ghanaian lady (Lady)
Ghanaian lady's mother (Mother)
Gabriel Symonds (Doctor)
Baby (a non-speaking part)

Scene 1. Doctor in his consulting room, on the telephone

DOCTOR: Good morning. How can I help you?
LADY: I'd like to have my son circumcised.
DOCTOR: How old is your son?
LADY: Three weeks.
DOCTOR: Why do you want him circumcised?
LADY: It's our custom.
DOCTOR: Even so, with all due respect, it's a very bad idea and I do not recommend it.
LADY: But it's our custom!
DOCTOR: Please come and see me and I'll explain why it should not be done.

Scene 2. The next day, in Doctor's consulting room

Doctor at his desk. Enter attractive young black woman with Baby at the breast, and a formidable looking older woman, her Mother. After the usual pleasantries:

DOCTOR: Why do you want him circumcised?
MOTHER: It's our custom.

192

DOCTOR: Even so, with all due respect, it will cause severe
    pain and should not be done...etc.

*Lady and Mother unsmiling, shaking their heads. Doctor shows diagram
of longitudinal section through normal penis and offers Mother a pencil.*

DOCTOR: Please take this pencil and show me how much
    you want to cut off.
MOTHER: I don't know...the normal amount.
DOCTOR: The only normal amount is none at all. Leave
    him as God made him until he's old enough to
    decide for himself.
MOTHER: But if he's not circumcised the other boys will
    laugh at him!
DOCTOR: Most boys don't go around showing their
    penises to other boys—that's why they're called
    private parts! Now, take this pencil and show
    me how much you want to cut off.
MOTHER: (*Despairing.*) I don't understand these matters!
DOCTOR: That's the point, you don't understand. Please
    ask the boy's father to come and talk to me.

End of play

The above play was performed only once. The father, needless
to say, never appeared.

A brief lesson in anatomy, physiology, and surgery

It's not only the Mother in the above true story who doesn't
understand about the foreskin. Ignorance of the structure and
functions of this organ is widespread, especially among those
who advocate and carry out its amputation. The following is for
the benefit of those who would like to be better informed.

    The Shorter Oxford English Dictionary defines circumcision

as: 'Cut off the foreskin of (a male), as a religious rite (esp. Jewish or Muslim) or for medical reasons.'

The foreskin is a complex structure and an integral part of the penis; it is continuous with the skin on the shaft. At the level of the coronal sulcus it consists of a double fold of soft skin lined with mucous membrane which is continued forward for a variable distance where it ends in a spout for the voiding of urine. *It contains one of the densest concentrations of nerves in the body,* and consists also of muscle fibres and blood vessels. It has been estimated that if the average adult foreskin were unfolded and laid flat, it would cover an area of 7.6 x 12.7 cm (3 x 5 inches). At birth the foreskin is fused with and inseparable from the glans of the penis which it covers and protects from friction, drying, injury, and contact with faeces. As the child grows, from a variable age starting around five years, the foreskin begins to separate from the glans after which it can be retracted to expose the glans. The process of separation occurs gradually and may not be complete till puberty or even later. The foreskin contains the above-mentioned rich nerve supply which, when stimulated during sexual activity, produces intense erogenous (pleasurable) sensations. Circumcision removes at least 10,000–20,000 specialised erotogenic nerve endings and 33–50 per cent of the mucosal tissue of the penis. Circumcision also partially or completely excises the frenulum. This is a highly erogenous structure on the underside of the glans that tethers the foreskin and allows it to glide back and forth over the glans and to remain in its forward position in the non-aroused state. The foreskin is thus an essential part of male anatomy; its removal destroys its sexual and physiological functions.

Cutting off the foreskin is widely carried out in the US for non-religious reasons, for social custom, or because of mistaken beliefs that its removal renders hygiene easier and has health benefits. The procedure commonly takes place in a hospital. For this purpose the baby is strapped down on a board moulded to the baby's shape. The infant penis, an organ about 3.6 cm (1.4 inches) long and narrower than an adult's little finger, will now have its foreskin cut off. First, the foreskin needs to be forcibly separated from the underlying glans to which it is attached. This involves grasping the end of it with forceps and inserting a probe between it and the glans and moving it in a circular fashion. This is extremely painful and usually is the point at which the infant starts screaming. Many people who have witnessed this or have heard recordings find it distressing. The screaming is quite unlike normal crying: the baby is clearly in agony.

A local anaesthetic may be used, though this is by no means routine. The administration of an anaesthetic is an admission that cutting off the foreskin is painful. If it is done, the usual way is by injecting the anaesthetic through the skin at the base of the penis. This of itself is painful, if only briefly. But why should the baby have to have a needle stuck into his penis and be injected with a local anaesthetic for non-medical reasons?

Some people claim babies sleep through the whole procedure and are more distressed by being tied down than by having part of their penis cut off. This is an error. The baby, overwhelmed with severe, apparently unending and, to him, incomprehensible pain, goes into a state of shock.

With or without the benefit of a local anaesthetic for this unnecessary operation, when the foreskin has been cut off, the baby has an open sore over his glans where the foreskin used to be attached. It takes about ten days to heal during which it is almost impossible to avoid all contact with urine and faeces. The mother, in addition to the demands of the normal essential care of her newborn son, now has the additional task of caring for a surgical wound and a fretful distressed infant who may be reluctant to feed and with whom this unwarranted assault may disturb maternal-child bonding.

But that's not all. Instead of a foreskin, the boy now has a permanent broad scar all the way round his penis proximal to the glans.

In a man whose foreskin has been cut off, sexual activity cannot but be impaired: the glans of necessity is now stimulated directly by hand or by contact with the vaginal walls—an abnormal and restricted form of sexual activity.

Cutting off the foreskin may satisfy the ritualistic or customary needs of parents or grand-parents, or the societal requirements of foreskin-removing cultures, but the person to whom the foreskin once belonged does not remain a baby for long. As he grows into boyhood and manhood, and for the rest of his life, he will have to live with the physical and psychological effects of a scarred, functionally diminished penis.

Guilt and denial

If someone posts on the internet a personal account about something and includes their email address, they should not be surprised if a member of the public responds. In fact, such a posting invites responses, does it not?

While browsing the internet one day I came upon an account by an American woman of her experience of giving birth to a healthy boy in Tokyo and then finding a doctor who agreed, no doubt for a large fee, to cut off part of the hapless boy's penis.

I make no apology for raising my voice about this matter whenever the opportunity arises, and I sent a mildly worded email to the mother saying I was sorry to read that she had had her son circumcised, that I hoped if she had another son she would leave him intact, and offered to discuss the matter with her.

A few days later I received from this good lady's husband the sort of email that it's fine to write—but not to send, at least until one has taken a little time to reflect on what one has written.

I had obviously touched a sore spot—to say nothing of the soreness that was inflicted on the poor baby. He said:

The decision to circumcise is a very personal decision…My wife and I researched for hours and read viewpoints from both sides before making our decision.

Circumcision is indeed a very personal decision—especially for the person on whom the procedure is performed. What did *he* have to say about this irreversible alteration of his penis that was inflicted on him and that will affect him for the rest of his life? The father continued:

I am circumcised and am glad that I am, my first son is circumcised and will have no issues with it, and my 15 month old son was also circumcised and things went smoothly. If we have more boys, they will also be circumcised, because that is our decision as their parents and it will not harm them.

His idea that circumcision will not harm his sons sounds like a classic case of denial. The physical, emotional, and sexual harms that non-consenting, non-therapeutic infant genital cutting causes have been widely documented. But if this father doesn't do it to his sons it will amount to an admission that what was done to *him* was wrong. He then launched into an attack on me:

The bigger thing I wanted to address with you is your complete overstepping of bounds and disregard for tact. I understand you are passionate about this issue, but that does not give you the right to email someone you have never met, someone who has never asked for your advice, and tell them (in a very classless manner I might add) that they have essentially failed their child. Please discontinue your pride-driven campaign of emailing people you don't know and offering unsolicited and guilt–laden advice. I'm saddened by the number of people that have likely left your office feeling guilty about a decision that really doesn't matter either way…

'Overstepping the bounds, failed their child, guilt-laden, saddened, feeling guilty…' I wondered if he was talking about himself.

One stitch or two?

In these days of greater openness about matters concerning the human body, I trust my readers will not take the following narratives as in any way indelicate.

As part of my training for general practice I worked for six months as a resident senior house officer in obstetrics. A woman had just given birth who came from a country where she had been subjected in childhood to the horrific practice known as female genital mutilation (FGM). Her labia were fused together and had to be surgically opened for childbirth to take place. The senior doctor who conducted the labour said, in an aside to me, 'I suppose we'd better ask her husband if he'd like her sewn up again.' I thought this remark was rather insensitive. What about asking the patient what *she* wanted?

I was reminded of this incident by a controversial case from 2012 which caused considerable grief to the trainee obstetrician involved. It concerned a woman from Sudan who, likewise, has been subjected to FGM in childhood. She attended hospital in London when already in labour but there was no way the baby could be born without surgical intervention. Therefore a midline incision through the scar was made to enlarge the opening so the baby could be safely delivered.

So far so good. But then there was a problem. Bleeding from the edges of the incision would not stop. The normal thing to do under these circumstances is to put in a stitch, or stitches, to stem the bleeding. Therein lay a dilemma.

The British FGM Act 2003 is quite clear: female genital mutilation is a criminal offence—except that:

No offence is committed by an approved person who performs a surgical

*operation on a girl who is in any stage of labour, or who has just given
birth, for purposes connected with the labour or birth.* (Paraphrased.)

This should be clear enough, but it didn't help the unfortunate
doctor who was involved in the above-mentioned case. The
doctor, a Hindu, said: 'I regard FGM as an abhorrent practice
with no justification in our society.'

If he had put in two stitches—one on either side of the
cut—the bleeding would have been controlled, and, incidentally,
something approximating to her normal anatomy would have
been restored. On the other hand, if he had used a single stitch
the bleeding would have been controlled and her infibulated
state (the labia minora being fused together) would have been
reinstituted.

Gentle reader, what would you have done?

Oh, and in case you're wondering, this woman is reported as
having had another surgical procedure some time previously to
allow sexual intercourse to take place.

I won't keep you in suspense any longer. The doctor used a
single stitch for expediency. However, unluckily for him, word
got about and—unbelievably—someone reported him to the
police!

Once the heavy machinery of the law is set in motion there
is no way of stopping it. The hapless doctor duly found himself
the recipient of charges brought by the Crown Prosecution
Service. This was potentially very serious. He was suspended
temporarily from the Medical Register and if convicted could
have been sentenced to prison for up to fourteen years!

Fortunately, however, at the end of the thirteen day trial,
common sense prevailed and the jury acquitted him as innocent
of the charge that he had committed FGM. At worst, the
problem was a training issue and clearly not a matter for criminal
prosecution.

There was much discussion about this fiasco in the medical

press and elsewhere. I also joined in the fray, but to raise a different, though related, matter. This is part of my letter that appeared online in the BMJ:

> *Performing or aiding and abetting female genital cutting is a crime under the Female Genital Mutilation Act 2003.* **So why are male infants and children not given the same protection from genital cutting (circumcision) under the law?** *As the FGM 2003 Act makes clear in Section (5), 'For the purpose of determining whether an operation is necessary for the mental health of a girl it is immaterial whether she or any other person believes that the operation is required as a matter of custom or ritual.' In the same way, it should be stressed that the call to end non-therapeutic non-consenting male genital cutting is nothing to do with an attack on any religion, but is prompted entirely by human rights concerns.*

Unfortunately, in spite of my letter and a few other like voices crying in the wilderness, at present there is no legal protection anywhere in the world for boys from having part of their penis cut off at the parents' behest.

Further foreskin problem
I made a home visit to woman who had recently given birth at maternity hospital run by a female doctor I knew and respected. She had seen the baby boy for a one month check-up when, to the mother's and baby's distress and my annoyance, she pulled the foreskin back. Apparently she believed this should be done, since unfortunately in America it is common practice, or rather, malpractice. Then the doctor recommended circumcision because the boy's foreskin was difficult to retract! I rang up my doctor friend and politely informed her that forcing retraction is meddlesome interference. It seems this is done from ignorance that the foreskin is normally adherent to the glans at birth and may not separate for a number of years; it should simply be left

alone. Fortunately, the doctor was glad of my advice and agreed to desist in future.

CHAPTER TWENTY-THREE
Sexually Transmitted Infections

A PLEASANT FIT-LOOKING 30 year old gay Englishman with close-cropped hair consulted me. When I examined him I noticed two curious 1cm (0.4 inch) silver pins inserted horizontally under his nipples. I wondered whether these were for decoration or sexual stimulation, or perhaps they were for both purposes. I had treated him previously for gonorrhoea. He told me that his current boyfriend was under a Japanese hospital for HIV infection, and my patient wished to be tested for HIV antibodies too, as he was clearly at risk. We discussed how he would cope if the result was positive: it was.

In my experience it is almost invariably gay men in this situation, as opposed to heterosexual men who are worried about recent casual contacts, who turn out to be HIV positive. However upsetting, they are not usually surprised because they are expecting this result.

Classic mistake

I don't always get it right first time. Once I made a classic diagnostic mistake, but subsequently was able to rectify it and take the correct action.

A young man came with a complaint of pain at his anus. He had what looked like a fissure (a split in the skin). This will usually heal on its own but using an anaesthetic gel can help in the meantime. Unfortunately, it made no difference so I referred him to a surgical colleague since sometimes a simple operation can cure the problem. The surgeon made the same diagnostic error and offered an alternative medical treatment: glyceryl trinitrate ointment. This relieved the pain but gave him a headache—a well known complication.

Ten days later the patient came again, being no better at his rear end and with a fever. He was also concerned about a blotchy rash on the palms of his hands and a faint rash over his trunk. The anal problem had progressed to three large painless ulcers and he also had enlarged rubbery non-tender groin glands. These are classic signs of secondary syphilis, with the primary chancres (ulcers) still present. This diagnosis was soon confirmed by a blood test. Therefore I started him on the standard treatment for this condition: daily intramuscular injections of penicillin. He was homosexual but denied penetrative anal contact, though that was an academic point. The moral of the story is always to keep other diagnostic possibilities in mind!

Fear of sexually transmitted infections

FAIDS is an unofficial abbreviation meaning Fear of AIDS. It refers to the situation where someone thinks they might have been exposed to the human immunodeficiency virus and becomes anxious; sometimes people in this situation become *very* anxious.

A 26 year old English girl came in an agitated state. She was worried about HIV infection because of condom breakage on a couple of occasions two years previously. Then recently she had developed symptoms which she thought were indicative of the onset of AIDS: tingling at her hands and feet, and a white coating of the tongue which she diagnosed as 'thrush'. Unfortunately she had seen a Japanese doctor who had performed a culture from a mouth swab. This grew the normal harmless bacteria to be found in the mouth but it was misinterpreted as an infection for which she was prescribed antibiotics and a mouth spray. I had quite a job persuading her that the culture showed only the normal mouth bacteria, there was no reason to suspect HIV infection, and her symptoms were due to anxiety. Her tongue looked perfectly normal to me. Nonetheless, as she strongly wished to have an HIV antibody test, I did this for her: as predicted the result was negative. This is partly a problem of the Japanese health insurance system. Doctors don't get paid much for talking with patients: they get paid for doing tests and prescribing medicines.

Then there was a wonderfully eccentric American lady who came to see me but before she arrived there were many phone calls presaging an interesting or complicated consultation. On arrival in my consulting room she made a dramatic announcement: 'I've been exposed to molluscum contagiosum!' She was a blonde middle-aged lady, smartly dressed in a business suit, and wearing glasses with thick black frames. She said how much she loved my cute British accent and how nice it was to see a western doctor. Her anxiety arose because she had a new boy-friend who had informed her, on withdrawing after sex (during which he used a condom), that he had been treated for molluscum contagiosum. This put her in a panic as she thought she had been exposed to some dread disease. We had long discussion about this disorder, but she was difficult to convince of its harmlessness.

'I was on a business trip and got drunk…'

Quite a few consultations start in this way, as if the patient needs to present me with an excuse for what will follow. One such person was a 28 year old Indian man whom I had seen before, who called me in a panic on a Sunday morning saying he was having difficulty urinating and had passed blood in his urine. I went to meet him at the clinic and he told me he also had a sore at the end of his penis for which he had consulted a doctor who advertised himself in the Yellow Pages as dealing with such disorders. I asked him why he hadn't come to me about this and he said he assumed I didn't deal with venereal infections.

The other doctor had done a blood test for syphilis and the result was indicative of the early stage of this disease. Indeed, he had a shallow ulcer near the urethral opening of the penis. The opening was partially blocked with dried secretions, and I thought that was why he had difficulty urinating. He also had enlarged groin glands compatible with early syphilis. In addition he had a positive urine test for chlamydia, the commonest sexually transmitted infection. Although injectable penicillin is the first-line treatment for syphilis it is not available in Japan—I had to bring it over from England in those days—so I gave an oral treatment with doxycycline for two weeks, which should have dealt with both problems.

At first he wouldn't admit to any sexual contact other than with his wife (which he had stopped as soon as the ulcer was noticed), but on more persistent questioning, he admitted to oral sexual activity in Thailand three months previously. He said he was drunk at the time and there may have been non-penetrative genital contact as well. So that explained that. It is simply idiotic to take such risks. The rule should be, if one wants to indulge in that sort of thing at all, to look but not touch. Then he had to tell his wife who also needed to be investigated. She tested positive for chlamydia but negative for syphilis. I followed them up for several weeks but then they left Japan.

Christmas ruined

I was requested to visit a 51 year old Englishman at an expensive hotel in Tokyo on one Christmas Day. He was in Japan on business and had brought along his wife and teenage son. The story was that about a month before that he had visited a pub in Singapore, and being under the influence of alcohol, had put his tongue into the ear (*sic*) of a woman he didn't know. Soon thereafter he felt discomfort at his tongue with a sour taste in his mouth and he thought his tongue looked abnormal. He went to a hospital in Singapore where he saw a young doctor who asked intrusive questions and did unnecessary tests for sexually transmitted infections including an HIV test. They were all negative except one for herpes type I antibodies. All this meant was he had had a herpes infection such as a cold sore at some time in the past, but it was a fine example of the common situation where an unthinking doctor does an inappropriate test and then misinterprets the result.

A wrong diagnosis of a herpes infection of the mouth was made and pointless treatment given with an antiviral drug called acyclovir. He had also treated himself with an over-the-counter gel to his tongue for oral candidiasis (yeast). The result of all this was that the poor man was in a state of severe anxiety about some dread disease he might have acquired from the tongue-in-ear jape and he was terrified of infecting his wife and son.

His tongue was normal, but it extremely difficult to convince him there was nothing wrong. I told him my best advice was to stop all medication, cease inspecting his tongue in the mirror, behave normally towards his wife and son and, as it was Christmas, to eat, drink, and be merry.

I was not surprised, however, when he came to see me at the clinic a day later. He was worried about a brown coating of his tongue and dryness of the mouth. Again, this was within the normal variation of the appearances of the tongue, and I thought was due to drinking coffee. To reassure him I took a scraping for microscopy which only showed cellular débris and no yeasts. I explained that in my view what he was feeling was not due to any disease but was due to anxiety which had been to a large extent doctor-induced. If one recommends an HIV test to a patient (other than as a routine) one should have a good reason for doing so because the suggestion will almost invariably cause disquiet.

FAIDS again

A pleasant Middle Eastern gentleman aged 35 called me at home late in the evening being very worried HIV. I arranged to see him the next day, and he told me an extraordinary story.

He was divorced and had recently split up with a girlfriend and was trying to meet women through internet dating. He was not interested in one night stands but was looking for a

Sexually Transmitted Infections

relationship, and had made contact with a girl whom he arranged to meet. However, he was concerned that she told him her sexual fantasies before they met, which he found off-putting: she wanted to have anal sex. (Then why did he go ahead if he didn't like the idea?) Two days before he came to see me they had met in a café in the afternoon and had a cup of coffee. She was just an ordinary Japanese girl and not even particularly attractive. She wasn't very responsive to his questions in trying to make conversation and seemed in a hurry to get to a 'love hotel'. (These establishments are found throughout Japan and rent rooms by the hour, anonymously.) This he found more off-putting, but she pressed him with 'What about my fantasy?' so he found himself reluctantly being drawn towards a love hotel—though he made several detours to make sure he was not being followed in case it was a set-up for robbery! In the hotel the woman undressed and wanted him to get on with it. Against his better judgement he inserted his *membrum virile* into her anus, then into her vagina. It was easier to penetrate the former than the latter, he said. But, having had second thoughts about the whole business and now being concerned about the risk of venereal disease, he withdrew to ejaculate. This annoyed the woman and she walked out on him. He also was left feeling very unsettled and worried about sexually transmitted diseases. I reassured him that the risk of HIV infection was extremely low but it was too early to do a test. However, there was a much bigger risk which was that of chlamydia infection, so I gave him a single dose of an antibiotic (azithromycin) to deal with this possibility.

Treatment by reassurance

An American man aged 25 came to see me. He must have had high expectations since he wrote on the registration form, in the space where patients are requested to say how they heard about the clinic, 'Some dude I met said this place was great.' I hope I

207

fulfilled his expectations. The story was of the confusion which commonly arises from going to see Japanese doctors. Partly, no doubt, it's a language problem but I think it goes further than that: the doctor's inability to recognise and deal with the real issue that the patient is worried about. Instead, the approach is often to order tests unthinkingly: this is a recipe for confusion and anxiety.

Five weeks previously the patient had had sex with a Japanese woman of short acquaintance and she did not want him to use a condom. He was very worried about this, and a few days later, his attention being drawn anxiously to his lower abdomen and genitals, he thought he discovered there was swelling of his left epididymis (the highly coiled tube above the testis) and it was tender to the touch. Then, from the internet he diagnosed himself as suffering from epididymitis and thought he needed a chlamydia test. He went to his local general practitioner, a woman, who refused to do a chlamydia test but did blood tests for HIV infection, among other things. He then consulted a urologist who apparently found no signs of infection but nonetheless prescribed antibiotics. This produced short-term relief only. In the meantime, he persuaded the original general practitioner to do a chlamydia test, which was negative.

When I examined him, his external genitalia were normal; the symptoms were due to anxiety. At no time had he had pain on urination or a discharge. He was feeling his own normal structures in the scrotum and they were tender from repeated prodding and poking.

The treatment was strong reassurance, and he went out a much happier man than when he came in.

CHAPTER TWENTY-FOUR
Birth in Tokyo

WHEN I STARTED working in Tokyo the clinic where I was an assistant was affiliated with a well-known foreigner-friendly hospital at which we had admitting rights. This meant I could admit patients there under my own care.

In those days it was not so long since I had done my obstetric training. For this reason, since I had been seeing an Englishwoman for ante-natal care, I offered to conduct the delivery at this hospital. She readily agreed. All went smoothly, and when it got to the 'pushing stage' she needed to get up onto the operating table. This was the normal style of delivery at that hospital where, for the convenience of the obstetrician, the woman would labour flat on her back with her legs in stirrups—it would be difficult to think of a more uncomfortable or unsuitable position in which to give birth.

However, when my patient had clambered up onto the narrow operating table, I encouraged her to adopt the position that came naturally to her for the actual birth: this was the kneeling position. Then, with the assistance of a midwife, the mother was safely delivered of her baby.

So all was well? It should have been, but when the mother and her new baby had been taken back to their room, the chief midwife suddenly descended on me with strong disapproval. She said, 'This sort of thing may be all very well for the middle of Africa, but we're not having it at this hospital!'

I believe they changed the system in recent times and natural childbirth is now the norm.

'Doing things' to a newborn baby

A charming American lady married to an Englishman, whom I had been seeing for part of her ante-natal care, had her first baby at the S— Clinic, a small maternity hospital. The chief doctor there had agreed for me to come in as the baby's paediatrician, since they had no resident paediatrician.

The S— Clinic had the great advantage over other places of birth in Tokyo since, unlike at other institutions, there was no routine separation of mother and baby and they did not have a nursery. The mothers stayed in comfortable single rooms with a *doula* in 24 hour attendance to help with breast feeding and general care of the baby. I got a call to come to the hospital because the delivery was imminent. There was a gap with my clinic patients so I could leave, and I arrived through the open door of the delivery room about five minutes after the birth.

I was confronted by the mother's bleeding gashed perineum as she lay semi-reclining on the operating table, with the cries of the baby coming from a side-room. There were about half-a-dozen green-gowned and masked people in the operating theatre, all busily moving around including the chief doctor and a nursing sister who were bending over the episiotomy wound. There was also a western woman who I think was the mother's sister-in-law. The doctor stopped his activities to greet me in a friendly and relaxed way and to thank me for coming. I went first to congratulate the mother and shake her hand. It emerged (pun intentional) that the baby had been pulled into the world with vacuum assistance because of suspected foetal distress in the second stage of labour—hence the episiotomy. Next door the baby was lying, pink and huge (4.0kg or 8lb 13oz) and screaming with her eyes screwed shut and arms and legs in the 'startle' position (as well she might) while a nurse—a young woman who obviously, I thought, had never had a baby herself—was busy *doing things* to her: measuring with a tape measure her length, chest and head circumferences; then she and another nurse gave her a bath to 'clean her up' during which the screaming somewhat abated as the baby must have felt more secure being back in the warm watery environment she had left only minutes before. I performed a quick general examination to confirm she was in normal health. After being washed with soap and water and vigorously dried with a towel, and the wonderful protective *vernix caseosa* (the waxy or cheese-like white substance found coating the skin of newborn babies) being all carefully removed, finally she was firmly wrapped in several layers of cloth. The nurse did all this, I thought, routinely and not particularly gently. At least I managed to stop her putting drops in the baby's eyes—an obsolete practice from the pre-antibiotic days when gonorrhoea was rife.

It occurred to me that none of the delivery staff had heard of, let alone read, Frédérick Leboyer's wonderful book, *Birth without Violence*. The title says it all: why do babies have to be pulled crying into the world, instead of being gently welcomed with a smile?

Pre-birth anxiety

Although anxiety over childbirth is natural, some couples cause themselves excessive worry by getting bogged down in details. I received a four-page fax from a couple I'd not previously met. I reproduce the beginning of it. (Emphasis in the original.)

> Dear Doctor Symonds
> My partner and I are expecting the birth of our first child in July next year and we are researching the options we have regarding where and how we can have the most comfortable experience from the first visit through to the birth of our child. Below we have listed many questions…this is a very important and **very expensive** decision for us…
> Basic fee per consultation…
> Please **list** any other tests which are necessary but not included in the price of the consultation and how many times each test would need to be done…
> Approximate **total** cost of hospital stay…

We live near S— Hospital can you deliver at this hospital? Yes/No

What do you charge for the actual delivery?

Are there any extra charges? I have heard some frightening stories that some doctors actually charge extra for delivering at night or on the weekend. This is not true of your clinic, is it?

What happens if you are unable to deliver the baby and the baby must be delivered by another doctor? What fee is charged?

Could you please list any other procedures which may possibly be requested or needed at the time of birth and their respective costs...

If for whatever reason another doctor must deliver the baby will this 'replacement' doctor a) Speak English? Yes/No b) Be fully briefed on our birthing plan and requirements Yes/No

Is there always a midwife present at the birth? Yes/No

Will she speak English? Yes/No

Is the father allowed to remain with the mother at all times during the birth?

Will the woman be allowed to move around freely during labour and give birth in **any position she chooses?**

Etc.

I replied saying these matters were too complicated to deal with in writing and invited them to visit me so we could discuss all their concerns properly. I never heard anything further. This fax reflects a great deal of anxiety about childbirth. It's a pity they didn't come to see me because I could probably have assuaged many of their concerns.

Breastfeeding mishandled

I made a home visit to see a baby born a week ago to an English mother. The story of the birth was interesting. She was born by

Caesarian section at full term because the labour was judged not to be progressing quickly enough after her waters broke. Because of this there had been a short delay in starting breastfeeding and then there was concern about the baby's falling weight. Therefore, bottle supplements were started.

The mother told me that it was a very deep-seated instinct to breastfeed, and she was almost in tears with disappointment and, indeed, anger, that she did not receive the right sort of support and encouragement in the early days, and that the reaction of the hospital staff was to switch to a bottle as soon as they thought the baby was not gaining weight as expected. When I saw the baby she was being breastfed with bottle supplements. The mother said the baby sometimes turns away from the breast in apparent pain, drawing her legs up, with 'wind', which is distressing to them both. I did not observe this behaviour when she breastfed at the clinic. (One can learn a lot by asking the mother to allow observation of breastfeeding.) The baby seemed perfectly normal to me, although her height and weight were not closely following those nice parallel lines on a growth chart. If one frequently weighs and measures and looks at charts one can get concerned. I asked the mother,

'Apart from her weight and so on, how do you think she's doing?'

'I think she's great'.

This was a mother's instinct speaking. I encouraged her to carry on breastfeeding as much as possible, using supplementary feeds only if necessary, and to stop timing, measuring, and writing things down!

This is a common story in Japan: interventionist obstetrics, leading as in this case to a Caesarian section, with resultant disruption of early maternal-baby bonding because of the inevitable (even if short) separation, and apparent excessive weight loss or failure to gain weight at the prescribed rate, with doctors' anxiety over this and the routine reaction of 'bottle' rather than trying to solve the problem.

High-tech birth

I made a home visit to see a newborn baby born to an English mother for a general check and a metabolic abnormality screening test done on a heel prick blood sample.

The birth had been the typical high-tech cascade of interventions. The labour was painful but manageable, and near the second stage she was asked to get up on the delivery table. She said she couldn't do it as it was too painful to labour on her back, and the obstetrician (an American trained Japanese) replied that he would be unable to deliver the baby unless she complied. So she was offered an epidural anaesthetic in order to get up onto the delivery table! Monitoring of the baby's heart was performed the whole time, and during the second stage it seemed that the baby's heart rate was falling, so she had a vacuum extraction. The third stage was 'actively managed', meaning the placenta was pulled out rather than being expelled naturally; the baby was taken away to the nursery for 'observation', and an hour later the mother had a post-partum haemorrhage. This might have been avoided if the baby had been put to the breast and suckled immediately, even with the cord still attached. Then another obstetrician had been called who did a vaginal examination with a 'quick feel around in her uterus' without any greeting or by-your-leave to the patient. Why didn't they give an injection of ergometrine to make the womb contract? And the midwives caused her considerable pain by pressing up and down on her abdomen in an attempt to 'rub up a contraction.' Unfortunately these practices are common, if not routine, in Japan.

Older mother

A 40 year old American woman who had recently given birth came to see me. The baby had been born at a hospital where babies are fed by the clock and they do pointless and obsolete test weighing before and after a feed to calculate how much milk the baby has received; then they make up any perceived deficiency of breast milk with formula! The baby had been seen at the hospital three times in the last few days because of diarrhoea (several loose stools per day) although he was otherwise well. Medicine had been prescribed with advice to continue breast milk and formula. I do not understand how anyone who calls himself a paediatrician can treat diarrhoea in this way. I advised the mother to stop formula and the medicine, and to give breast milk *ad libitum*. Unfortunately the baby had had part of his penis cut off. This upset me for the rest of the morning.

Premature labour and stillbirth nightmare
The wife of one of the staff of a large international bank had been pregnant with twins and had gone to see a Japanese woman obstetrician. Unfortunately, she had started in premature labour at 28 weeks and was referred to a specialist hospital. There, they had taken an X-ray (it's not good for unborn babies to be irradiated), apparently not believing the evidence of the scan and fearing there might be triplets—only twins were seen. Then she had a Caesarian section, but one baby died and the other developed breathing problems.

I was asked by the husband to visit his wife and the surviving twin in the hospital. Seldom have I have heard such a nightmarish tale. For the Caesarian section she was given a spinal anaesthetic but it was ineffective and the poor woman was screaming in agony. Then the female obstetrician panicked and fainted in the middle of the operation! When I spoke to her she was defensive about the anaesthetic, but she admitted she did faint in the operating theatre because of the tension with the patient screaming and her husband's alarm—he was present in the theatre. It is inexcusable that the surgeon should have been unable to control events in the theatre, and the husband should not have been allowed in—it is not uncommon for fathers to faint under these circumstances. Further, I find it extraordinary that the operation took place with inadequate anaesthesia, and it was indefensible that the surgeon and the anaesthetist were one and the same. If an epidural or spinal anaesthetic fails, someone needs to be on hand to administer a general anaesthetic. I also saw the baby who weighed about 840g but was in a stable condition, and I thought the standard of care in the paediatric intensive care unit was acceptable. Overall, the outcome was as good as could be hoped for under the circumstances of the premature labour.

CHAPTER TWENTY-FIVE
Psychiatric Cases

A TALL GOOD-LOOKING Englishman in his thirties came to see me. I'll call him David Wellworth. He appeared rather grim and tense and spoke softly in a monotone while looking down at the floor. His problem was over his current girlfriend, a Japanese divorcee ten years his senior. They had just returned from holiday together, but it had been ruined by his retrospective jealously over her previous relationships. She was frightened that their rows might escalate into physical violence, and he was then overcome with almost suicidal remorse at having caused her so much distress.

Why do some people feel they have to control others—even their past lives? Why could he not let the Japanese girlfriend be herself and not care about her past? It was as if he could not exist as an independent person without the affirmation of total devotion of this ageing mother figure.

In the end I referred him to Dr Smith, a clinical psychologist with a PhD, because at that stage in my career I had neither the confidence nor the time to take on such a complicated psychological problem.

Two weeks later he came again for a routine check-up. He was still depressed and obsessed with fantasies about the sexual activity of his girlfriend with her previous partners. He had been seeing Dr Smith but had not liked her, nor had he liked another psychotherapist he had seen independently who he thought was gay. I suggested that he might come for informal counselling with me. This he angrily dismissed saying he didn't want a 'talk over a cup of tea', but he needed treatment for his obsessive problem. When I asked what sort of treatment he thought he needed, he was unable to tell me. I suggested I could try to find a different counsellor with whom he might get on better since it didn't seem I could do much for him. Perhaps he was the kind of patient who, in a sense, needs incompetent doctors: 'No one can help me.' With his permission I called Dr Smith to discuss his case. She said she wasn't happy about treating him anymore, for which I couldn't blame her, as he had told her that he had once literally ripped the clothes off a previous female therapist in a fit of anger!

As he seemed seriously depressed and possibly suicidal, I prescribed an antidepressant and managed to get a same-day appointment with yet another counsellor, Dr Jones. When I told David about the urgent appointment I had arranged, there was an outburst of anger directed at me: 'What the fuck am I going to do between now and 11 o'clock?' Later he apologised for this and asked if I thought he was aggressive. I replied diplomatically that I thought his behaviour was understandable under the circumstances.

Six weeks later there was a further crisis. Dr Jones called me to say Mr Wellworth was indeed suicidal and he had sent him to a nearby large government hospital where, not surprisingly, he was not admitted. David came to see me the following day and said he just wanted to talk but he didn't want me to ask any questions. He said he also needed advice about some practical matters. He was wearing dark glasses and spoke in his usual quiet voice. There was a feeling of suppressed violence about him which might explode at any moment. The immediate problem was that he had pressured his girlfriend to 'confess' to him all the terrible things that had happened to her ten years previously when her ex-husband allegedly molested her; it was these mental pictures which had reduced him to a state of despair. In spite of his prohibition I asked a rhetorical question, 'I wonder why this is still affecting you so badly?' With barely controlled irritation he dismissed this question: he did not want to get into any discussion of the whys and wherefores.

So we got onto the practical matters he did want to discuss.

He had five possibilities in mind: 1) try to carry on as he was; 2) be admitted to hospital; 3) go home to England (but this wasn't a good idea because the last time he was there his father had threatened to kill him!); 4) go away to America where he had a friend he might be able to stay with; or 5) commit suicide. I felt that the third-mentioned suggestion was the most appropriate, as it would remove him from the source of his distress, and with some time and distance he might feel better. It also would also remove him from me, but there seemed to be little I could do for him. I thought he was someone who cannot live in himself and is so full of anger he doesn't want to try and understand his problems.

A month later I got a call from the girlfriend to say he was in a private psychiatric nursing home in England and the doctor there wanted background information about him. I told her that David would have to call me first to give permission to talk to the doctor.

David came to see me on his return to Japan after discharge from the nursing home. He was taking a different antidepressant and said he felt better. He told me he had sent his girlfriend to a therapist. This was an interesting example of the psychological phenomenon of projection: it was *she* who needed treatment. I heard later that he was even trying to control and direct the therapy by frequently phoning the therapist!

I continued to see him periodically. He was coping better overall but still had episodes of worse depression, terrible rows with his girlfriend, and remorse afterwards. In spite of this they were still together. Somehow they needed each other.

Patients sometimes get better when they stop the treatment
The Ambassador of a South American country came to see me. This was on the recommendation of a psychiatrist in Hong Kong who had called me about him a few weeks before. He wanted me to refer him to a clinical psychologist and prescribe Prozac, the wonder drug that abolishes unhappiness.

The patient was an intelligent, young looking 55 year old man who talked a lot. He had been well till three years ago when he developed a severe attack of vertigo which lasted two weeks. He was then in Malaysia and was treated inappropriately with anafranil (an antidepressant) from which he suffered unpleasant side effects. Then he was treated with alprazolam (a tranquilliser) which helped. The problem was that he had continued to take alprazolam—a notoriously addictive drug. He felt well when taking a high dose but became dizzy and unwell if he attempted to reduce it. In the meantime he had been 'investigated by neurologists in five continents', as he put it, with brain scans and other tests but the results were all normal. The psychiatrist in Hong Kong wanted him to increase the alprazolam and take Prozac in addition. However, it was perfectly clear to me that he was suffering withdrawal symptoms from this excessive medication and what he needed was slowly to reduce and then stop the alprazolam, not continue it and add another drug.

Medicine and manners

I believe inter-collegial courtesy is of the highest importance in medical practice. If it is not observed it may have unfortunate consequences for the patient, as well as for the professionals involved. 'Unfortunate' is putting it mildly: it could have been fatal in following case.

A patient who was suffering from depression came to see me and I referred him to the above-mentioned Dr Smith for psychotherapy. Then I heard nothing further until the patient turned up again three weeks later with severe bruising all down the right side of his body. What had happened?

It turned out that Dr Smith did not have enough confidence to treat him herself, and without telling me, *referred him on* to a Japanese psychiatrist. The psychiatrist, in the way that psychiatrists do, prescribed an antidepressant. Unfortunately, he omitted to take an occupational history, that is, ask the patient what he did for a living. Or maybe he did ask but failed to take this information into account in his prescribing.

The patient was a professional racing driver. I have known several racing drivers in my life; they were all rather interesting, introverted people. It is a highly skilled job that requires athletic physical fitness combined with intense concentration; you need the ability to make split-second decisions. Yet it is quite a lonely sport. You are most of the time strapped into the cockpit of the car with little direct human interaction. The 1966 film, *Grand Prix*, shows this rather well, I think.

What is absolutely clear is that when you're driving at speeds which may exceed 320 kph (200 mph) there is no margin for error. Your mind must be unclouded—or the result could be fatal to yourself or other people on the track.

Antidepressants all have side effects including sedation. This may not matter too much in ordinary life but they are absolutely contra-indicated (must not be used) in a racing driver! He was fine in the car even though he was depressed; it is a kind of meditation, for when racing you cannot think of anything other than the job in hand. The patient had been in a crash and nothing worse had happened than the severe bruising. He was lucky.

Why, oh why, did Dr Smith take it upon herself to refer the patient on to someone else without conferring with me? Did she think that because of my well-known reluctance to use mind-drugs including antidepressants, the patient was not safe in my hands? Apart from the potentially fatal outcome from her failure to refer back to me, this was a failure of common courtesy. Needless to say I never sent her another patient.

This incident highlights another problem that is especially evident in Japan: the lack of a general practitioner who is recognised as being in overall medical charge of the patient. It often happens that a patient independently consults specialists at different hospitals, but there may be little or no communication between them. This fragmentation of care can result in reduplication of tests and treatment, or inappropriate prescribing. Also, hospital doctors often work in rotating training schemes and the patient may not see the same doctor twice. If there is a query, whom should the patient approach? Who will provide continuity of care?

A mild case of arrogance

A patient was referred to me by a certain Dr Robinson, a psychiatrist working in Tokyo. He qualified in another country and does not have a Japanese medical license, but nonetheless he may see patients for psychotherapy. But what happens if Dr Robinson thinks a patient needs medication, since he cannot prescribe it himself? He has to ask a licensed physician to take on this responsibility.

For this patient I agreed with Dr Robinson that he would probably benefit from an antidepressant, so I duly prescribed it, and in the meantime he continued psychotherapy with Dr Robinson. So far, so good. But then, perhaps inevitably, with Dr Robinson trying to wear two hats at the same time, he wanted me to prescribe in addition to the antidepressant, a stimulant, Ritalin, to help the patient get going in the mornings! I said I would be reluctant to do this as Ritalin is not licensed for use in depression and is potentially addictive. Nonetheless, I said I would discuss it with the patient at his next attendance.

However, when the patient came for his follow-up appointment he admitted he had already obtained Ritalin from another clinic. So now we had one patient being treated by three different practitioners for the same problem. I didn't want to upset him and as he had already started with a second drug, and I said I would continue it. But I felt moved to write the following letter to Dr Robinson:

> I thought it would be as well if I put in writing some concerns I have had in connection with patients you have referred to me.

I understand that it must be frustrating for you, as a psychiatrist, to be unable to prescribe drugs in Japan and to have to follow a more limited, if no less important, role as a psychotherapist. Under these circumstances I am happy to collaborate and to prescribe drugs if *in my opinion* they are appropriate, while you see the patients for therapy.

However, if we are to continue to collaborate in this way, I must ask you to have confidence in my ability to assess patients' needs for drugs and to monitor their progress from this aspect, making changes as I see fit. While I appreciate your suggestions for drug treatment, I must make it clear that I am not necessarily going to follow them. Perhaps I may remind you that I have had extensive experience in treating all kinds of psychological problems in the foreign community, including acute psychiatric emergencies.

In the case of Mr—, although I agreed that an antidepressant was appropriate, I was not happy about adding Ritalin. As you know, the indications for this drug are hyperactivity in children and narcolepsy. While I am in general reluctant to use drugs in an unorthodox way, I did not entirely rule this out and would have been happy to discuss it with the patient at his next attendance.

However, I think it is quite wrong that you apparently entered into a conspiracy with the patient so that he obtained the Ritalin from another practitioner. He is entitled to do this, but then I would normally expect him to receive all his drug treatment from the practitioner of his choice. I do not think it is in patients' best interests to be treated by two or more doctors independently for the same condition. But as he admitted what had happened and I did not wish to upset him, I agreed to continue treating him.

I hope that you will take these comments in the constructive spirit in which they are intended, and that we can continue to have a good—indeed better—professional relationship.

A few days later I received a reply from Dr Robinson. Some extracts:

> You are obviously not as well equipped to handle certain psychiatric problems as is a psychiatrist who has completed a residency in psychiatry...even if a patient has already engaged with you, if...in my opinion you are not able to provide care that I think is warranted, then I will recommend that patient seek care elsewhere.
>
> You would have also much to learn from me on the use of psychopharmacologic agents...it would be prudent of you to realise your limitations in this field. Not only did you not do a residency in psychiatry [this is a wrong assumption: I did a psychiatric residency as part of my general practice training] nor are you board certified in this specialty, but it is impossible for you to keep up on all the latest literature...as only those in that specialty can.
>
> You are not able to listen to or learn from others in an open sense...If you humbled yourself a bit your relationships would go better.
>
> I would be happy to discuss what kind of role you could play in the psychopharmacologic management of patients who come to see me. If you are interested in discussing this further you are welcome to come to the institute here to meet with me.

Obviously, cooperation with him was then at an end, and I sent no reply.

Stress-induced symptoms

An Englishwoman aged 31, a teacher at a Japanese high school, complained of dizziness. This can be a challenging symptom to sort out. She elaborated that the feeling was 'as if looking through a dirty pane of glass, and almost a headache'. She had been seen at hospital by a neurologist who thought there was nothing wrong except stress, and he prescribed a benzodiazepine tranquilliser, but it had upset her to be labelled, as she thought, as a psychiatric case. She was under stress because of difficulties at work and being due shortly to return to England. I found nothing wrong when I examined her, so I advised stopping the tranquilliser and to keep in touch if she was still unwell.

A week later she came again with the same symptom. In addition, that morning she was almost overcome by a wave of dizziness which made it difficult to continue teaching her class. She started to cry as soon as she entered my room. I found nothing to indicate a physical disease and tried to reassure her. Nonetheless, to be thorough I thought we should do some basic screening blood tests, but I told her that her symptoms were suggestive of an anxiety state. It then came out that, although she had managed well in the last two years under all sorts of pressures at work, the original problem was 'of course, because of a man'. It seemed to help her to be able to tell me this, and I said that it was as if she had coped 'too well' with this disappointment, and now it was coming out near the time she was getting ready to leave Japan. We discussed how she might come to terms emotionally with this major disappointment.

It's easy to collude with a patient that there 'must be' an organic cause, especially in the face of strong pressure to pursue such an approach. The neurologist she saw originally was correct but mishandled the situation by prescribing a tranquilliser. It's a matter of finding the right balance: over-investigating someone with psychological symptoms on the one hand, and on the other hand not doing enough through forgetting the dictum, 'All neurotics die of an organic disease.'

A cure for drug addiction?
A 31 year old Englishman working for a major foreign bank came to see me. He was a well-dressed young man speaking in a lower middle class accent who admitted he had a drug problem and wanted help.

Three years previously he had started using cocaine in America and had gradually needed larger and larger quantities. He dosed himself every few days, but it would take several hours till he felt the effect so he had to take time off work. In addition, he needed to borrow money to buy the stuff, and the problem was getting out of control. Also, cocaine dealing or even possession is a crime in Japan and can land one in serious trouble. His difficulties were compounded by the fact that he was depressed, and this seemed to be as a result of the drug use. He had tried to come off a number of times and had attended drug rehabilitation programmes, but without success. He had also seen a counsellor and a psychiatrist; the latter had prescribed antidepressants, without benefit. In a further attempt at self-help he had read books on the problem, but this had made him more depressed, especially with all the emphasis on the 'recovery process' as if addiction is an illness for which you need a long convalescence to get over. He described his life as one of anhedonia, that is, having little or no capacity to feel or look forward to anything with pleasure.

On the assumption that all drug addictions are basically similar, I thought I would try the same approach which I have used successfully with nicotine addiction. He didn't need to 'use' every day, so the physical withdrawal symptoms were mild or non-existent. The reason he continued to poison himself with cocaine was the belief, or hope, that he would experience a 'high' which would take him out of his depression. This was because when he took cocaine he felt mild relief for about half-an-hour, though this was nothing more than to make him feel 'neutral', as he put it. But then he felt worse: more depressed, angry with himself, and guilt-ridden. I thought he was pining for the remembered euphoria he experienced when he first used cocaine. But why did he feel depressed all the time? The answer was that this is a mental withdrawal symptom of the drug. Therefore, the way to be rid of this feeling is to cease putting it into your body. He then realised there is no point in using cocaine. The anticipated high no longer arrives and the expected benefit, such as it may be, is illusory. Thus he was helped to understand that the conflict of being tempted to use cocaine was unnecessary. He could be rid of the conflict by reminding himself that the drug no longer did anything for him. The result of this insight was that he then had no difficulty in refraining from something he no longer wanted to do.

He came again two weeks later to say he was much happier, had no more desire to 'use', and didn't think he would ever want to again. We went over a few points, such as whether he needed to avoid bars and the company of people he knew who also 'used'. I told him he didn't need to make any other changes in his life unless he wanted to. The key to success was to keep in mind how marvellous it is not to be a drug addict, and to remind himself about the reality of the situation if he ever felt tempted to try this drug again.

A very specialised practice

A Canadian man aged 27 came with a letter from a doctor in Canada which stated at the top: 'Practice limited to attention deficit disorders, hyperactivity, epilepsy and learning disorders.' The letter gave the patient's history which included difficulties in speaking when aged 3 or 4, and having to work hard all the time to achieve good school grades and obtain a university degree. I wondered what was so remarkable about that. He was married and supporting himself as a teacher in Japan. In other words, he was outwardly successful.

He saw the doctor in Canada after a car accident two years previously which he felt was due to lack of concentration. An EEG had been done which was said to show a 'partial epilepsy equivalent syndrome', whatever that is, for which an amphetamine was prescribed. The patient felt better able to concentrate while taking this drug, but was concerned about feeling tired when he stopped it (hardly surprising). In the last eighteen months he had taken Ritalin (a milder kind of stimulant) while he had been working in Korea where apparently amphetamines were unavailable, and he requested a further supply of Ritalin.

We discussed the whole situation and I told him I thought he had normal difficulties which had been medicalised by the Canadian doctor who, with such a narrow speciality, was very likely to prescribe long-term medication and recommend regular follow-up. I advised that he stopped the Ritalin, putting up with the withdrawal effects for a while and then being free of them for good. I also mentioned that he should have confidence in his own normal good health and not be burdened with the groundless belief that he had a medical illness which needed to be controlled for the rest of his life by taking a chemical drug! He agreed to try and cut down gradually although he wanted to continue at the current dose for another two months. I pointed out that, as with any addiction, there was a self-perpetuating desire never to stop. He then asked about referral to a specialist: a psychiatrist or neurologist who might know more about the chemical mechanisms involved or who could advise about an alternative to Ritalin. Anything to avoid facing the reality of living without drugs! Nonetheless, I agreed to give him a further short-term supply.

Some years later in Japan, because of the abuse potential of Ritalin, the rules were changed so that only specially licensed psychiatrists can prescribe it.

Repatriating a disturbed mental patient

From time to time I would be asked if someone who was suffering from a mental illness should come to live and work in Japan. I generally advised that if the patient was in a stable condition and the drugs being taken (or equivalent) were available here then it might be reasonable.

For some foreigners, however, coming to Japan for the first time can be quite stressful.

Even ordering from a menu in a restaurant can be challenging. Though many people enjoy this and are stimulated to learn Japanese, I have seen not a few patients with mental problems deteriorate when they come to live in such a different environment from the one they are used to.

Although there are good English-speaking general practitioners and psychiatrists in Tokyo (the rest of Japan is another matter) who can usually take care of patients with mental illnesses in the community, if someone deteriorates and is in severe distress, being unable to work or take care of themselves, it can be a nightmare trying to find a hospital to admit such a patient, though if someone is clearly out of control the police may become involved.

What happens if a foreigner in this situation is admitted to a Japanese mental hospital? The policy is to keep patients quiet and tractable by filling them up with drugs. Note the plural. For example, I have seen patients suffering from depression treated with a cocktail of seven different drugs: two kinds of antidepressant, an antipsychotic, a tranquilliser for day-time use, a sleeping tablet, a drug to prevent side-effects from the antipsychotic, and a tablet to prevent stomach upsets from all the other drugs. No wonder these patients are wondering around like zombies. Locked wards are the rule. There is little attempt at rehabilitation or occupational therapy. For foreigners, especially if they are not fluent in Japanese, there may be nothing to do all day but await recovery or escorted repatriation when the condition is sufficiently improved. A family member, friend, or medical escort usually needs to be arranged in collaboration with the airline; this can be difficult and time-consuming.

Although each case needs to be considered on its merits, in my experience it is better that someone with a potentially unstable mental condition be advised not come and work in Japan, as the following case illustrates.

A well-known European theatre company was performing

in Tokyo some years ago. One of the troupe had a history of schizophrenia and was showing signs of disturbed behaviour. My services were requested to decide whether he was fit to perform on the last night. I determined that he was. The performance was flawless but later that night I received an urgent call that this person was out of control, running around partially undressed and shouting nonsense in the public areas of his hotel. By luck I managed to get him promptly admitted to a mental hospital, and it fell to my lot to escort him back to his own country when he was deemed fit to travel a few days later. Unfortunately, the hospital had omitted to ensure he took his sedative drugs on the morning of departure. I collected him at the hospital with two colleagues from the troupe and by the time we got to the airport things were starting to deteriorate. He refused to take any medicines. What to do? It seemed the only sensible thing was to get on the plane and hope for the best. The airline was aware of the situation and I carried injectable sedative drugs with me just in case. This was a wise precaution because subsequently his behaviour became unruly to the point where it was causing concern to other passengers. In this situation the captain's word is law, and he ordered me to give an injection to the patient in spite of his resistance. Four cabin staff were needed to hold him down while I did my bit. After that we had a quiet flight and an ambulance was waiting for him on landing. It was interesting that he was more comfortable in the fantasy world of the theatre but couldn't cope with external reality.

CHAPTER TWENTY-SIX
Child Psychology

AN ENGLISHWOMAN BROUGHT her 18 month old daughter who had been pulling her hair out. The history, as usual, pointed to the heart of the problem. The birth (in England) had been induced for post-maturity and a difficult labour followed. There was monitoring of the baby's heart and much anxiety from premonitions of disaster from the attendants. In the event, the birth was normal and the child healthy. However, two days later a dislocatable hip was found and she was put in a special leg splint for six weeks. When she was 3 months old her paternal grandfather aged 62 collapsed in front of them and died soon afterwards in hospital. Unfortunately a health visitor, who was a nurse, told the mother this meant there was a serious risk of heart disease in the family and advised her and her husband to have their cholesterol levels checked. A nurse is not qualified to give medical advice of this kind. Shortly thereafter they came to Japan, but the father was away a lot on business trips.

The hair pulling was especially noticeable when the child was put in her crib to sleep at night. She didn't have a security blanket and apparently didn't like soft toys. The mother usually let the child cry herself to sleep. Earlier on the same day that they came to see me they had consulted a Japanese paediatrician about the hair pulling, who alarmed the mother with talk of 'hair balls' in the stomach and had recommended an ultrasound scan. The mother was also told this was a symptom of a serious psychological disturbance which could progress to the stage of pica (eating substances other than normal food) and head-banging, and that she should see a child psychologist. On hearing this, the mother came to me for a second opinion.

The hair pulling was a symptom of insecurity in the child. This was understandable because of all the recent family upset and worry the mother had been put through. I reassured her and we discussed how she could help her child to feel more secure, in particular by not letting her cry herself to sleep, and cuddling her when she wanted and needed to be cuddled. I told the mother that she herself was the best psychologist for her child.

Pain in the neck

A similar situation showed itself in another patient. I was requested to visit at home a 6 year old American child with pain in his neck because the mother said the pain was too severe for her to bring him to my clinic. The previous day he had had a minor accident on his bicycle but had walked away apparently unhurt. However, this morning after getting up he came into the living room and lay down on the sofa on his left side. Any attempt to get him up or change position made him scream in seeming severe pain. He indicated the site of the pain at one small area at the left side of his neck. He had eaten and drunk a little during the day and had urinated into a potty from that position.

Examining him as far as I could, I found he had no fever and there was no inflammation at his right ear-drum. I could not look at the other ear as he was lying on it. He was reasonably cheerful and playing with a toy though keeping the left side of his face to a cushion the whole time. I managed to persuade him to bend and straighten his neck, but any attempt to get him to turn to the right seemed to be very painful. Although it is said that children of this age do not suffer from psychologically-induced symptoms, I did not think he had a serious physical disorder. Then, with the mother's permission, I raised him up to the sitting position. During this manoeuvre his screams were maximal and but somehow indicative of distress rather than pain. The mother held him to her and placed her hand over his left ear as he wanted, and I managed to examine the left ear-drum—it was normal.

Then the following story emerged. He had come to Japan with his mother and siblings (a toddler and a babe-in-arms) a month ago, but his father had come two months in advance of the rest of the family. The child was unhappy here, missing his friends. Thus, normal family life had been disrupted. The mother said she was not a very sympathetic person and had a rather matter-of-fact attitude. She expected the children just to get on with things themselves, as she has a great many practical matters to attend to. This seemed to be the clue to the problem: there was no evidence of neck injury or ear-drum inflammation, and the behaviour of the little patient was unlike that of a child in severe pain—it seemed exaggerated.

I discussed this with the mother, saying I could find no disease or injury to account for the pain; it seemed to be literally a cry for help. Then the boy said something extraordinary for his age: 'I wish I'd never been born,' and 'I want to jump out of the window.' I thought he was greatly unhappy and needed his mother's physical presence and attention. She mentioned getting professional therapy for him but I said, as with the child discussed above, the best therapist he could possibly have was herself.

Recurrent headaches

Another case where the history revealed the cause of the problem was that of a 7 year old girl, Amelia, whom I saw because of recurrent headaches. The mother was from New Zealand and the father from Germany. They spoke English at home. There was also a younger brother. The family had come to Japan five years previously. Amelia first attended a kindergarten and then a Japanese junior school in the last year. That was when the headaches started. Sometimes she was free of headaches for up to ten days, though they occasionally woke her at night. She was otherwise well.

Amelia looked unhappy and clearly there was a problem

connected with the school. I asked the mother why she went to a Japanese school: it was because they wanted her to learn Japanese. It seemed she was self-conscious being the only foreigner at the school—a blonde blue-eyed girl. Although she was accepted by the other children she was under stress due to being in a foreign language environment.

My impression was that the parents were forcing this child to do something she found too difficult. Although she was trying hard to fit in with her parents' wishes she was in a conflict, and that is what was producing the headaches. It seemed the parents had some rather inflexible ideas about schooling and were not sensitive enough to the child's needs. I wondered why they didn't send her to the German School in Tokyo and why the father didn't speak German at home. I suggested Amelia should have some time off school, but the mother was reluctant to take her out before the end of term, so she had to endure another week of it. The mother also said, tellingly, 'She just wants to be at home with me all day.' Of course she did, rather than being the only foreigner, the odd one out, in a school where she was struggling with the language.

Hyperactivity caused by boredom

Sometimes it seems schools are too quick to raise the possibility of whether disruptive behavior in a young child is due to the so-called disorder of hyperactivity. One such child I saw in the clinic was a 6 year old boy attending one of the international schools in Tokyo. He had been seen by an educational psychologist, with inconclusive results, though they found his IQ was 138. The mother had not noticed any hyperactive behaviour at home, and said he concentrated well while being read to and was good at reading himself and at maths.

I found a lively boy who was growing normally. He showed an intelligent interest in my weighing scales, eye-testing equipment ('Can anyone read the bottom line?' he asked), auriscope, and torch. He also remarked that the second hand of the wall clock in my room was going faster than an ordinary clock: it had a sweep second hand which appeared to move smoothly around the dial.

I thought this very smart boy was not being stretched enough at school—in other words, he was bored—and I suggested the parents take this up with his teacher.

Normal behaviour misunderstood

I had another illustration of how a child's normal behaviour may be misunderstood by adults. A mother of Indian extraction came to see me with a respiratory infection, and brought her 2½ year old son who also had a cold. I thought the behaviour of the child was interesting. He was running around in my room, looking into everything as children are wont to do. The mother kept telling him to 'behave' and to 'calm down', no doubt out of respect to me. But from his point of view he was having a great time and his behaviour was perfectly reasonable and intelligent. He took my stethoscope off its hook where I kept it at the side of a cabinet, tried to put the ends into his ears, then tried to put it back on the hook, but it was upside down so he turned it the correct way up to replace it. Then he went over to the steps by the examination couch and immediately figured out what these were for. So children's behaviour which might be annoying to adults is often the normal way they learn about their environment.

Imposing adult wishes on children

A young American mother brought her 15 month old son to see me with a cold. She had another son aged 3. She was concerned about the child with a cold because she was planning a three day trip to Hong Kong with her husband. I suggested that he would miss her and she him. She readily agreed. So I asked why they didn't take him with them. She replied that it was the first time she would have left him, it was the only holiday she could have since the birth, and he wouldn't enjoy shopping in Hong Kong—in other words, justifying leaving him from her adult point of view. But why do some mothers want to abandon their children while they go off with the aim of enjoying themselves? Obviously, the little boy, and no doubt his elder brother too, would be very unhappy if their mother disappeared for three days. Then it emerged that she was pregnant again, and we started discussing antenatal care and choosing a place of birth. I mentioned that I could do shared care with at a nearby maternity hospital. But she said she couldn't come to me because she knew my views on circumcision from the leaflets and posters in my waiting room and a letter on the subject I recently had had published in *The Japan Times*. Although she wasn't keen on the idea, her husband was adamant that if they had another boy he would want to have part of his penis cut off! It seemed he wanted this done because he thought the normal (intact) penis looked unaesthetic, and he wanted to protect his son from possible locker-room teasing. I briefly explained some of the reasons for not have this mutilation performed, lent her a book entitled *Say No to Circumcision!*, and offered to discuss the matter with her husband.

It turned out, however, that the question was academic because she had a miscarriage. Naturally, she was in much distress and came to talk to me afterwards about this unfortunate event.

CHAPTER TWENTY-SEVEN
Complaints

I HAVE ALWAYS tried to do my best for all my patients and to practice medicine at the highest level. This has been very rewarding but occasionally there have been complaints. I hasten to say these have not been many. Out of the thousands of patients I saw every year perhaps once in two years someone complained.

If you only get praise you learn nothing. On the other hand, complaints can be considered a precious gift: there's usually a reason for them and they can point to ways in which one can improve one's practice and give a better service to patients.

A woman aged 31 attended with her husband. I had not seen them before. Her last period was only one month ago but a home pregnancy test was said to be positive. She wanted a letter to confirm the pregnancy because she wished to have the baby in Australia under the care of an obstetrician who, apparently, required such a letter before he would book her into his hospital. I said I was willing to do this but would need to do my own test first. I might have made some mildly humorous comment to the effect that the obstetrician must be incredibly popular if he required such early booking. Also, I pointed out that a urine pregnancy test might not be positive at such an early stage, and if we did a blood test it would take a week to get the result. However, she wanted a test today, so I did one. The result was equivocal, as would not be unexpected very early in a pregnancy, but she was incredulous. I suggested that she return for a repeat test in a week's time, but she suddenly stood up and walked out of the room, saying 'Thank you very much'. The husband, who had said not a word throughout the consultation, followed her. They paid the bill for my consultation fee and the test on their way out.

Soon afterwards I received a letter from the patient in the style of Disgusted of Tunbridge Wells:[22]

> Dr Symonds,
> I am writing to express my extreme dissatisfaction with the consultation my husband and I received on [date].
> I found your demeaning, argumentative and judgmental manner deplorable and unethical.
> My husband and I will actively discourage members of the expatriate community from attending the Tokyo British Clinic.
> Appalled,
> (Signed)

This was upsetting, and I thought her statement of her intention to damage my reputation could be actionable. Unfortunately, she didn't say what it was in my manner or speech which she found demeaning, argumentative, judgmental, and deplorable. (She must have been at the Thesaurus.)

I called my medical defence organisation in the UK and they sensibly told me to ignore this letter: not to reply or even acknowledge it. They added that if she slandered me on a public platform that would be different.

Out-of-time

Then there was an extraordinary phone call from a patient I had seen only once, four years ago. He was from Saudi Arabia and of black South African parentage. When I saw him he had been in Japan for two years and was working part-time in a restaurant. His complaint was of a tingling or pricking sensation at his arms

---

[22] A satirical generic name, derived from the pseudonym of a person who lived in the conservative middle class town of Tunbridge Wells in Kent, England, for someone who writes to newspapers in a tone of moral outrage, said to date from 1944.

and chest, and he had been investigated at various hospitals with normal or negative results, including an HIV test. I found he was a fit young man and reassured him there was no evidence of physical disease. I discounted my fee as he seemed to be of limited means. Today, that is, *four years later*, he rang up to complain about the fee, in particular being disappointed that he received no treatment. The receptionist explained that the fee was for the consultation, but he insisted on speaking to me. I told him that being so long after the event his complaint was absurd, and I cut the conversation short.

Sued

For most of my career at the Tokyo British Clinic I was single-handed. This had advantages and disadvantages. Having no one working with me I could avoid personality problems which can sometimes arise with colleagues in the same practice, but I didn't have anyone with whom I could discuss patients and other medical matters during a coffee break. And taking holidays was difficult—if I wasn't there no money was coming in!

From time to time however, I did have an assistant. In two cases these were British doctor wives of businessmen who had been posted to Tokyo. They had had to pass the same licensing examination that I took and this involved time, trouble, and expense for the clinic. After they started work it was difficult sometimes for them to realise they were not still in the NHS. One part-time assistant I took on was involved in the only occasion in which I have been sued.

I was away on a brief visit to London and this doctor, an experienced and highly qualified woman (I'll call her Dr Harris) was holding the fort. As soon as I arrived back I was told of a problem.

A 24 year old Australian woman who was visiting Japan had come to the clinic. She complained of a severe headache in the previous few days with occasional vomiting. Headache can be difficult to diagnose. There is always the worry whether the patient might have a brain tumour, rare though this is. Unfortunately, in this case the patient *did* have a brain tumour.

Dr Harris made as good an assessment as might reasonably be expected at a first attendance. No diagnosis was made but she was given pain-killers and advised to come back if the headaches persisted. With hindsight it is always easy to be critical and say that the sudden onset of a bad headache with vomiting is a red flag. However, in subsequent correspondence with my medical defence organisation I was informed that failure to make the correct diagnosis at a first attendance in general practice would not of itself be regarded as negligent.

The young woman patient was not happy with Dr Harris's handling of her case and two days later betook herself to the Jikei University Hospital. In Japan anyone presenting to an emergency department of a large hospital with a headache is liable to have a CT or MRI scan performed there and then as part of the clinical assessment, or often, it seems, instead of the clinical assessment.

The patient was admitted straightaway and an emergency procedure performed to relieve the pressure inside her head. Then arrangements were made for her to fly back to Australia for definitive treatment as soon as she was fit to travel. The patient's mother had immediately flown to Tokyo and was understandably very upset over her daughter's illness and, not so understandably, upset with Dr Harris. What to do? It seemed to me that however excusable it was that my colleague had missed the diagnosis, the inescapable fact was that she *had* missed the diagnosis. Therefore I felt the only decent thing to do was to go immediately to the hospital—it was just after the patient had had the emergency procedure—to meet the mother and the patient and apologise to them both. Obviously, Dr Harris should have gone, or we should have gone together. But would she? No. 'I was taught never to apologise,' she said. So, once again, Muggins had to go. I even took with me some flowers that my nurse, bless her cotton socks, bought with her own money—she had felt sorry for the patient when she came to the clinic.

So off I went to the hospital, met the mother and patient and apologised on behalf of Dr Harris, and I returned the consultation fee. The mother was not impressed.

In due course I received a letter from a solicitor in Australia claiming damages for the delayed diagnosis, pain and suffering, etc. She was intending to sue Dr Harris and the Tokyo British Clinic jointly and severally. The matter was placed in the hands of our defence organisation—we belonged to the same one in the UK. Although they agreed that a delay of two days would have made no difference to the outcome, they decided to settle out of court for a not inconsiderable sum of money: they didn't want to take on the potentially large expense of defending an international suit.

I felt that a large part of the mother's annoyance was due to the lack of a direct apology from Dr Harris.

Unreasonable complaints
An American girl who said she had fairly severe low back pain came all the way to see me from Sendai, two hours from Tokyo by train. Her back movements were unrestricted and elicited no more than mild discomfort. I advised manipulation but this she declined. To try to reassure her I said that her disorder, in mechanical terms, was relatively slight. Her response was, 'I find that offensive!' Presumably she thought I was making light of her pain. But what is the matter with some people that they are so touchy? I suppose one can't please everybody all the time.

Another complaint that occurred occasionally was of the following kind. A patient would come with a cold. I would examine him carefully and diagnose that he was suffering from—a cold. Then I would offer symptomatic treatment and advise him to contact me if he didn't soon recover. I would hear nothing until two or three weeks later when a letter or email arrived saying, 'I came see you on [date] and you told me I was suffering from a cold. But it got worse so I went to see Dr —. He took an X-ray and told me I was suffering from nearly pneumonia (*sic*)! How come you missed it?'

Back pain and pending litigation

As it was my intention to provide the highest level of service to the community, I have never turned anyone away. On rare occasions this has backfired. A few patients have been troublesome, particularly over payment of fees. In such cases, with hindsight, there have usually been warning signs and if I had heeded them I might have saved my staff and myself needless trouble.

A Japanese woman made an appointment to see me at 3.30 pm one day in connection with a back problem. Before arrival she telephoned as many as four or five times to speak to my nurse for reassurance that I would be able to interpret the X-rays she was bringing and that I was familiar with back problems.

She turned up *two hours late*, at 5.30 pm when we were about to close the clinic for the day. Admittedly, she had come from Chiba, the neighbouring prefecture to Tokyo, and there had been a thunderstorm—a premonition, perhaps?—but she didn't call to say she would be late. Having had all the prior indications that this was not going to be a straightforward consultation, and as she had arrived so late, I should have asked her to come back on another day. But out of a wish to be helpful my nurse and I stayed on after the other staff left. The nurse was in my consulting room with me all the time as a chaperon and witness, which turned out to be a wise precaution.

The patient was a petite, anxious, unsmiling Japanese woman aged 31 who lived with her mother in Chiba. She had not worked for a year. The first problem was that she would not say what her symptoms were, but she wanted me to look at the X-rays and scans of her back which she had brought along. I did so. They appeared normal to me. It was very difficult to elicit her medical history because she would not answer any questions in a straightforward way, but instead, repeatedly told me what other doctors whom she had consulted had told her. She wanted my opinion on their opinions. I said I could not comment on what other doctors had said until I had made my own assessment.

Eventually the following story emerged. Two months previously she had been shopping in the Mitsukoshi department store in Chiba. She had sat down at a rest area where there was a massage chair with electrically-operated rollers. Such rest areas with demonstration models of massage chairs are common in large department stores in Japan. I have tried these contraptions myself; they are pleasantly relaxing and are under the direct control of the user. The patient said the next day she had such severe pain at the whole of her back that she couldn't walk, though she did not stay in bed. Two weeks later she had recovered sufficiently to go on a trip to Belgium but the pain was bad on her return to Japan and since then it had been constant. She had complained to the department store and to the manufacturer of the chair, and it seemed there was litigation pending. When I had got that far in eliciting the history of her problem I was still unclear what she wanted from me: help to be rid of her pain, or to be provided with a certificate, or both? She wanted my opinion. I said I would need to examine her back first but she was very reluctant for me to do this. I said I could not proceed otherwise, and then she consented.

On examination, apart from a pronounced lumbar lordosis (excessive concavity at the lower back), I could find nothing wrong: all her back movements were normal and painless, there was no weakness of the muscles of her lower limbs, and I found no signs of nerve compression such as from a slipped disc.

It is essential to have an open mind to patients' problems, but the story of severe persistent back pain immediately after using a massage chair is dubious. A patient with a genuine physical disorder is only too glad to have found an attentive and inquisitive physician, but her reluctance to tell me her symptoms or to be examined was suspicious. It was, nonetheless, strange that the physical examination was completely normal.

I had then to give my opinion. This was that whatever damage might have been inflicted by use of the massage chair, it had recovered and I could find no cause for her continuing pain.

At that point she became angry and said, 'I am very disappointed,' and she accused me of not being a specialist. I raised the question of stress or depression as a reason for her continuing pain but these she denied. Part of the problem seemed to be that what I said conflicted with what other doctors had told her, such as that the pain was due to the vertebral spinous processes touching each other from the excessive concavity of her lower back.

Then she produced five medical certificates from other doctors which she wanted to have translated into English, in writing. This I declined on the grounds that we were not a translation service. I think what she really wanted was for me to write a certificate which she could use as evidence in her contemplated litigation against the chair manufacturer. I told her I regretted I was unable to help her in the way she wanted.

She refused to pay the bill on her way out. Later we called her mother in Chiba who said she was not surprised to hear what had happened and she offered to pay the bill on the patient's behalf.

It is always problematical when litigation is pending or unresolved. If the patient's pain has recovered they will get less or no compensation, and therefore there is an incentive to allege the pain is persistent.

Dr Cyriax described such patients. He would tell them that he thought the worry was exacerbating the pain, and they should return when the litigation was finished. If reassessment confirmed the absence of a physical cause for the pain, he would then offer a short course of some harmless treatment, such as electrotherapy or massage, to give the patient an excuse to recover without loss of face.

Floating asthma inhaler

There was an interesting interaction with a patient, an American woman aged 38, who came with two young children. She asked if I minded if the children had their snack while we were talking. So they started munching on biscuits and cheese and drinking juice. This was a bit unusual though I didn't find it objectionable. They seem very well-behaved and quiet, perhaps too quiet. Now, most patients come straight to the point and say what is troubling them, but although this woman went on talking I had difficulty understanding why she had come. She said she had been to another clinic run by foreign doctors, but my clinic was nearer for her—not exactly a compliment. She had asthma, and I think she probably just wanted a refill of her inhalers. These I provided after a brief examination including checking her peak-flow readings—a test to see how well asthma is controlled. She mentioned that she had been advised to place the canisters in water and if they floated it meant they were nearly empty. I pointed out that that this was an unreliable way of checking how much of the contents of the inhaler remain and is not recommended. To treat her asthma she was using both a bronchodilator ('reliever') and a steroid ('preventer') inhaler regularly, and I said that that probably meant she was not having enough of the steroid. Then she became red in the face and started crying, saying that she need these medicines to keep functioning to look after her children, and it was upsetting that I was implying she was over-using them. This was not the case: I meant their use might have needed adjustment.

In my experience, if a patient becomes upset over a misunderstanding it is very hard to retrieve the situation. Nonetheless, I was as sympathetic and helpful as I could be, and offered to see her again at greater length to go more into her problems. This made things worse: she became angry again and accused me of thinking she was just a neurotic mother. By then I was over-running the time and had already been reminded by the receptionist that other patients were waiting, but she didn't seem in any hurry to leave. I had to stand up to encourage her to go. On the way out I again offered a further appointment, but she said we didn't have the right rapport, so I quietly said that I understood, and that ended the consultation. Even so, she stayed for a further twenty minutes in the waiting area, reading a book to her children.

Nine days later I received a letter from the husband of this neurotic woman, demanding return of the consultation fee. This was because he claimed I had given her bad advice in that I had assured her that her inhalers were not empty, when according to him they were, so her asthma had became worse and she had to be treated elsewhere with oral steroids. I replied denying this groundless allegation.

CHAPTER TWENTY-EIGHT
Swindled!

NATURE HAD BEEN kind to Tristram Norriss.[23] He was tall, good looking, and spoke with a reassuringly pleasant British public school accent. There was, however, something wrong with him. It was revealed in a comment by an eminent graphologist, Mrs Marianne Jacoby, to whom I showed a specimen of his handwriting: 'If this man's job is swindling people,' she said, 'he'd be very good at it!' Unfortunately, by then it was too late.

No self-respecting graphologist will attempt a handwriting analysis without knowing two basic facts about the writer: age and nationality. I merely told her that he was a 36 year old Englishman and, after a brief discussion of how she arrived at the above damning characterization, she contemplated the writing for a short time more. Then she added, tellingly, 'This man is boring. I don't want to talk about him any more.' A devastating, spot-on description of his personality.

Some years previously I had read in a medical news magazine that the advice often given to salesmen was that the best investment they could make was to buy a copy of the British *Medical Register*. In the days before computers this was a two-volume tome containing registered doctors' names and addresses. The reason? 'It's the biggest list of mugs in Britain.'

One hazard of working as an expat is that, being relatively wealthy but too busy to study the financial markets or the complicated business of investing, one is prey to being approached by so-called financial advisors.

Tristram Norriss was introduced to me by a colleague who had bought a life-insurance scheme from him. I later discovered this was mis-sold and it was only with difficulty that he had

---

[23] His real name is used.

got his money back. Apart from the question of why, under these circumstances, Norriss was recommended to me at all, it should have been a warning sign. The only consolation, as I discovered later, was that I was not the only intelligent person who had been taken in by him! To my knowledge, some dozen people fell victim to his fraudulent schemes. In retrospect, red flags there were aplenty. For example, at the beginning of our association, I visited his office in Okayama, a city some distance from Tokyo. There were the usual office paraphernalia: desks and chairs, cupboards full of insurance company brochures, a computer and printer, etc. And the office was clean—too clean. On reflection it was obvious that no serious work, or work of any kind, took place there; it was just for show.

Similarly, although as it turned out later his marriage was hollow, Norriss liked to present himself as a family man. Had a Japanese wife and a child, and his father-in-law, a retired school teacher, had invested his savings in Norriss's business.

To cut a long story short, I naïvely thought Norriss was a useful man to know as someone to guide me in investing my savings. Although I am embarrassed to say it now, I was induced to place a not inconsiderable sum in his company on the promise of a share in his business, a yearly dividend, and the return of my capital after three years. Also, as he was then an agent for a well-known medical insurance company, he agreed to give me a share of the commissions paid to him if I introduced patients who subsequently bought this company's policies. Then he sold me a single-premium life insurance policy, helpfully offering to fill in the details himself to save my time, just getting me sign the document at the bottom of the page!

No dividends or share of commissions were paid, and—most surprisingly!—he declared himself unable to return my investment when the three years were up. Also, the life insurance policy was deliberately mis-sold since he ticked the box without my knowledge where I agreed to pay increasing premiums every year, so it was not the single premium policy I wanted. (This was later corrected by the insurance company.) When this came to a head, as was all too obvious in retrospect, I had been the victim of a deliberate fraud. I took him to court. Norriss's meagre defence was that the payment into his company was an investment and I was just unlucky because the company failed. The judge didn't agree and ordered him to pay me back in installments. However, when he had paid about half he skipped the country and disappeared, abandoning his wife and child.

I later discovered that the 'failed company' defence was something he made a habit of claiming. His modus operandi was to persuade people to invest in his latest company and, when the expected returns didn't materialise, he lied that he was very sorry, but the business, as businesses sometimes do, went bust. Tough luck. This happened with some fifteen different entities set up in his name—and these were only the ones I knew about. Norriss is also wanted for questioning by the British authorities in connection with a sum of several million pounds that passed through his hands and was then unaccounted for, after a large occupational pension scheme went into liquidation.

Eventually I ran him to earth in Hong Kong where I discovered, among other charming facts about this man's life, that he had bigamously married a Chinese woman after falsely stating on the marriage licence application that he was a bachelor, and he had a child with her. Subsequently, this wife and child were also abandoned. He is now wanted by the Hong Kong police for questioning in connection with alleged bigamy. The latest information I have about him is that after a year on the loose in Malaysia where he pursued women through social media dating sites, with his ill-gotten gains he has bought himself a nice little house somewhere in France. Now it is probably only a matter of time before his creditors and the UK Serious Fraud Office catch up with him.

Annoying though it is, I was fortunate in the sense that I

could afford to lose the money I put with him. Some of the other people he swindled were not so lucky: they had their life savings stolen.

CHAPTER TWENTY-NINE
Memento Mori

ONE OF THE greatest privileges of being a doctor is to be involved from time to time with patients who are dying. Death is the ultimate mystery, but it will be revealed to us all.

Sudden death in an adult

I was asked to visit a woman at home whose husband had died suddenly at the age of 41 from a massive heart attack. They had a delightful, highly intelligent and articulate 5 year old daughter who showed me her toys when I arrived and wanted to play with me. She knew her Daddy was dead. I did my best but it was terribly sad. It seemed to me that life is like walking a tightrope across a chasm: with reasonable luck we will get to the other end and die of old age—or we may fall off at any moment.

Cot death

On another day at 6.30 am I was called to one of the saddest events a doctor ever has to deal with: a 'cot death', now called sudden infant death syndrome (SIDS). Twin boys had been born by Caesarian section for maternal hypertension two months previously. It was the first night the parents had put the babies to sleep in a separate room, and when they went to them in the morning, one was dead. An ambulance had been called, and the family was taken to a hospital where the formalities were carried out. The next day I attended the funeral since I wanted to support the parents as best I could.

Why do some infants suddenly and inexplicably die? Certain factors contribute to the cause, such as a mother being under 20 years of age, maternal smoking, and being a twin as in this case, and the infant being put to sleep face down. My own theory is that it's unnatural for infants to sleep on their own. A newborn baby needs the constant physical closeness of its mother. Perhaps the baby awoke in the night. Where is mother? He doesn't understand she is only seconds away. Maybe he just gave up? It is said that bed-sharing can increases the risk of SIDS, but this may be because of other factors, such as an unsuitable (too soft) bed surface for an infant or too much bedding resulting in overheating. Room-sharing, with the infant's bed or bassinet next to the parental bed, is recommended. In traditional Japanese homes the family all sleep together on a futon. This provides a firm sleeping surface and no-one can fall out of bed because it's already on the floor. Another advantage is that the baby is right next to the mother and can suckle even without her being fully awake. This practice has great advantages for the problem of the infant who won't sleep. It's only in some western cultures that we expect babies and infants to sleep alone.

Dying in a Japanese Hospital

I received an urgent message from one of my patients mentioned previously, Mr Hulot, about his mother-in-law. She had been living independently until two months previously when she became increasingly breathless and needed hospital admission.

As the matter seemed urgent I took time off from the clinic to visit the hospital with the patient's daughter and my nurse. We drove there in my car which took about an hour. When we arrived it seemed to me that the poor lady was in a terminal state. She was barely conscious but did respond to her daughter's voice. She had an intravenous feeding tube since she had stopped eating and drinking, and was undergoing dialysis as well. As a visitor to the hospital it wasn't easy for me to examine her, but I spoke to the doctor in charge, a sensible and pleasant man. The worrying aspects of the patient's condition were her reduced level of consciousness, a temperature of 38.5° and a cough with purulent sputum. They were giving intravenous antibiotics and dialysis. The daughter had found a bed for her a large hospital in central Tokyo and wanted my opinion on her suitability for transfer there. I said that one had to face the fact that she may not recover and I could see no point in transferring her because they would not be able to do more for her there than where she was. It was a very difficult situation: she was dying because her kidneys, heart, and lungs were failing (shutting down).

Japanese doctors seem automatically to want to investigate and treat all such problems even when the chance of recovery is virtually nil. Rather than using their judgement and advising on what they think is appropriate, they seem always to be influenced by the relatives' wishes. Naturally, the relative will usually beg to have everything possible done that might save the patient's life, and the doctors are reluctant to point out when such treatment is futile. I asked about stopping the dialysis and the doctor said he would if *the daughter* requested it. This was, however, an academic point because the patient died the next day.

Dying peacefully

I was involved in a similar case with a patient, Kenneth Woodroofe[24], whom I first met in 1993 when he was aged 84. He was a much loved professor of English and was still active with teaching and writing. Although he never married and as far as I knew had no living relatives, he had a loyal following of students and friends. In November of 1993 he suddenly collapsed unconscious in the street and was admitted to hospital. After he had been there ten days I was asked to visit and advise on his condition. This I did, with the agreement of the hospital.

The diagnosis was a stroke complicated by multi-organ failure. I found him drifting in and out of consciousness, on a respirator (breathing tube), and undergoing dialysis. Of course, if there is any reasonable chance of recovery a patient should be treated to the best of the hospital staff's ability, but the prognosis looked

---

[24] His real name.

grave. A week later I visited again. Although he was off the respirator, by that time he was worse overall: unresponsive, with a cough and sputum from bronchopneumonia, and fever. As in the previous case, the dialysis was continuing and he was receiving intravenous antibiotics.

Regrettably, in this kind of situation Japanese hospital doctors often seem unwilling, or maybe they feel unable, to advise on prognosis; they are prone to continue treatment even if it is pointless, and leave life-and-death decisions to the relatives, or friends in lieu. I found the friends—there were about a dozen of them—had formed themselves into two groups: one of mainly Japanese people who urged that everything possible be done in the hope of saving him, and a mainly western group who were in favour of letting the poor man die in peace. I thus found myself in the difficult position of having to adjudicate on this matter.

I spoke to the doctor in charge and, although the answer was already only too clear to me, the following conversation ensued:

'Please tell me what you think the patient's chances are of recovering.'

'I can't say there is zero chance.'

'Look, he's not going to walk out of here, is he?'

'Ah, no, I suppose you're right.'

Five days later I re-visited and he was in a terminal state: unconscious, with laboured breathing. But at least the doctors had accepted that they would not try to resuscitate him, and would desist from further dialysis or breathing assistance. Still, they couldn't resist giving a blood transfusion when he coughed up a small amount of blood that morning.

He died peacefully the next day. Three of his friends (one Japanese and two western) were at the hospital keeping watch over his last hours to ensure that no futile heroic measures were undertaken, and to be with him at his passing.

The scandal of terminal care in Japan

The following case is an example of a situation in Japan which occurs all too frequently. [25]

The Japanese wife of a western man had the misfortune of developing stomach cancer and was treated in a university hospital in Tokyo. Her stomach was removed and for some months she was reasonably well. Then her condition deteriorated: she lost weight, could hardly eat, and her abdomen swelled from spread of the cancer. A doctor from a local hospital looked after her at home, visiting once a week. It has to be said that this treatment was not of the highest level, with the prescribing of multiple drugs some of which were inappropriate and caused side-effects, and drugs which were needed for effective relief of pain and discomfort not being used. The poor lady's condition progressed to the point where re-admission was unavoidable.

But what happened then? Was there someone in charge of her case who explained to the patient and her husband what the situation was and what they were trying to do about it? No. Her care, if you can call it that, was shared between a team of doctors, none of whom appeared to know what was going on.

But the worst failing was reluctance to use a proper pain-relieving drug, that is, morphine. Was this *difficult*? Did it require *specialised knowledge*? No. It required basic knowledge of terminal care, easily available to any doctor. The husband in this case had to make a thorough nuisance of himself before the staff would bestir themselves to give her morphine. Fearful of what might happen if he was not there, he would not leave her side. Although she was in a single room, would they provide a bed or futon for him? No. He had to make do with two chairs. Were the staff concerned enough to ensure he could leave to obtain some

---

[25] This problem was highlighted by a Japanese doctor, Fumio Yamazaki, in a book, the English edition of which came out in 1996, called *Dying in a Japanese Hospital*, published by The Japan Times.

food for himself and then return to the hospital? No. The place was locked up at night.

The principles of pain relief in this situation are that *morphine must be given in an adequate dose to relieve the pain and it must be given regularly in order to prevent return of pain.* It can be given by mouth or injection. The common practice in Japanese hospitals of using a morphine-like drug by a skin patch is unreliable since it is impossible to get an adequate and easily adjustable dose into the bloodstream by this means.

The patient, or her husband, should not have had to beg for morphine. Were the hospital doctors afraid that a terminally ill patient may become addicted? Were they afraid that such a patient's life may be shortened? Are there rules that limit the dose and frequency of the administration of this merciful drug? Were the doctors incapable of understanding that when someone is dying, treatment aimed at cure or prolonging life is futile and the focus must change to assist the patient to achieve a pain-free death? This is nothing whatever to do with euthanasia. In practice, with skilled administration of morphine, when a patient's pain and distress are relieved, they may well live longer and die peacefully, no more wracked by pain.

Where is the decency and humanity of those who have, or should have, the ability and the means to relieve another human being's suffering, but fail to act effectively? How long will it take in Japan before high quality palliative and terminal care are routinely available to all who need it?

ACKNOWLEDGEMENTS

I should particularly like to thank the following Japanese specialists who have unfailingly provided prompt and skilled attention for the patients I have referred to them, and without whose help it would not have possible for me to run a successful practice: Dr Fumito Akasu, Dr Reiko Akasu, Dr Kenichi Akiyama, Dr Hiyoshi Amano, Dr Atsushi Amemiya, Dr Osamu Doi, Dr Yasuyo Kasai, Dr Komei Kumagai, Dr Kiyoshi Kumano, Dr Teruyuki Kurihara, Dr Hisami Matsumine, Dr Kazuo Matsushita, Dr Seibu Mochizuki, Dr Masafumi Nakakuki, Dr Yoshihiko Takao, Dr Fumiyaki Ueno, Dr Minoru Yamato, Dr Jun Yano, Dr Yuki Yao, and Dr Kazuhiko Yoshida.

In addition, I offer my special thanks to Mr Colin Bamford, Sir John Boyd, the late Mr Iain de Staines, the late Sister Barbara Anne Hogan, Mr Kaoru Kataoka, Ms Chikage Mizuno, and Mr Klaus Naumann for their help and encouragement in setting up and supporting the Tokyo British Clinic.

I am also grateful to Mr Roger Brookin and Dr Chris Fagg (an old friend from medical school who gave me the idea of writing this book) for checking the manuscript and for their helpful suggestions.